D0757004

Inheriting Our Names

An Imagined True Memoir of Spain's Pact of Forgetting

C. Vargas McPherson

First Published in the Unites States.
Copyright © C. Vargas McPherson 2020
All rights reserved.

PUBLISHER'S NOTE

This is a memoir based on some historical facts and plenty of imagination.

ISBN 978-0-578-80094-3

www.vargasmcpherson.com

cover photo reproduced with permission:
David Pérez Navarro
www.graphicnatural.es

for John, Madeleine, and Benjamin
and for my sister, Patricia

Inheriting Our Names

An Imagined True Memoir of Spain's Pact of Forgetting

"Let me go and look for my past life,
so that it can deliver me from this present death."

Sancho Panza
Cervantes' *Don Quixote*

"Our memory is our coherence, our reason, our feeling,
even our action. Without it, we are nothing."

Luis Buñuel

Prologue

I was born on the only day God is dead. Jesus is crucified on Friday, and he is forever and eternally resurrected on Sunday, the third day. But the interminable Saturday between, that second day, he is stone cold dead, in the tomb, behind that great rock they rolled over the entrance. It is the ultimate Sabbath, when all things cease and give way to a great sadness, a great stillness and silence. And in Sevilla and amidst the staunch Catholicism and tyranny of Franco's Spain, it was a day between despair and hope. A day of watchful waiting.

On the day I was born, this church, the Basilica de la Macarena in Sevilla was cloaked in black. Ordinarily aglow with strong Spanish sunlight, the windows were draped with long black veils, the statues and paintings were overlain with shrouds, and my grandmother, my *abuela* Aurora, wore *traje de mantilla*, with a black *mantón* covering her head. That Saturday, between Good Friday and Easter Sunday, my grandmother prayed the *Mater Dolorosa*, the rosary of Mary's Seven Sorrows. Those Seven Sorrows that trace the life Mary witnessed as Her son was hunted, lost and then found, wept over, crucified, buried, and anointed, were always my *abuela*'s entry into the Virgin's heart and, eventually, into her own.

That Holy Saturday, my *abuela* Aurora sat in this darkened church, at the feet of the Virgin de la Esperanza Macarena, the effigy of the Holy Virgin artfully carved from sweet-smelling sandalwood and ancient cedars. Carved as if its heart were flesh, and on it were etched all the expressions of human grief. I can almost hear my grandmother ruminate on how in 1658, nearly complete, the statue lacked only one last intercession when the artist, la Roldána, finally administered the special preparation. Carefully, la Roldána measured, mixed, and dispensed the elixir known as *encarnado*, a color that gives the impression that the wood has become incarnate. Here, in la Macarena, are the Seven Sorrows made flesh in a mother's body.

That day, my *abuela* sat quietly in this church, in the Macarena *barrio* of Sevilla, reflecting upon all that had come before: the years of war, of hunger, of continued oppression under Franco, of want and need, and finally, what constitutes enough. She thought of her children: those who survived, the one who didn't, and her daughter – my mother – who tried to escape the ghosts of home but found she carried the haunting always with her. My *abuela* imagined me as well, on this day in which the greatest mourning is being transformed into the greatest joy, as a butterfly is created within the milky quiet of its chrysalis. Quietly and unseen.

In this sanctuary, the day I was born, the air was thick and heavy. And although the candles remained unlit on that day, the cloying scent of melted wax from all the many that had burned the day before lingered in the solemn still air. The fragrance of glossy-leafed orange trees in bloom and from the creamy carnations that adorned the processional floats, added top notes to the multilayered perfume. My grandmother rocked back and forth on the wooden pew until she remembered what brought her here, again, to the feet of the Virgin. Twisting each bead of her rosary, murmuring softly words only la Macarena could hear, she whispered her fears. "This baby will not save her from her sorrow. She must save herself. We can only save ourselves." She knew full well the vast sadness of her daughter's heart because it reflected her own – as hers reflected la Macarena's.

Peering into the eyes of the elaborately jeweled and clothed statue, my grandmother beseeched, "*Señora*, she is all alone there. Her letters reveal nothing. I think she is trying to protect me." My grandmother pulled in a ragged breath and reached out to the Virgin. My *abuela* knew that she and I would never meet. She would never hold her second grandchild. We were an ocean apart, but also a lifetime. Her lifetime.

~

Pooled in my palm as I sit in her church – my mother's church and my grandmother's church, but not my own – are the blackened rosary beads my *abuela* Aurora fingered almost every day of her life. But they are foreign to my touch; I roll them as an archeologist might, hesitantly, detached, but respectfully. I am just beginning the prayer cycle of the Seven Sorrows of Mary, the *Mater Dolorosa*. I am trying to learn how to use the Seven Sorrows as a map, some kind of chart where I can pinpoint the few facts I know and follow the paths toward some understanding, some meaning from this family legacy of unspoken grief. This, too, is an inheritance from the years of Spain's stifled secrets.

Here in Sevilla, I am seeking something familiar, something that could explain our family and the distance and space between us. I am seeking all my grandmother buried, all my mother rejected, all that Spain has silenced since its brutal civil war. It is my mother's abandoned life – her family, home and country – that draws me like an anthropologist or an historian to this place where I follow in her footsteps, stare through the bars on the gate of her girlhood school, walk through the bank that was built upon the wreckage of her family home, and wonder how and why. Here in Sevilla, I am seeking my inheritance.

So, without any claim or passport or inherent sense of homecoming or *patria*, I have traveled across the Atlantic to witness the pageantry of Holy Week in Sevilla. For one week, I have followed my *abuela*'s beloved Virgin de la Macarena through Sevilla's marigold-strewn streets. I've walked my mother's *paseo* of acacia trees. And I am piecing together a history of a time before my birth. Today, I will sit here, like my grandmother, twirling these beads, reciting the *Mater Dolorosa* like an incantation, calling on all the ghosts. On this Holy Saturday 45 years after my grandmother pleaded with la Macarena, I will sit vigil for these lives that have gone before. And on my own Holy Saturday, I will attend to the quiet and unseen transformation and pray that the metamorphosis is happening within me as well.

Stored in the names of my family are an historical memory held back by the clench of a nation's teeth, the hardened jaw, and ulcerated gut of generations sentenced to silence. This is my fiction derived from few facts. Here is my handful of names. And it seems only right that this story begins with the beginning, the dawn, with Aurora.

The First Sorrow: Prophesy

"... and Simeon blessed them and said to Mary his mother, 'Behold, this child is set for the fall and rising of many in Israel, and for a sign that is spoken against (and a sword will pierce through your own soul also), that thoughts out of many hearts may be revealed."

Luke 2:43-45

My grandmother first gives her heart to la Macarena on December 18, 1925, when the first *Besamanos*, the ceremony to kiss the hand of the Virgin, is celebrated. Aurora is fourteen, thoughtful and mostly kind. Though she is tall for her age, her gait is not ungainly; she is not awkward or uncomfortable in her body. She carries within an abiding knowledge that she is fully loved.

Aurora watches the world around her, wondering about those things that can't be seen. She is earnest and without judgment. Curious. Constantly questioning why things are such as they are, why things are done the way they are done, why these parents, this family, this city, this *barrio*. She could have been anyone, anywhere at all, but she is Aurora. She is her mother's wild child: always asking questions, always, "why can't I go to school like my brothers? Why do they always get the bigger portions at meals? Why do we give money to the Church when they are already so rich, and we are not?" Aurora's mother is often exasperated. So many questions.

At the *Besamanos*, the statue of the Virgin Mary la Macarena is wearing Her gold crown, a white *saya* embroidered in gold, as well as Her long luxurious black lace *mantilla*. She stands quietly as the mass is performed, yet la Macarena is not rooted on Her high altar. Instead, She is standing outside Her church, still within the gates of the courtyard, yet on the terra-cotta tiles amongst Her people. It seems everyone in the Macarena quarter has come to kiss the Virgin's hand, and from before dawn, the line snakes all through the working-class *barrio* in Sevilla.

Aurora waits in line, not patiently, but dancing on her toes to catch a glimpse of the Virgin as She extends Her hand to be kissed. Aurora's initial reticence has been replaced with a growing excitement. She sees that her friends are in line, everyone is. Even the men are waiting for this first ever opportunity to gaze, eye-to-eye, into the face of la Macarena. But the line is so long, and time is passing so slowly. Aurora starts a prayer, a mantra, to sing under her breath. "*Estoy aquí. Vengo*," more to remind herself that she is here, in this historic moment, the first *Besamanos*. Aurora is imagining touching Her hand, resting her lips however briefly upon Her sacred hand when Ana joins her. The two begin whispering back and forth just as they used to when they were in school together, before each had to start working in the dress factory.

"Does la Macarena have hair beneath Her *mantilla*?" asks Aurora as she flips her own dark curls with the backs of her fingers.

"Does She have ears?" Ana giggles in reply.

The girls are harshly shushed by the adults around them. So, they gather their restless hands in a knot between them and place their foreheads together as they imagine seeing, up close, the delicate stitching on Her robes, and wonder whether they might be able to touch the fabric, feel the heft. How will the embroidery compare to their own handwork? Perhaps someday they could get work in the famed Elena Caro Embroidery Studio, where the delicate *mantilla* for their beautiful Virgin was created.

Ana's mother calls and the girls kiss before she skips off leaving Aurora once again to her thoughts. The swelling crowds, the slow pulsing movement forward, the low hum of whispered prayers begin to fill Aurora. She rocks slowly, feeling the rounded curves of the cobbles beneath her feet, the soles of her espadrilles conforming to the stone.

It has been three hours, and Aurora is still waiting in line. Thankfully it is not raining, and it is not too cold. But still Aurora sways upon the hard stones beneath her rope-soled shoes, perhaps from fatigue, perhaps from her intent and purpose. She struggles to remain focused on her slow pilgrimage forward. "*Madre de Dios*," Aurora continues chanting, "*estoy aquí. Vengo.*" Over and over Aurora tells la Macarena that she is here, she is coming. Soon the words are not touching her lips, not moving her tongue, but simply swelling with her breath. The words become her breath. Aurora breathes in, "I am here." She breathes out, "I am coming." While shadows lengthen, Aurora continues breathing the words, "I am here. I am coming." She becomes less aware of time. There is a stillness within. She steps forward when the line moves forward. Yet she is still, completely still, even as she steps forward.

From an unfathomable distance and yet so near as to seem inside her, words. "*I hear you. Not much farther. You are nearly with me.*" The words sing softly in Aurora's ear. She feels the scented breath against her cheek, moving her hair.

Aurora turns to see who might have spoken to her, but there is no one. The women around her are either whispering quietly amongst themselves or they are locked away in their own private reveries. These women, stout black bundles bracing themselves on the ancient city walls or rocking upon the cobbles, seem oblivious to Aurora. Yet the words she heard were clear, unmistakable.

"*Señora?*" asks Aurora in the smallest whisper. A rose-scented breeze lifts, and the women around her pull at their shawls and tug at their beads. Aurora feels the perfumed air fill her lungs, an easy breath, nourishing.

Again, quiet but clear, "*I hear you. You are nearly with me.*"

She cranes her neck and peers over the shoulders of those ahead of her. Even in the movement, Aurora feels foolish. She thinks that she must be hungry or more tired than she realizes. She's hearing voices, smelling roses, and now looking over the shoulders of those ahead of her, to see what? Who?

But as soon as she sees the Virgin she knows. La Macarena de Esperanza is looking right at her. Her eyes are steady, penetrating, as though seeing something important in Aurora. And She winks. There is no mistake.

That evening, at eight, the order comes from the Bishop to close the gates of the church and prohibit entry to any more people. But his edict is futile for there are over 1,000 people still waiting to pass through the Macarena Gate and into the church courtyard.

As Aurora nears at long last, she wonders if the wink she saw was perhaps light glancing off one of la Macarena's crystal tears. She watches the Virgin's face, studies the shadow and light as it caresses Her jaw and glints off Her cheekbones. She admonishes herself for these doubts, but still she wonders, "why me? Who am I?"

Creeping closer and closer, she waits. As each person ahead of her takes their turn, Aurora looks for a sign that will prove beyond doubt la Macarena saw *her*, spoke to *her*.

At last she arrives, and she can hardly breathe. She is surprised to discover that she and the Virgin are nearly the same height. La Macarena always seemed a tremendous figure, a larger-than-life representation of Mary, the Mother of God. And yet here She is. Her hand reaching out to Aurora. Her posture slightly inclined as if to embrace. La Macarena's crown towers above them both, and it is at this gold aura that Aurora is staring when she feels la Macarena's eyes searching out her gaze, pulling her in. "*I am not this gold crown. I am not this fancy dress. Aurora, I am here. With you.*"

"You know my name?" her voice barely a breath.

"*I have always known your name.*" La Macarena is smiling an invitation.

Aurora is quaking now. She is afraid to take the statue's extended hand, but somehow, holding her gaze to la Macarena's tender face, Aurora reaches out and bends low touching her lips to the outstretched fingertips. She feels a tremble and a warmth radiate to her lips. Again, she smells a sweet perfume not unlike the roses in the María Luisa Park. Aurora feels the push and shuffle of those behind her in line. They have waited their turn and are nearly unable to contain themselves. They are so close. She hesitates perhaps a bit too long, and low grumbling begins.

"*Hija, anda.*" Voices are urging her to move along. "*Muévete.*"

She wants to turn to them, apologize and ask them to wait just a moment more, but her voice is lost to her and she can't take her eyes off those of her beloved Macarena. Aurora's breath is hinged in that moment between inhale and exhale when she hears the quiet voice again. "*Go now. Go home, and we will talk later.*" And with a slight nod from the Virgin, Aurora is released.

The way home is difficult. Aurora's legs threaten to buckle, and she leans heavily on the remnants of the stone city wall. Many of her neighbors are in tears, overjoyed at their own intimate exchange. Everyone is talking about the scent of roses that surrounds the Virgin, about the warmth of Her touch that seemed much too tender to their callused hands. Aurora, too, smelled the rose perfume, she too felt the warmth emanate from the Virgin, she too feels close to tears. But she doesn't hear anyone mention they heard la Macarena's voice.

~

It is estimated that more than 10,000 *Sevillanos* went through the gate to kiss the hand of la Macarena in 1925, and my *abuela* was one. It was the beginning of a relationship that would span decades. For Aurora, the *Besamanos* was the dawning of a sisterly bond that would sustain and guide her for the rest of her life. For the remaining 40 years of Aurora's life, she will come to la Macarena to tell Her everything. Not as a confessant, not seeking absolution or forgiveness, but as a friend might whisper secrets and concerns to her closest confidant. As Aurora chooses a husband, as she marries him in front of her family and friends, her most important witness is la Macarena. As each of Aurora's children is born, she will bring them to meet la Macarena. They will be christened beneath Her gaze, and She will be their most important godmother, their very special *madrina*. Through marriage, children, war, hunger, death and dictatorship; through all of her life, la Macarena is here.

~

Aurora's beads are now in my hand, and I clumsily and self-consciously caress each one trying to recite the first sorrow of the *Mater Dolorosa*. The beads are uneven, handmade from boiled rose petals that were rolled, then dried, and carefully strung with simple silver decade beads. A slender, silver cross with only the pierced hands and feet of an ebony Jesus is still attached. These beads, or others very like them, were effortlessly twirled in the fingers of every woman in my mother's family.

I read the first sorrow from the little book I purchased in the gift shop, Simeon's prophesy of the sword that will pierce through the mother's soul so that many thoughts out of many hearts may come to light. I wonder what this means for those in my family, and in all of Spain, who have left so much buried in the past, unspoken, unnamed, unclaimed, unresolved, unabsolved. Looking at la Macarena's tear-stained face, I wonder why, despite being troubled by the prophesies, She kept all these things buried, pondering them only in Her heart.

I imagine that when my *abuela* held these same beads that Holy Saturday the year I was born, the rosary slipped easily through her fingers. The silver decades cool between her callused fingertips in the late afternoon sun, and she rocked almost imperceptibly while her breath shaped the words of the first sorrow. "Behold, this child ... and a sword will pierce through your own soul also."

A slight shudder passed between her shoulders and she wrapped the black fringed shawl tighter before moving to the first rose petal bead and the Hail Mary, "... *Santa María, madre de Dios, Ruega por nosotros, Ahora y en la hora de la muerte. Bendita tú eres entre todas las mujeres. Bendito el fruto de tu vientre, Jesus.*"

~

These same words cross her lips as she worried these beads in 1936, the year before my mother was born, the year of the election, the war and the cold, brutal winter. This was her daily office, her habit shared with la Macarena. She did not attend the daily Mass at the church of San Gil, but my grandmother always arrived early morning, well before Mass, and sat at la Macarena's feet and prayed the *Mater Dolorosa*. Aurora took comfort that la Macarena, too, is a mother. Together they could commiserate and console, each a witness to the other. The Virgin knows how the day presses and how there seems not to be enough sometimes, and yet, at the end of the day, there is. More often than not, there is enough.

My grandmother, in 1936, is still a young woman of barely 25. Her eyes are framed by brows that demarcate a fierceness if need be, kindness always. Dark and absorbing, her eyes don't linger long before moving onto the next *cosa del día*. While they may seem to flit from one thing to another – for her days are full – her gaze is deep and discerning. Manuel often feels she is finding his very soul when she looks at him. But she tells her husband that it is not his, but her own soul she sees deep within his eyes. His parents always call him the pet name "Manolo," but she prefers his given name, Manuel, because it means "God is with us," and this she believes without reservation.

Her waist is still trim after bearing two children: her firstborn Esperanza, and little Manolito. Her narrow shoulders are stronger than one might imagine. Her softness shows around the edges of her lips, her stubbornness along her jawline. She is half a head shorter than my *abuelo*, but when she wears her comb, *mantilla*, and heels, she is his same height, and they stand shoulder to shoulder, eye to eye.

Together they are forging their family. They have two small children who are healthy and beautiful and bright. Times can be hard, but they are mostly good. Manuel works in a foundry, and she takes in washing and mending when ends don't quite meet. Their working-class neighborhood is full of family and friends, and they feel blessed.

On the morning of February 12, 1936, Aurora goes to church, leaving the children with her neighbor. There is nothing unusual about the day. The morning air is cool and slightly damp from the breeze off the Guadalquivir river. The humidity curls Aurora's hair along her temples, and if Manuel were walking alongside her, he would wind his fingers through the ringlets and gently tug. A slow smile passes across her lips.

She is smiling as she walks down the street, past the gated courtyards and patios, past the crowded homes of her neighbors, and toward the church. She pulls her shawl about her shoulders and takes care that her head is covered. The lace of her veil snags in a hairpin that is threatening to slip, and she deftly pushes it back into the tidy chignon. But the stray curls framing her face will not be contained.

Aurora steps onto the cool marble floor of the church leaving the early morning bustling sounds of vendors off to market: those loud men coaxing and coercing their mules and oxen with songs or switches; the beasts bawling out their protest; chattering women at the pumps, filling pitchers and buckets, gossiping. It's wash day, but she allows herself this moment to forget the cold slap of the wet laundry. She is anticipating her morning peace with la Macarena.

Having this time to herself, with the Virgin, brings a center to her day. So much of her life seems running after the two little ones, preparing meals, cleaning, mending, racing around in circles like the spokes in a bicycle wheel. But this time with la Macarena pulls her into the hub. After just a short time, Aurora can feel the knots in her shoulders loosen. She can notice a more soothing note to her voice. She always breathes easier. After her morning here, Aurora feels she can move outward from her heart, the core of her being.

As Aurora plunges her fingers into the icy bowl of Holy Water, she senses that something is wrong. The rings radiate outward from where her fingers touched, and Aurora's gaze also moves over the surface and is lifted from the edge of the basin to the sanctuary and the halos of incense circling overhead. La Macarena is not there. My grandmother's stomach coils at seeing the barren place where the statue of la Macarena should be. Aurora looks around as if perhaps She has stepped away from Her position of honor within the church walls. She has moved before, but usually not before Aurora starts praying. Always the scent of roses, always the gentle breeze, and always the simple clarity of knowing.

However, this time, la Macarena is nowhere in the church. A

quick scan of the nave, chancel and apse admits to this. But more, Aurora feels Her absence. It centers around her breath. Instead of the deepening almost intoxicating draw of incense-laced air into her lungs, Aurora's breath is abbreviated, high up in her chest. The others who have arrived at this early hour are looking at the emptiness and crossing themselves quietly. Aurora feels somewhat assured ... she is not the only one who doesn't see la Macarena.

My *abuela* starts to hear pieces of the conversations happening all around her. "It was for Her own good."

"Of course, it is only right! She must be protected."

In the narthex, there are the hushed whispers of looting as the women cover their heads with lacy *mantillas* and dip their fingers into the bowl of Holy Water.

"A fire would destroy Her."

"Do you really think it will come to that? Our own Macarena?" This last question is met with silence that brings Aurora's focus to her children, her family.

Lately, many churches as well as some homes of the affluent around Sevilla are being torched in late night marauding. Many of the city's poor and working class are at the end of their patience with the once again broken promises of reform, steady work, and raises in pay. The idea of a fair wage burns brightly in their hopes, and the well-fed priests and the rich landed gentry need to see the light; perhaps feeling the heat will help. And, the workers of Sevilla and all of Spain need to be reminded that in a few days, and with their votes, the election can change everything.

Aurora starts for home wondering, "but where is She?"

~

I know from my research that cloaked in darkness, just before dawn on February 12, 1936, one year before my mother's birth, the sculpture of the Virgin of Hope, la Macarena de Esperanza, was secretly moved from the parish church of San Gil to the private house of Don Antonio Román Villa, at 6 Orfila Street. Of course, no one knows that is where la Macarena has gone. That will be a closely guarded secret for many years, a secret that Her brotherhood, the anonymous confraternity, will keep even from their wives.

~

Five days later, the morning of February 17, 1936, is the morning after the general election, and tensions are running high as everyone waits for the results. The count has not been released, but the people had come from all over to vote. The surrounding villages, the poorest *barrios*, even those who are usually working too hard to take the time, voted. The streets are full of farmers, ranchers, workers from near and not so near villages awaiting the results. They sleep in doorways, they camp in parks, they crowd the bars and the plazas. And they wait for their voices to be heard.

All radios are tuned to Radio Sevilla. They are broadcasting loudly from windowsills and patios so everyone can hear when the news is announced. There is a stereo effect of sound as Aurora walks home from the church. She has been going every morning just to see if la Macarena has returned. She has not. Aurora knows that her vigilance does not go unnoticed, but she feels untethered, nonetheless. Her mornings with the Virgin have been her anchor. She feels dizzy, adrift. The radio announcer's voice bounces off stone walls and stone streets adding to her feelings of vertigo.

Once home she pulls her very own Esperanza close and sinks her face into her daughter's hair. Esperanza squirms and wriggles in her mother's embrace until she is turned face-to-face with her mother. She places her small hands on either side of Aurora's face and looking into her mother's smiling eyes Esperanza nearly sings, "now I can see you!"

"There is this," Aurora thinks to herself, this daughter who takes in the whole world through her dark gleaming eyes, only to give it away with a smile.

Aurora sits calming her jangled nerves and smells the dark unruly curls of her firstborn, her daughter named for Manuel's mother, but also for the Virgin de la Esperanza Macarena. It is Aurora's secret that in her heart, this daughter, her beloved Esperanza, her very Hope, is named for la Macarena and not for her mother-in-law.

There is not much time for these moments of tenderness – idle such as they are – and almost as soon as she embraces Esperanza, Aurora is scooting her away to go play with little Manolito who is sounding the beginning of his day from his crib. Esperanza grabs the baby doll she calls Francisco José and skips off to the bedroom she shares with her little brother. Snuggling her doll next to Manolito, she begins singing:

Tengo una muñeca vestida de azul
Con su camisita y su canesú
La saqué a paseo, se me constipó
La tengo en la cama con mucho dolor

I have a doll dressed in blue
With her little shirt and her lace shawl
I took her for a stroll, she caught a cold
I keep her in bed, she is in pain

Manolito claps along, his plump little fingers more often than not missing their mark. Aurora can't help but pause and smile at the two before making breakfast. She wonders why it is that nursery rhymes are so often about sickness and death. But she finds herself singing along with Esperanza:

Y esta mañanita me dijo el doctor
Que le de el jarabe con un tenedor
Dos y dos son cuatro
Cuatro y dos son seis ...
Ánimas benditas me arrodillo yo.

This very morning the doctor told me
To give her some syrup with a fork
Two and two are four
Four and two are six ..
Blessed souls, I kneel down.

Aurora stands and inhales deeply, pulling the air as far into her lungs as her persistent asthma will allow. Today is a good day, but she chews the aniseed anyway, one of the habits she believes helps her coughing fits. She ties the apron around her waist, protecting the flowered housedress she wears everyday but Sunday and begins to slice bread to fry in olive oil and garlic for Manuel's breakfast. She has set aside a pinch of sugar for Esperanza to sprinkle on her bread. Manolito is still mostly nursing.

~

I imagine, had I met my *abuela*, she would have pulled me close into her broad soft lap and held me as long as I wanted, playing with my hair, singing funny little songs with me, sprinkling sugar on my bread. She would have marveled at how I look like her second Esperanza, her little blond one with blue eyes. The one who lived. She would have encouraged my curiosity, my sense of wonder, all my many questions. She might have recognized herself in those questions. And these would not overwhelm her or frustrate her. Instead, these would have been qualities to celebrate. Grandmothers can nurture such inquisitiveness and enter into the discovering. Grandmothers can comfort like that. They have time enough, patience and love enough. Mothers are often busy, and the workday is never ending, and while there may be love enough, there is never time enough.

~

After my grandfather Manuel works his 12-hour day in front of the blazing furnaces of the foundry, he walks into his neighborhood bar. Rain is now splattering hard against the cold cobbles of the plaza. My grandfather is broad backed, with gleaming black hair and a jaw set against a mounting tension. His eyes are blue, like mine, and they shine like beacons from his soot-darkened face.

He sits in a whitewashed room at the back of the bar with his *vecinos*, neighbors, other men who have been anxiously reading pamphlets before burning them in late-night fires. Their conversation is low and strained as they talk about a world without the dictates of the Church or an imposed government. A world where each man alone would be his own private governor. Would it be so?

"Many turned up for the election," Manuel whispers as he pinches the pungent tobacco from the pouch he carries in his shirt pocket.

The radio, crackling, echoes, "The Spanish people came out in droves on Sunday, the 16th of February 1936. Nearly 10 million out of a possible 13.5 million voters cast their ballot, and the Popular Front won 271 seats out of the 448 in the Cortes." The announcer's voice registers an enthusiasm and gains volume as he resoundingly proclaims the election, "a clear victory for the Republic!"

The Popular Front promised amnesty, and the working-classes of Spain voted for that freedom and deliverance from centuries of oppression. In the bar, the men's voices also begin to raise in confidence, "¡*Oye, cállate*. Listen and be quiet" Manuel's hand is suspended over the pouch of tobacco, "there's more!"

This, at last, is the official result they have been waiting for, broadcast on the radio for all to hear: "the socialists are awarded 89 deputies, the Republican Left is awarded 84, the Republican Union has 37, and the Communist Party is awarded 16." All under the People's banner! It may be a volatile cocktail of leftist parties, but it is the beginning of democracy. Finally, a People's Republic.

Manuel strains his ear to hear more, squinting against the smoke and staring off into some middle distance, concentrating on the announcer's fading voice. But it is useless. The boisterous celebration only gains momentum and volume as the radio continues proclaiming victory for the working class and landless peasants.

My *abuelo's* friend Ignacio, his hat tipped to the back of his blond head, leans in as he pounds his empty glass down, "*¡Ahora!* Now, our government will bring about a change for our farmers, for our workers, and for us! Eh, Manuel?" His hat falls back behind him as he exclaims, "*¡Ahora es tiempo nuestro!* It is finally our time!"

Manuel is economical with his tobacco. It is a luxury he affords himself only after work is done, and he takes his time making his cigarette. He leans back in his chair and glances down only briefly to see that a leaf has escaped his grasp. He presses his forefinger on the stray leaf and flicks it onto the brown paper. Then rolling carefully back and forth, he presses the leaves into a densely packed twist.

Faces bloom blood red as cigarettes are lighted. The air in the bar quickly becomes blue with smoke. Dots of fire grow and diminish in the hazy light. The acrid smoke fills the bar, and Manuel's eyes water as his own cigarette smoke dances before him. Conversation is almost peripheral to this rite of smoking. The workday is over, and this moment is for exhaling. And the men like to see their breath. It reminds them they are alive.

All these men are laborers, workers in factories or foundries, holding two or more jobs. All are hopeful that the new government will allow for a distribution of wealth that is more equitable. All have not much else besides *esperanza* – hope – to hold onto. With families to support and wages so low, the rumblings of change seem to indicate a map, a topography of a land they do not yet know but are desperate to reach. A promised land, not of milk and honey, but perhaps a living wage.

Ignacio amplifies what each silently harbor, and his voice is resonant with hope, "Here, finally, is a chance to control one's own life and possess one's own soul." His arm is upraised, bent at the elbow, his fist pummeling through swirls of cigarette smoke.

~

My *abuelo* is not a tall man, but he carries himself as a towering figure. Not imposing but assured in his place and well-regarded. His jaw is square and broad and always lined with dark stubble no matter how often he shaves. He wears the uniform of every workingman, blue coveralls over a collarless shirt. A black felt *boina* covers his dark hair. The work at the foundry blackens his hands beyond the scope of soap and water, and his forearms are thick and heavily veined. The hair on his arms is singed so that he always has the scent of standing too close to the fire. His blue eyes beam from his darkened face, the lines radiating from the corners outward like star shine. His eyes are clear, a glass of cold water, and my grandmother Aurora loves how she can look into those eyes and feel nourished, completely quenched of a thirst she never knew she had.

When I first met him, I was eight, and I loved the smell of him. Tobacco, sweat, and that slightly singed smell, a burning incense that clung to him even after he bathed. It was the first time our family had returned to Spain since my parents and sister left in 1959. My mother's father, brothers and sister wrapped around her in a long overdue embrace that was breathtaking to witness. It was a homecoming as they reached out to include my sister and father. They hadn't seen each other in so long and much had happened. During those eleven years, my father had reenlisted in the Air Force, I had been born, we had moved from Oklahoma to San Antonio, my father had served two tours in Vietnam, and my *abuela* had died surrounded by her husband, her four sons, and my mother's younger sister. Those eleven years had folded like a fan they could tuck away, even if just for that embrace.

This was also the first time I heard my mother speak in her native tongue. Her voice was an exhalation of vowels like open arms, a silvery strand of song; her words escaped in an ephemeral fluency far from the halting confluence of consonants in the foreshortened phrases of our shared language. She and I had learned to speak English – my first language, her second – together. But I did not understand what this meant to our conversation until we arrived in Spain where I heard her trill her *Sevillana* tongue into words that wound around her family in something like warm laughter. This language provided an easy and effervescent return to someone everyone but I knew.

Sevilla was her city. For 22 years, Spain had been her country. Those strangers were her family. That, the home where she grew up. She seemed to come alive as soon as we arrived in Sevilla. My father smiled in recognition of his bride. My older sister, too, was embraced as the prodigal granddaughter returning to the city of her birth. My grandfather wept. Here was a place I had never been, a genealogy I did not know. Was all this mine as well?

Long practiced in the art of invisibility, I shrank to the shady corner of the courtyard where the pots of fuchsia bougainvillea overflowed in a fountain of riotous color. Watching these demonstrative people – my mother's family – pour out so much affection, I felt as though I might drown. Never before had I seen so much hugging and kissing; tears and laughter and voices colliding; it was overwhelming. I was overwhelmed. I stood there in the shadows and watched as my mother smiled, laughed and cried all at once. She moved differently. She was more fluid, loose and generous, embracing and touching, exhibiting a tenderness that was confusing to me. Her voice and hands were animated and alive in a way that pulsed a rhythm beyond what I knew. And I didn't understand.

Here was a warmth and intimacy that was missing in our exchanges in English. It was a familiarity that comes from sharing something fundamental like a language, home and history. Her taut jaw softened, and the hard lie of her mouth opened and then curled like the petal of a blossoming rose, and her tentative hollow voice filled with something resonant like happiness, something like song. I didn't recognize her, and this frightened me. I didn't understand anyone. I didn't recognize anyone. My mother, father and sister were wrapped in an embrace I felt no part of. But just as I had nearly completely faded into the stucco walls, the tendrils of bougainvillea wrapping around my arms and snaking through my hair, my *abuelo* turned and stepped towards me, took my hands in his and whispered, "*no te preocupes, preciosa.* Don't worry, I see you." And he danced me into the middle.

I was enchanted by this man, a complete stranger who I couldn't understand, who could see me. His eyes winked at me when no one else saw; his eyes drew me into the circle that surroundsed my mother and sister, a Venn Diagram in which he alone was the intersection. His eyes were like some expensive antique china with a blue pattern fading a little around the edges, bleeding into the white porcelain. I, like my grandmother before me, looked into those eyes and knew love.

~

Like many men in the Macarena quarter of Sevilla surrounding the church of San Gil, Manuel leans on the polished chestnut bar, smoking his hand-rolled cigarette and drinking his tumbler of *Jerez*, listening as the radio spits the news. The bar is dark. The air is thick, electric with expectation, with anticipation, and cigarette smoke. It will be an uneasy letting go of all the years of waiting. Waiting for something to happen, waiting for deliverance, for salvation. Yes, this new elected government is a People's Republic, and the people are out in the plaza now, beginning to openly speak about their newfound power. But underlying this new freedom is a tension.

Manuel remembers back in 1932, not a full four years ago, when tensions were just as high. Artillery surrounded a tavern frequented by known communists in his *barrio*. It was reduced to wreckage with more than twenty rounds of rapid fire. Children screamed as the oddly flat and deceptively benign sound of gunfire ricocheted against the plaster walls. Aurora, a new bride and just beginning to ripen around the middle in this first of an eventual seven pregnancies, raced indoors. She began pulling the washing off the lines that stretched across the patio from her kitchen window before closing the shutters against the violence.

In 1932, my *abuelo* was 22. He was old enough to be working in the foundry alongside his father, and he was keenly aware of the dangerous propaganda that circulated. Leaflets of clandestine origin, calling for the implementation of strikes, were being distributed in Sevilla. *Fist and Sickle, Revolution, Strikes*, were words one read in dark alleys four years ago but in 1936, they are whispered in bars just like this.

Manuel's hand is steady as he raises his tumbler and announces with the strongest voice he can muster, "Yes, anything is possible now. Everything can be within reach!" But his eyes are darting to the door, to the shimmering eyes of his friend, to his glass half-emptied. The cigarette smoke curls dusky halos around their heads.

~

The next morning, Sevilla shimmers white and gold. Everything reflects the feeling of a new start. The sparkling light bounces off the low, rolling waves of the Guadalquivir river. The river reflects the Torre del Oro in soft ripples, and the sunlight is only more blinding as it strikes the Giralda Tower. The Giralda chimes the hour and reveals to all who gaze upward the curvature of its Moorish minaret beneath the imposed bell tower. It once was an astronomical observatory, but now it is the bell tower of the colossal Cathedral whose intricate and lofty spires reach for the sky. It is said that from the top of the Giralda, one can just touch heaven.

Sevilla at heart continues to be indifferently Moorish. In its more affluent neighborhoods, the white houses with fountains quietly burbling in their courtyards gleam in the brazen southern sun. The massive wooden doorways studded with bright brass nails protect inner graceful arches and polished tiled mosaics. In the gardens and parks surrounding the Cathedral, the swaying palms and aromatic oranges that line the golden pathways are remnants of its Moorish past. But in the early dazzling light, the vast Cathedral looms, casting a slanting shadow over the plaza. Solemn and silent, the Cathedral is not yet bustling with the gypsies selling their blood-red carnations and prophesies. Only the partridges and sparrows flutter about brazen in the knowledge that they are safe from the hunters and the hungry as long as they don't stray from the porticoes and flying buttresses of the Cathedral.

Tuesday is market day, and everyone is out early in hopes of fetching the best their meager *pesetas* can buy. The neighborhood is a mixture of medieval grids, winding alleyways, and laundry lines stretching from window to window, linking buildings, linking the very lives of the inhabitants of the Macarena *barrio*. The narrow, twisting little streets enclosed by whitewashed houses with balconies crowded with pots of blood-red begonias and bougainvillea, all eventually wander to the marketplace. Carts pulled by emaciated horses or sharp-boned mules and oxen, and laden with onions and ropes of braided garlic from the surrounding country farms, lumber through the serpentine streets toward the market.

The air is a curious mixture of smells. The *panadería's* sweet yeasty aromas of fresh bread and pastries waft lazily through the streets only to be overwhelmed by the fish-monger's stall or the pile of dung left by the oxen pulling the poultry man's cart. Aurora walks through these streets noticing all these smells, but her expression does not change. These are the scents of her life.

Aurora squints her dark eyes against the glare of the morning sun, sidesteps a steaming pile left by some farmer's ox, and marvels at how the market seems differently busy. It is bustling with people talking, calling out to each other, clapping each other on the back and laughing loudly, emboldened yet still self-conscious, as though someone is watching. She likens the freedom and the feelings of liberation she herself feels to the release after an asthma attack, when the bands around her chest loosen and her breath succeeds in sustaining her, all the while knowing that the next attack will come again. It always does.

Reaching for the optimism that she sees all around her in her neighbors' faces and in their greetings to one another, Aurora pushes a wisp of her ebony hair out of her eyes. She sings, "*Buenos días*" to the fruit vendor perhaps a bit more forced than she would have liked. He bows low and offers his goods with a sweep of his arm. The Moroccan blood oranges and plump sensuous dates tempt Aurora, and she imagines offering tiny bites to her children but in the end, she nods her daydreaming aside and shrugs off toward the vegetable stand.

The fish monger calls out his *sardinas y boquerones* in this neighborhood. They are his least expensive offerings. The rag man is ringing a small bell to announce his arrival on the square. His wagon, rife with knotted scraps of old clothing and twists of cloth, in just a few months will be emptied. The knife-grinder shrilly whistles several long metallic notes that slide up and down Aurora's spine. Her knife, though somewhat dull, slices well enough for now. The coal merchant just stands idly in this neighborhood. He knows that in this *barrio* not many can afford coal for their braziers. These people will wait until he leaves, sending their sons and daughters to collect the small unsaleable pieces that fall from his cart.

Aurora pushes Manolito in the pram. Esperanza, ever her mother's little helper, points to the chicken coop and wonders aloud which will meet God today. "Chickens go to heaven, right *Mamá*?"

Inwardly, Aurora smiles at this little one who wonders about so many of the same things she herself thought about at that age.

She corrals Esperanza towards the vegetables and buys onions, garlic, and a pepper at a stall where a sullen old man slowly moves a smooth pebble from one side of his toothless mouth to the other. She knows this habit as her father used to do the same claiming it prolonged the taste of his drink. As a little girl, she tried this trick herself with a lemon drink she shared with her brothers and sisters. Of course, it didn't work. But taking a small sip and holding it under her tongue would fill up her mouth with the deliciously tart taste of lemons as if she had taken a mouthful. She still likes the pucker and shiver of lemons.

The vendor barely acknowledges Aurora's wide-open smile of good morning. His voice, gravelly and short, nearly bellows, "Take my word for it. All this is too new. We do not know how to breathe this air. Soon we will be as those fish." He points to the fish monger's stall, at the mackerel arranged there with mouths open and no air anywhere that can sustain them now. He mimes the gasping open close, open close, and laughs harshly at the bewildered look on Esperanza's face.

"But the people voted. We followed the procedure ..." Aurora begins to defend the new government and those who elected them, trying to push aside the mounting unease.

"This has nothing to do with the elected government," interrupting and nodding his head to a group of blue-shirted workers moving off toward their work at the factories. Manuel is among them. "They don't know these waters. And the oars are out of our hands, just like always."

She hears the vendor continue to mutter as she walks away. "There are already many cripples in Spain. And soon there will be many more. All we've done with this election is invite war."

Aurora moves her small brood to rejoin the others in the plaza. A low-slung freighter sounds a resonant note of lament as it sluices up the Guadalquivir. The dirge falls heavily upon Aurora.

~

That evening, during the *paseo*, Manuel laughs at Aurora when her hesitations threaten to dampen the festivities. Reveling in the news now feels premature to Aurora, like a pregnancy in the early weeks. But she takes his offered arm as they walk.

All through the neighborhood, children are running and singing. Everyone is talking loudly, laughing as if proclaiming this happiness, this hope, to the heavens. Manuel is holding Aurora's hand now, and he tickles her palm forcing a smile to dance across her face. The elation that is spreading throughout the *barrio* is contagious, and after a short while Aurora relaxes enough to take part. It is true, she thinks. They voted. The numbers are in. It is an overwhelming win for the Republic. She can't argue with the facts.

All the neighbors are out this evening, walking and talking in the soft air. The only difference is in the posture of the men. They seem to be taller, broader somehow. And the women, sensing a renewed vitality, are clucking about their boastful roosters. The friends stop a moment to stand under a lamppost. Conchi, Aurora's dearest friend and neighbor, is more like a sister. Just as their apartments share a common wall, the two share everything: childcare, food, soap, laughter, gossip. And Susana, like a beloved aunt who lives across the courtyard, dotes on the children with only the faintest hint of deep sadness at never being blessed with motherhood herself.

"You'd think they themselves were elected!" Conchi nudges Aurora and gestures with her chin at her husband. "Emilio says he helped sway the election when in fact I had to boot him out the door to go with me and vote!"

Susana chimes in, "So true! We are more responsible for the win by getting our men to fill in their ballots, not to mention voting ourselves!"

Aurora knows it's true. It wasn't easy getting Manuel to vote on Sunday because he, like so many men, had been working nonstop and wanted nothing more than to rest. But for her, it was the first time she had ever voted. Women had only been granted the vote five years ago. It was thrilling to fill in her ballot, to place it in the box, and to know that her voice counted. It was validating and magnificent. She feels taller herself.

Laughing and laughing, Esperanza can hardly contain her glee at seeing her parents smiling and joking. Her skirts are fluttering about her thighs while she runs circles around the adults as if she could lasso the moment. As if she could hold everyone together just like this. Aurora knows just what her daughter is doing because she, too, is spinning a gossamer thread around this moment of joy. But unlike Esperanza who is the embodiment of her name, Aurora knows a new day brings new moments, a new dawn. Aurora, too, is the incarnation of her name.

~

It is late March now, and my *abuela* is wearing her Sunday dress scooped modestly at the bodice, exposing her strong clavicle and just a hint of her ample bosom. Against her breast lays a fine gold chain with a medallion of the Virgin that slips under her dress. She is holding Manolito who has been fussy with teething these last days. The baby, just over one-year old now, plunges his little hand down between her breasts looking for the gold disk and drools a slow stream down her dress. Her hair is neatly combed back and gathered in her usual chignon. It is fine and textured, and the little curls that Manuel loves have escaped their pins. She has tucked a rose behind her left ear.

The orange and almond trees are blooming. The aroma is nearly intoxicating with the profusion of white, fragrant, night-blooming jasmine – *dama de noche* – and blue flowering plumbago climbing the stone walls. It is now well and truly spring, and Esperanza races ahead reaching for the falling petals and gathering them in her skirts. Esperanza whirls around, spinning round and round with her arms out, crying out that the earth is spinning, as if she is the still point. Aurora and Manuel walk side-by-side and in-step as Esperanza collects then tosses petals like confetti.

It is in this park that Manuel and Aurora first walked together not so many years ago. Chaperoned of course, but by a conspiring older cousin who looked away as they stole behind a rose covered trellis or behind a fountain. Aurora recalls stolen kisses and a line from a poem Manuel recited to impress her: "even the water inebriates us." Even when the rest of the city is dry, the park flourishes, and Aurora covets the roses. So many roses, all in the beginnings of their bloom at this time of year.

But closer to home they pass a man carrying a small coffin up on his shoulder. Aurora quickly looks away and crosses herself. Outside a neighborhood shop, small boys sit on the dirty stoop and sew hemp mats, their hands raw and blistered from the coarse rope. She squeezes Manuel's hand and pulls her Esperanza close.

~

Even today there is a photograph of Aurora that my mother keeps on her dresser. In it, my grandmother is standing alone in a rose garden in the María Luisa Park in Sevilla with her hand up to shield her eyes from the sun. The acacia and orange trees seem to leap from the image and spill their perfumed petals, beckoning to me. A single blossom plays against my *abuela's* ebony hair tinged with steel. She is older in this photograph. She has had all her children, and she has watched most move into their own lives. In the photo, her eyes are still and focused, reaching out to me, the granddaughter she never knew. The rest of her is blurred, wispy at the edges, as if she will not be contained within the borders of a print. Only the blossoming trees surrounding her and her gleaming eyes seem tangible. The photographer snapped a candid shot of her, perhaps called her name because she turns to the camera, arm upraised against the glare, and her eyes, vivid with a spark of menace mixed with anger, harbor a deep love.

Perhaps it was my *abuelo* Manuel who snatched that image of her. Or maybe my mother. I don't believe that she would have allowed any formal portraits to be taken of her. Photography was for the dead. To capture a living soul in a photograph, she would think impossible. A person is a living, changing being. Alive and new in every moment. And I understand her point; as soon as the flash fades, that moment is past, and both the perceived and the perceiver are changed, albeit subtly, by the moment preceding. But in truth, I've never seen a more soul-filled, vibrant photograph than that one of my *abuela*. I wish I had known her.

~

My grandmother pounds garlic under the steel blade of her knife. After a few strong whacks and some coarse chopping, she tosses it into the pan of shimmering olive oil. Her eyes water as she chops the onion. She crosses herself, glancing conspiratorially at the picture of la Macarena de Esperanza, kissing her thumb and tasting the sweet bite of onion. "These tears are nothing but onion," she whispers to La Macarena. "*Gracias por todo, Señora.*"

Aurora misses her interludes with la Macarena in the church. Every morning and for just those few moments when they knelt together, Aurora could feel full and at the same time empty. She was not *Mamá*. She was not wife and daughter and friend and neighbor. She was nothing at all, yet immensely full and whole, brimming. There is the church-sanctioned photograph of the Virgin curling along the edges that hangs above the doorway in the kitchen, and Aurora likes the photo to be in the kitchen since that is where she spends most of her time. It is in the kitchen that she cooks, washes clothes, bathes children, and of course, prays. She finds these womanly things bring her to a meditative place. The routine of scrubbing floors, chopping garlic, rinsing dishes, stitching up tears, or weaving together the frayed edges of moth holes becomes a ritual wherein her mind can hush. The picture of the Virgin is not breathing with the passion she feels when they are together in the nave but for now, she manages with the photograph. It is all anyone has.

After their supper of garbanzos in the weak mutton broth she has made from yesterday's leftover leg bone, Aurora and Manuel go out into the plaza beside the church to watch *cine*. All the neighbors are out; some having staked their claim of pavement well before dinner so they would be guaranteed a clear view of the evening's film. Manuel spreads a cloth and uses his jacket to nest a space for Esperanza and Manolito as they settle down beside Aurora. Aurora brings out some mending in anticipation of a little extra light from the projector, and it is her hope that the children will sleep while she and Manuel watch the film.

Sevilla, founded so long ago, was once a walled city with seven gates. There is a well-preserved section of wall in the Macarena Quarter where Aurora and Manuel live. Originally Roman, what remains of the wall is 12th century Moorish, a reminder that Sevilla was once the capital of the Moorish kingdom in Iberia. Once upon a time, Sevilla was one of the most strongly fortified cities in Europe. The walls were designed to defend the city against enemy attacks, but also to protect the inhabitants from frequent floods from the Guadalquivir. The Puerta Macarena is one of three remaining gates in the city.

These same ancient city walls that border the northern edge of Sevilla near the Macarena gate come into a more modern use on this late spring evening in 1936. A cotton sheet is hung from one of its pillars onto which a faltering shaft of light, flickering from an opposite window, projects the film.

The entire neighborhood, or so it seems, has turned out for the free show, some carrying buckets they will overturn to use as stools. Most like Aurora and Manuel, carry blankets. Still others look on from their windows or balconies. Children flock to the rooftops cooing and clucking like the homing pigeons housed up there. They hang in bundles from the trees; their dark heads shining like polished chestnuts. Esperanza is too wide-eyed to lie still and sleep. She watches the older children crack *pipas* between their teeth, eating the salty sunflower seeds and spitting the husks as far as they can. A competition ensues and bets are wagered, and Esperanza laughs and laughs between trying to spit.

Aurora wipes the dribble from Esperanza's chin and tries half-heartedly to rein her in. "*Mira, mija,* your doll. I think your baby Francisco José wants to lie down awhile. Why don't you come help him fall asleep."

"*¡No mamá, es una fiesta!* We are not tired. See, look at Francisco José. His eyes are awake!"

After the brief struggle, Aurora settles herself in beside Manolito who is snoozing happily in his little blanket cocoon.

The film they see is *Morena Clara,* a comedy in which a beautiful young singer, Trinidad, and her brother are judged because of their obvious poverty and homelessness. The crime they are accused of would mean imprisonment or perhaps even death. As the tension mounts and lives are hanging in the balance, the entranced audience hushes. And when the prosecutor walks on screen, the neighborhood heckles and whistles their displeasure. But when Trini dances on stage, everyone shouts "*guapa, guapa*" in appreciation of her beauty and her passion for life. She is a ready heroine for this crowd, courageous and full of heart.

As Trini's brother presses his cheek against his guitar and begins the rhythmic thrumming, Trini paces, tiger-like, across her stage, leading from her ribcage as if it were indeed a cage in which she is trapped. Her hand rests below her breast, and a subtle movement begins to travel from her clavicle down her spine to the soles of her feet. Trini sings and dances through her fears and finds that there is hope in just the act of dancing. While she moves through the complex cadence of the familiar dances, the women in the audience rise from their blankets and stools and begin their own unconstrained accompaniment, dancing the *sevillanas* with their cinematic heroine.

Aurora pushes aside her mending, stands and raises her arms to dance. She watches as her own little Esperanza mimics the movements. My *abuela* takes up her skirts in a grip that is strong and feels the music pulsing along with her own bodily rhythms. All movement is controlled in the staccato steps that raise small clouds of yellow dust, and her widely arced arms are supple and sinuous and fierce. Aurora feels fierce as she touches her core and allows the reverberations to quicken her step. Beads of sweat glisten on her brow, her upper lip. Moisture collects at her collarbone and finally succumbs, slipping between her breasts. Just when it seems she might lose control of her dance, she reins in the energy, concentrating it so that it becomes a forcefield around her, an invincible shield. It continues like this, a release and return, an unraveling and tightening, a yielding to the world all around her and then pulling that world deep within.

At the end of the dance, Aurora opens her eyes and she is standing breathless among all her friends and neighbors, her daughter laughing and twirling pirouettes around her still. Everything is as it was. Everyone is where they were. But glancing around self-consciously, she tugs at her dress and tucks a stray strand of hair behind her ear as she finds her seat next to Manuel.

The story continues and the crowd settles back in for the culmination of their hopes and dreams that have come to be embodied in the young protagonists: Trini and her brother. Thankfully the prosecutor fails to gain a conviction when the judge, won over by Trini and her authenticity, grants her a pardon. Then Doña Teresa, the mother of the accursed prosecutor, also charmed by Trini's singing and dancing, organizes a grand fiesta and invites her to stay as long as she likes.

As the end of the movie unfolds, the entire neighborhood, including Aurora and Manuel, are once again dancing and singing. The women swirling, arched backs and chins set, the men clapping out syncopated, percussive rhythms and shouting their encouragement. "*¡Anda, anda!*" and "*¡Olé!*" The revelry acquires a momentum too great to be tampered with. It is a gradual crescendo building over and against the established rhythm, a freeform expression without denouement.

For Aurora, the dance is a defiant stance stamping out worry and fear. It is the bold movement of staking out the ground beneath her feet. Each pound of her heel, "We live here!" Every strike of her toe, "I live here!" There is a posture of vindication the entire audience adopts as the music abruptly ends: chin up, chest forward, and shoulders squared. Backs become bridges arched over and beyond this moment here. Arms encompass family, community, city, life itself. Eyes spark defiantly. These friends and neighbors are, for the moment, assured that those with power, those with money, will come to realize the value of Trini and, by association, perhaps even the working-class people of the Macarena *barrio*.

The Second Sorrow: Persecution

"... behold, an angel of the Lord appeared to Joseph in a dream and said, 'Rise, take the child and his mother, and flee to Egypt, and remain there till I tell you; for Herod is about to search for the child, to destroy him.' And he rose and took the child and his mother by night, and departed to Egypt."

Matthew 2:13-14

The people's government sets to work to rectify centuries of neglect of the country's poor. In retribution for this new government's measures, the wealthy landowners take vast sums of capital out of the country. The exodus is devastating. An economic crisis ensues, and the value of the *peseta* rapidly declines damaging trade. With the cost of living rising, workers demand higher wages. Manuel's earnings barely feed his small family. Yet for others it is much worse.

Many factory owners attempt to blackmail the new leftist government by decreasing the work week to three days. There is less productivity, less revenue, less economic leverage. And because the workers were already struggling on full-time compensation, they are now literally starving. The leftist political parties and unions who fought to win seats during the election start organizing a series of strikes in Spain. The workers are caught in the middle of a devastating tug of war.

Even Manuel, who had pushed Aurora to believe that change was indeed possible and immanent, feels that something is stirring that is bigger than the plans of the newly elected government. Old and new organizations are sprouting up all over with propaganda of their own: the PSOE, Spanish Socialist Workers' Party; the PCE, Spanish Communist Party; the UGT, Socialist-affiliated Trade Union and more, all promising great changes through their collective efforts. For a while the working population stomach their hunger pangs with the knowledge that the owners and those in power are also not making any money off their labor. The union leaders instigate the strikes by explaining that loss of income is the only thing that will convince the factory owners to return to a full work week. But soon enough, the workers realize that the owners have more money than they need and can hold out without revenue much longer than the workers can live on no wages at all.

It goes on and on like this. A slow education in reform. A slow burn as rations are cut, wages are cut, food supplies are cut. My grandparents, like many of the poor and working-class people of the Macarena neighborhood, are wary of the different faces this reform takes. This new government has so many facets: communists, socialists, nationalists, fascists ... each vying for their position using the working class as collateral.

The days when the foundry workers strike, Manuel seeks work elsewhere so he can feed his family. But more often than not, he only finds more comrades spreading revolutionary ideas. He comes home with his pockets bulging with pamphlets and leaflets, but no money. The tracts are crudely printed on ash-gray paper made from old rags, coarse and so porous that the ink bleeds along tiny capillaries on the surface. But the pamphlets could have been the golden tablets handed down to Moses by God himself from the way they had been handed to Manuel. There is an urgency to the exchange, as if this simple transfer of information could change the world.

Hammers and anvils are evident everywhere. "Strike while the iron is hot," is the motto heralded in the factories. Manuel laughs his bitterness down because he is an ironworker. He works in a foundry. Striking iron while it's hot is what he does for his living. And his laughter turns bitter because there have already been strikes, and what have they produced? Nothing so far. In fact, everyone is in worse shape than when shorter work weeks were implemented. If there is another strike, then there will be no money at all. No money, no food. But Manuel cannot deny the call he feels from the bold drawings of heroic workers and the empowering intrepid messages on the posters plastered on the barber's window and on the city's wall at the Macarena gate. They seem to forge a new horizon to which he is drawn.

For so long Sevilla and all of Andalucía has been a squandered country of arid land. Acres and acres held by a mere handful of surnames. Generations of men whose vast estates have hardly been diminished since the Roman Empire continue to press laborers into service for less than a living wage. The reformers, both socialist and communist, are stymied when their proclamations and promises fall on bewildered and disbelieving ears. They haven't yet realized that what has been centuries in the making won't be easy to eradicate.

The spirited advice on the reorganizing of farms, fisheries and factories is exciting to Manuel as it is to all the laborers who work from sun-up to sun-down. The bucolic images in the pamphlets and posters speak to an archetypal aspiration within the workers. But do they dare to believe all this is possible? Rich golden harvests? Irrigation? Loaves and fishes enough for all to have a belly full? A full day's pay for a full day's work?

Yet the pamphlets and posters pasted on walls and buildings don't stop at showing the glowing golden fields of wheat; they also tout that the workers are completely divorced from any ownership of the means of production. The posters inform, if somewhat pedantically in Manuel's view, that the workers are divested from the power and material possessions that are rightfully theirs as fruit of their labors. This harsh exploitation of workers, he is instructed, is the cause of the workers' degradation to what the socialists regard as a mere "animal-like existence of eating, sleeping, procreating, and working." Thus, the workers are alienated from not only material goods and possessions, but from themselves. Heady proclamations to those who live the reality.

Manuel holds this tension and tries not to bring his apprehensions home to Aurora. Sometimes she worries so much that her asthma acts up. Sometimes she is all questions, not satisfied with the answers he can give. He thinks it's better this way. But she always empties out Manuel's pockets before folding his work clothes over the chair. She sees the neatly folded tracts and does her worrying anyway.

Later in the evening, Aurora burns the pamphlets in the brazier. She is afraid of so much change and of taking it for granted. She is afraid of the cost. Afraid of what the vendor with the pebble in his mouth forewarned. Who were they, after all – the people, the workers – to expect so much? She burns them for the little warmth and the comfort they offer, and because there is so little else to burn.

~

On April 5, 1936, the statue of La Macarena is returned to San Gil. Again, Her movement is under the night sky. And Her movers are darkly cloaked, with the long hoods of the penitents. Upon Her return, there is no great fanfare, no welcoming parade. However, the entire *barrio* is electrified with the news. She is just where She belongs, on the morning of the fifth, as if She never left. Easter is on the twelfth this year, in just seven more days, and there is much to do to prepare for the Virgin's pilgrimage through the streets of Sevilla. But before all that, before Aurora can think about Holy Week, she rushes out of the house, towards San Gil, to sit with la Macarena. There is so much to talk about.

As soon as she sets foot in the church, Aurora can feel la Macarena's presence. The church is abuzz with activities as the floats for la Macarena and *Jesus de la Sentencía* are decorated with countless white roses, carnations and four-foot tall ivory candles. The *Hermandad*, the confraternity that cares for and supports la Macarena, is busy counting the hundreds of cartons of candles. Some of the brothers will hold the tall pillars as others stoop below the float to carry upon their backs the Virgin as She journeys through Her city during the *Madrugá* on Good Friday.

Her *paso de palio*, the float and the canopy that protects Her, is supported by slender silver columns that sway gloriously as She is carried through the streets by Her *costaleros*. Aurora thinks of these men, barefoot, hunched over, carrying such an enormous weight and an invaluable treasure upon their backs. For twelve hours the men slowly amble over the cobbled streets, resting now and again as the crowd roars their devotion or as a *saeta* is sung in Her honor. Aurora imagines the weight on her shoulders, her feet curving on the cobbles ... what she would give to be able to carry la Macarena.

"*You carry me in your heart. That is where it counts.*" It's a voice Aurora hasn't heard in two months. The Virgin is laughing as She climbs off the altar and over the velvet ropes. "*Besides, I'm too heavy! These robes!*"

"Yes. I do, but these past months, I thought ... I haven't been able to ..." La Macarena's absence was real, and the absence was in Aurora's heart as well. Aurora takes la Macarena's arm so She doesn't trip over the stanchions placed to protect Her. "Be careful!"

"*I know,*" the Virgin comforts. "*Estoy aquí, I am here, Aurora. Tell me everything. Anything at all.*" She sits right next to Aurora. Removing Her crown, She turns Her neck this way and that to loosen the strained muscles.

Aurora explains about the posters and propaganda. She confides that she is worried for Manuel, afraid that he thinks he has something to prove. Sometimes he crosses the strike line when they have run out of money. Then there are the arsons, the looting, the strikes. "The *guardia civil* has ramped up their numbers and they think nothing of random searches and midnight rides in their trucks. No one ever returns. People are disappearing. You disappeared!"

"*Yes.*" Her voice is soft and emanates from inside the walls, the floor, even the air within San Gil. Aurora almost feels Her voice, more than hears it. The slow vibrations like gently yielding waves of light against her skin.

"They took You away because there were threats to burn the church. Other churches have been burned to the ground. Everyone is so angry that reform is taking so long. And so afraid, too." Aurora reaches out as if to touch la Macarena's robes, "I am grateful nothing happened, but mostly that You are safe."

Morning light filters through the windows. Within the slanting shafts of light, motes of dust shimmer and spark, and the smoke from incense and candles twists and turns like spirits overhead.

"*I am. I am here now. With you always.*"

Aurora shifts slightly in her seat. She so wants Her to understand. "Yes. But I feel the world is changing. Something is happening and people are restless for the election to mean something. I can feel the earth tremor." Aurora looks up at the Virgin's crystal tears, "whatever is coming, it has a heavy, menacing footstep."

Aurora closes her eyes and slowly exhales, deepening her breath, trying to slow her heart. Inside she is so still but her heart beats on, her heart pulses and her lungs fill and empty. Her breath comes and goes. This juxtaposition within her body astonishes her, the stillness and the stirring. An unflagging flame beneath the flutter of wings.

La Macarena shifts Her weight and Her embroidered robes undulate into a dizzying pattern. "*We can bear almost anything when we know we are not alone. Even these times of trouble. They come and go. Only connection lasts. It is what sustains us.*"

They are quiet for a time while Aurora basks in the comfort of being with la Macarena again. She touches her beads that are always in her pocket and starts the Seven Sorrows of the *Mater Dolorosa*. But today my *abuela* can't seem to get past the second sorrow in the litany. Over and over the words play across her mind: "Herod is about to search for the child, to destroy him." The only lesson she can glean is that it's always the children. It's always the children who suffer most.

~

Sitting in my grandmother's church, I pause over this second sorrow. I roll the silver decade between my thumb and forefinger imagining the devastation my *abuela* will endure. Her life will meet and follow the same course as the Virgin's for a while. She will experience the loss and pain, and eventually – and for a long while – she will lose the hope that la Macarena embodies.

It is always the children who suffer and when children suffer, so do their mothers. I think of my *abuela* and my mother. Their pain is present still despite their attempts to bury it; I ache with it. Sitting here in the basilica of la Macarena, I want to hold their anguish and their grief so that I can better understand the legacy that has shaped me. But I also want to be held. I want to be swept up, claimed, validated.

I know I am tired. It has been a long week full of Holy Week processions and pageantry and nagging jet lag. The repeating words of the rosary are whirling. The heavy thick scent of candle wax is overpowering. I don't know if I belong here. I don't know where I belong.

I return to the second sorrow, two generations removed, a lifetime apart. The only difference is that I know some few facts of what is to come: loss of life, loss of hope, loss of faith. And then a turning, returning to what sustains. I sit just where my *abuela* sat, in the same pew at the foot of the statue, and I ache for her. If I could console, if I could be comforted in turn by her, what might be different? What might have been different? I wallow in the second sorrow until I am distracted by a light glinting off la Macarena's crystal tears.

~

Holy Week in 1936 is especially poignant. Not only are churches being burned and looted, but statues are being defaced by the frustrated and hungry workers. Jewels have been stolen right off some of the famous Virgins. Gold and silver from the *pasos* stripped and sold, probably for food or medicine, but still, my *abuela* cannot abide looting in this way, whatever the reason.

The morning she sits with the Virgin, it is clear my *abuela* is troubled. *"Aurora, is your heart so big we can't fill it?"* La Macarena teases as She steps off Her altar.

"Sometimes I'm so angry I lose myself. I lose you."

"I am never lost and you, Aurora, are a fish swimming about in sustaining waters always thirsting for more," la Macarena laughs as She nudges my grandmother with Her elbow.

But Aurora thinks la Macarena doesn't understand. She tries to explain how she saw their neighbor Pacheco atoning publicly like everyone else on Palm Sunday. "But he is the one who is handing out papers calling for violent revolution. He is the one who is saying that bloodshed is the only way to seize the farmlands, that our government is moving too slow. And he denounces the Church for being complicit in keeping the working-class poor. Maybe he is burning the churches!"

"Does Pacheco seek peace?" the Virgin replies, shrugging. *"Does he need absolution? I think he belongs just as much as any of us."*

"You had to go into hiding! Do they deserve solace?" Aurora can barely contain her exasperation and scrapes her fingernail along the wooden bench.

La Macarena takes Aurora's hand and squeezes hard, *"Aurora, you come to me, but not to mass. You confide in me, but not in the confessional. Tell me, are you loyal to the Church?"*

"But I don't go around burning churches!" Aurora pulls away to face la Macarena fully.

"No, of course not," la Macarena stares right back.

"And do You think they won't do it again? They will. Statues are being burned. You might be next!" Her fingers grip the rosary, straining the links to the point of breaking.

La Macarena leans back against the pew and tilts Her face up to the ceiling. Closing Her eyes, She asks, *"Is your concern for the state of these men's souls, the Catholic Church, or is it for me?"*

Aurora's head aches with questions she can't answer. The Church commissioned the sculpture of la Macarena. The Church teaches the story and provides the lesson, but it also thrives by turning a blind eye to the needs of the faithful. It preaches against sin when stealing food is the only way some can eat, including Pacheco and his family. The Church pronounces pious ideals as their priests live warm and well-fed lives while many have no coal, no stove, no bread. How does one reconcile these discrepancies?

"You are my church," Aurora whispers at last, knowing that she is not the only person who holds this faith. Her hands fall open in her lap, her rosary lank across her lap.

La Macarena nods as She takes the rosary from Aurora and works a cat's cradle that transforms into a chalice, "*There is a reciprocal relationship between God and you, and you choose to mediate through me, through our relationship. Your emotional response to me opens a dialogue between you and God deep in your heart. It is so for everyone in their own unique and individual way.*" She weaves the rosary on Aurora's fingers showing her how to make the chalice.

"I don't understand. Relationship?" Aurora copies the fingering easily.

La Macarena reaches in and pinches a strand and flips the rosary back into Her hands showing the chalice turning into a flower that opens petal on petal. "*You yourself, your heart, sharing your heart with others is your church. That is church. Everything begins and ends with you.*"

~

I arrived in Sevilla on the Saturday before Palm Sunday. As I handed my blue U.S. passport to the official, I smiled. It's probably a default reflex all over the world: when in an unfamiliar situation, smile. But he didn't look up as he thumbed through the pages. As he scanned the passport, he asked if I was visiting Sevilla for business or pleasure. I fumbled my response and said, "neither."

At this he paused, and I held my breath while berating myself for not choosing one of his very simple options. He looked at me over his glasses and with one bushy eyebrow cocked in question, "Neither? Then why are you here?"

"I am here for Holy Week. *Semana Santa?*" I stuttered as I pulled my house keys from my purse and then dropped them in again. I wouldn't need them here.

His expression softened, and he pronounced me a pilgrim. "There are many of you, people not from here but not quite tourists. Like you said, 'neither.'"

He found the first page and opened it wide before stamping it with such force and flourish that I jumped. He laughed at me and wished me a good stay. "*Gracias*," I said as I turned to walk through the terminal and toward the taxi stand.

But I am not a pilgrim, and this is not a spiritual journey. By rights I should be equally at home in Spain as I am in the United States. Stepping off that plane should have felt like a homecoming, but it didn't. I should be able to understand the taxi driver, but I can't. I should know my way around these streets, but I don't. I didn't tell my aunts, uncles, and cousins I was coming because I've only met them once a long time ago, and I needed to be here alone. I needed to feel this earth beneath my feet. I needed to find my grandmother who died before I could know her. I felt like the foreigner I am. I felt like a tourist looking for home.

I held these beads when I watched yesterday's Good Friday processions, the *Madrugá*. I imagined I was following in the footsteps of my *abuela* as I followed la Macarena through the streets. I fingered them as la Macarena made Her *salida* carried aloft by Her confraternity. As She swam above Her adoring devotees, they parted around Her like a current allowing Her to pass, then deftly again filled in Her wake. She seemed to shimmy and sway to the trumpets' blaring fanfare. Her face was aglow with the candlelight, and when She passed through the gates, thousands applauded Her beauty.

On coming out of the Cathedral near the Giralda, I saw the golden light of dawn caress Her brow. For so many, this is the procession to be followed the length of its entire route as She levitates around the Plaza de la Encarnacíon, down Feria Street, and in the great square opposite the Central hospital. I think of the men who carried la Macarena for twelve hours yesterday, the *costaleros* who bore the *paso* through the streets, through the darkness. I wonder if those men felt their burden ease as the crowd reached in. For a moment during the *Madrugá*, it appeared as though the *pasos* were borne on the shoulders of every man and woman in Sevilla. I, too, tried to walk along with Her, pausing at times for a *saeta* to be sung, holding my breath as She traversed a particularly tight alley. But also, and more, because my grandmother so loved la Macarena. She walked this route, and I wanted to walk in *her* wake.

~

The heat is beginning to stifle Sevilla. In 1936, the big fiesta and horse fair that is the Sevilla Feria is smaller, less joyous than in years past. Men trudge about with loosened collars, seeking out the shady side of the street. The women carry their fans and wave them across their bosoms, moving the still air like hot breath across their skin. In the evenings, the doors of the houses open and everyone comes out on the streets to sit in the cafés or sit out on the pavement on chairs they've brought from their homes. The scent of the small green flowers adorning the night blooming *damas de noche* wafts in through opened windows. Jasmine overwhelms the thick evening air.

Weeks pass before Aurora first hears the words "war" and "revolution," but within 24 hours of that first anguished whisper, people begin preparing for the worst. First-aid kits containing gauze, bandages, topical ointments, iodine, and antiseptic creams are sold on the streets as the hawkers take advantage of the hope turned to fear. The rag man quickly runs out of discarded cloth to tear into bandages. Neighbors begin to salvage clothing, bed linens, anything cloth that might staunch the bleeding. Guns are smuggled from house to house in an effort to thwart the *guardia civil.*

The foundry is firing full force now. My *abuelo* is commissioned to repair the weathervane on top of the Giralda. I know poets have described the Giralda as a *Mudéjar* tower with a Christian crown. And this crown is called "*giraldillo.*" The slender bronze statue is said to represent Faith, but most in Sevilla call her Santa Juana. She holds a flag in one hand and a palm leaf in the other to indicate the direction of the four winds.

From the top of the Giralda, my *abuelo* watches twilight deepen over Sevilla as the sun sinks. He doesn't notice the delicate lace work of brick that covers the four walls of the Giralda. He doesn't notice the architecture that seems to defy gravity. Instead, he stands amid the pinnacles and spires he has seen all his life and looks out over his city. He sees his *barrio*. He follows the streets to San Gil and then south to the Maestranza district where his fires are burning. On the way, he passes the Cathedral's carved lace stonework in the classic *Mudéjar* lozenge pattern called a "*sebke*," a confluence of Roman, Moorish and Catholic design. Despite these layers of history, my *abuelo* sees only his home.

The sky over Sevilla is gold and red with a dusky purple where the slanted light lays upon the faces of the crowded houses of his neighborhood. The huddled houses of the Macarena *barrio* look as if they have been dusted with golden pollen, so a soft haze dulls the slicing light of the setting sun. There below him are the houses and apartments of his neighbors and his family, and he is here, strapped onto the Giralda repairing Santa Juana's palm leaf, wondering what new era this wind will usher in.

The next day, my *abuelo* gets word that the Bishop has requisitioned wrought iron gates for all the side chapels in the Cathedral.

He wants *rejas* to be placed as iron gates in front of the priceless art and artifacts: the sculptures and silver- and gold-plated altars of the Cathedral. The wealth of the Cathedral nearly outshines the sun in Sevilla. Aware of the mounting antipathy the poor have for the wealthy Church, the Bishop chooses avarice instead of compassion.

Manuel shares in the frustration and disappointment his *barrio* feels in the Church. The chasm between those who have and those who have nothing is vast, and he see no way to build a bridge. But as a result of the talk of war and revolution, he is promoted, given a small pay increase, and is commissioned to design the wrought iron gates that will protect the Churches' vast riches from disgruntled workers just like himself. The Bishop has specifically requested Manuel be the chief blacksmith on the project, proclaiming "his artistry as a *rejero*, his excellent use of symmetry, and his sweetness of line." My grandfather will be able to feed his family.

"It's my job, Aurora. It's what puts food on our table," he knows the argument Aurora is about to make as she collects their dishes from the table. He tilts his chair back and begins to roll a cigarette. He will patiently listen as she gives voice to his own struggles.

"But for the Church to ask the foundry for such a thing ... instead of helping us ... it's beyond me how they can make such a request of the people they have ignored and continue to neglect. Don't they see the children with their ribs like the bars they want you to make?" Aurora places the dishes down and fills a pot with water for washing.

"You're right. But for them this is national treasure, not a pocketbook of *pesetas* for the poor." Manuel's hands are thrust deep into his pockets, and he finds a hole there. He makes a mental note to tell Aurora later when she is not so angry.

"That's not the point. By commissioning bars on our national treasures, by spending money to protect our altars, our chalices, instead of feeding us, that's the point. If they used that money to feed our children, they wouldn't have to protect *their* gold." Aurora stokes the ashes in the kitchen fire and puts the pot of water on to heat.

"I will be working, Aurora. I know it is a hateful thing, but I will be able to work." He rocks his chair forward and lights his cigarette. The irony is not lost on him.

~

The coming coup against the elected Popular Front government will be comprised of the Church, the Spanish monarchists, fascists, landowners, Adolf Hitler and Benito Mussolini: money, might, and muscle.

On May 10, 1936, the duly-elected leftist president Manuel Azana assumes his new position, replacing Alcala Zamora. Not many days after, Spanish Army officers, including a small rotund General named Francisco Franco, begin plotting to overthrow the newly elected president. The weeks leading towards summer are hot under the glaring sun, and except for the radios in the bars crackling with political speeches, the city is stony silent.

After his first full week of work in months, Manuel goes to the bar. A beggar at the door holds a withered arm against his breast and his other hand outstretched, palm up. The infirm and maimed never find work in times like these. There are too many able-bodied men who are hungry. The sight of blind and maimed people leaning against a wall or sitting in front of doorways or shuffling through the streets at all hours and in all seasons is nothing new. Because there is no aid for the indigent or ailing or unemployed, these men and women and even children are left to beg their existence on the streets. Most are homeless or live in the shanty towns on the outskirts of town. What taxes are paid go directly into the pockets of the ministers instead of into public assistance. It is common to see the poor selling lottery tickets, contraband cigarettes, matches, trinkets, "a small service for a small coin." But with war imminent, their plight can only worsen.

My *abuelo* leaves a small coin in the outstretched hand of the bent man at the door. It's not that Manuel feels generous, he just knows that so many have even less than he. His work has increased, but most are still on shortened weeks or on strike, or somehow broken like this man.

The man bows low and coughs out his beggar's blessing without raising his eyes, "may your shadow never grow less."

Manuel's shadow, once just his own, now encompasses his wife, his two children. He appreciates this blessing now more than ever. "*Gracias, hombre. Gracias.*" Manuel searches out the man's face. The creases around his eyes indicate a life lived merrily despite the now vacant cast.

Entering the bar, Manuel hears immediately the concerns of his friends, "even the Church is rallying to the fascist cry!" Paco's voice is rough, angry. "What of our election? What of our government?" Manuel knows that his coworker has been frustrated. Paco is a young man barely 20-years old. He is brash and sometimes arrogant, but he was active in campaigning for the socialist reforms. And he is anxious to see results. For this, Manuel gives him due respect and some allowance for his passions.

The barkeeper nods in Manuel's direction and pours him *un dedo*, a finger's width of *Jerez* in a small glass. "Did you read about Franco this morning? He was reported to have been seen just beyond the Macarena gate." As Juan fills him in on the discussion, Manuel opens his pouch of tobacco slowly, allowing his eyes to adjust to the dim light. Juan keeps the chestnut bar front polished, and it glints sharply from the sun when the door opens. Across the bar top, there are rubbed depressions where countless forearms have rested. Manuel fills the paper with tobacco more from feel than from sight.

"Ah, he's only here because we have the finest riding horses not to mention the most beautiful women. Too bad he missed la Feria. He could have seen the best of the best," says Ignacio, winking conspiratorially at Manuel and finishing his drink.

Placing a napkin around the neck of the bottle, Juan pours another drop into Ignacio's glass. But not too much because Ignacio runs a high tab. "Have you heard he's now saying that he was christened in the Cathedral? It's not true, of course. He just wants to be a native son," replies Juan.

"Yeah, but who doesn't?" asks Ignacio, downing the pour in one gulp, grimacing and shuddering as the burn fills his core.

"No, don't you see? He thinks we're easily duped. He wants a way to win us over without a fight," says Manuel as he dips his finger into his glass of *Jerez* and runs it along the rim. A shrill ethereal song lifts from the glass.

The door opens and the intensity of the sun outside flashes their faces casting their features in deep chiaroscuro. "Only because he knows we'll give him a fight. One he won't easily forget!" Hammering the polished bar, Ignacio grabs at the front of his pants and thrusts his hips forward, "this is how we'll get things done in this country! With *cojones*!"

"Oh, is that true? Have yours descended yet?" Juan can't help poking fun at Ignacio who remains unmarried despite countless introductions and his careful attention to grooming.

The bar explodes into laughter. Yet the tension is high. Manuel can feel it in the atmosphere like the cigarette smoke. "All the papers call him *El Caudillo*, the boss. If Franco takes over the army, he will bring his friends the Moors," Manuel adds. "Not to mention the Italians and Germans." His finger still circles the rim of his glass, though the sound has faded.

"Well, he speaks Arabic like a native. All those blood-thirsty Moroccan troops will be on his side. They cut off heads you know," shudders Juan, crossing himself. "God help us."

"God has nothing to do with this! This is for us, the people, to fight," argues Ignacio, raising his fist. His hair falls forward into his eyes and he quickly runs his fingers through in a practiced and fluid motion.

One thing about Ignacio, his spirit and love of Spain are undaunted by the rumors and reality all around them. Manuel envies him this. Ignacio succeeds in mustering enthusiasm in the quorum. Grunts of affirmation give way all around as they take on their enemy in imagined battles that swirl with the cigarette smoke.

But Paco, in a voice that silences them all, says "the day Franco is accepted as *Caudillo*, there will be war."

~

Aurora stops often in the plaza, staring up at the sky as though expecting to see some great proclamation written across it. The gypsies collecting and hovering at the edges all buzz with premonitions of doom as well as potions, elixirs, and talismans to keep dear ones protected. The regular card-readers and fortunetellers performing in the markets and in front of the Cathedral have switched from telling the sex of the coming baby to prophecies concerning the coming war. Will your family survive? Will your home be destroyed? Will Sevilla fall to Franco?

"They sell death in one hand and salvation in the other,"

Aurora thinks to herself as she hurries past the gypsies careful to avert any stray evil eye. But still, she glances back over her shoulder knowing full well that most in her neighborhood would say the same about the Pope. At least the gypsies display their wares on the street corners, out in the open.

~

Some thirty-five years later, when I lived as a child with my family in Spain, my mother warned me to be good, to be quiet and not attract attention, "the gypsies like blond, blue-eyed children. They may come in the night."

The idea of a gypsy coming in the night to steal me away was both terrifying and exhilarating. I would burrow under the blankets and stay as still as a cornered mouse, barely breathing so the covers wouldn't rise and fall and give me away. I knew the stories about gypsies: that they wandered in caravans and slept in camps, that they didn't belong, that people like my mother didn't like them, that they had no real home. But I also wondered what life I might have with them. Would I learn to dance? Play the castanets? Would I get to wear those ruffled dresses? Would they really want me?

My mother's warning always left me feeling alone, alienated from her, but thrilled that the gypsies might want me. I always imagined my sister being safe from these threats, being dark like my mother, with similar flashing hazel eyes. She seemed to belong to my mother in a way that I never could – the two of them in a fierce embrace. The gypsies wouldn't dare take my sister.

~

All that spring and early summer of 1936 there is a flurry of fact and fiction to sift through. Aurora hears rumors of General Francisco Franco leading rebel uprisings. Then there is other news of his death, brought down somewhere over the Alboran Sea. Some attest to his being arrested and assassinated after being accused of all sorts and sordid crimes. Others say he is in Morocco sleeping it off with his harem.

Aurora's worries keep her sleepless many nights. She imagines foreboding origins to the various sounds of the night. A cat yowling is a desperate cry for help. An engine backfiring is gunfire. Often Aurora races to the window only to see the lamplighter making his rounds.

One such night, well before dawn, Aurora sees la Macarena outside her bedroom window. The Virgin is wearing only Her white linen undergarments, no gown, no mantle, no gold crown. And Her hair is unbrushed and hanging in Her face. My *abuela* is startled to see la Macarena not wearing the fine cloak of heavily weighted silk intricately embroidered in green and gold. Aurora imagines that the mantle weighs so much that la Macarena must be glad to be out of it, not to mention that six-pound gold crown. "But to be out at night in only Her underclothes and with Her hair exposed!"

When Aurora was much younger, la Macarena did not have the magnificent robe that She now wears. She wore a mantle everyone called a "*camarona*," so coarsely woven that many likened it to a shrimp net. Aurora remembers when every family received a highly embossed letter from Her Royal Highness Doña Esperanza de Borbón petitioning each Macareno and all of Sevilla to help pay for la Macarena's new *mantilla*. She had commissioned the esteemed embroidery artist Juan Manuel Rodríguez Ojeda to create a masterpiece for Sevilla's most revered Virgin. And Aurora put all she could from her sewing money towards the collection to replace the ugly *camarona*. *Centimo* by *centimo*, enough was raised in the poorest *barrios* of Sevilla to purchase the fine mantle for la

Macarena. She wore it for the first time in 1930. Since then, la Macarena is rarely without Her mantle of emerald green and gold. And no one except Her dressers has ever seen Her in Her fine lace undergarments. Until tonight.

At first, Aurora is not sure if she is dreaming. Pinching the back of her hand, she looks down and sees her rough cuticles, the ragged nails. Washing laundry and scrubbing floors takes a toll, but sewing, too, dries out her cuticles making them sharp little thorns that catch on the cloth. Tucking her fists inside her sleeves, Aurora again looks out the window and sees la Macarena, like a ghostly manifestation, flipped onto Her belly and slung over someone's shoulder, racing away in the otherwise dark and deserted night. Her long chestnut hair falling across Her face. Her pale articulated arm rising and falling as if She is blessing Aurora. Or waving goodbye.

She hears la Macarena call. *"I am in good hands. Don't worry."*

But of course, Aurora will worry. The Virgin is never without Her mantle and cloak, and never without Her entourage, the hooded anonymous Brotherhood. And She is trailing scattered rose petals in Her wake; anyone at all could follow Her. The intentional soundlessness that fills the night is discomfiting. Aurora's breathing becomes shallow and a lightheaded feeling brings her back to bed. Aurora breathes a Hail Mary. She prays it is the *Hermandad* who are carrying Her over their shoulders like a kidnap victim. She prays la Macarena isn't being stolen for some other purpose.

Just before daybreak, and just after Aurora again finds sleep, she and Manuel are awakened to the sounds of gunfire. Cries pierce the calm and peace of the morning. The sounds of running echo across the sleepy *barrio*. La Macarena's church, the church of

San Gil built in 1691 for the Brotherhood of la Macarena near the ancient Roman Macarena gate in Sevilla, is the target of firebombs, an arson that destroys it. After a roaring blaze that awakens the entire *barrio* and burns until mid-morning, only the church walls remain standing. The ceiling is caved in and everything, though bathed in hazy sunlight, is blackened beyond recognition. Those responsible are never caught.

Aurora and all of Sevilla take some comfort that la Macarena cannot be found amongst the charred ruins of the church. There is just a small collection of roses under the burnt altar, but no one sees these. Among the ruins, the sculpture of the crucified Christ by the renowned artist Pedro Nieto is found. The eminent effigy that had been processed every *Semana Santa* dating from 1630 is burned almost beyond recognition. A neighbor Aurora thinks she recognizes as one of la Macarena's kidnappers (or is it rescuers) is helping to dig through the debris. His hands are blackened by soot, and he has a deep burn on his forearm. It is he who discovers the Christ beneath the smoldering wreckage. And he is the first to weep. Aurora wonders if he returned to the church after escorting the Virgin to safety. She wonders when he got burned.

Everything was turned to firewood or fuel in that one night. Even Aurora scavenged for pieces of wood that might be used in her stove. Children set out on a treasure hunt seeking out molten puddles of silver glinting in the scorched remains. Not that there was much to find. It was obvious that whatever silver and gold had adorned San Gil had been taken before the blaze. Nothing will ever be the same.

~

On July 17, 1936, right-wing military leaders meet in Spanish Morocco to collectively declare insurgency against the elected government.

~

On July 18, after a leisurely lunch of gazpacho and oily sardines at a hotel in the center of town, one of Franco's men, Gonzalo Queipo de Llano, dons his starched uniform, smokes a cigarette on the terrace of his room, then departs for the military's divisional headquarters on Jesus del Gran Poder street. With little more than verbal opposition, he arrests General Villa-Abrille and takes over command.

Queipo de Llano repeats the maneuver at the infantry barracks next door. There he finds he has only 130 men to do his bidding because summer leave has depleted the army's presence in Sevilla. It would seem many of the troops he was counting on for his coup are vacationing on the Costa del Sol. While he is surprised at himself and at Franco for not thinking of this possibility, he is not daunted by the lack of manpower at his disposal. With these 130 men, he marches into the city to proclaim a State of War.

A few blocks away, near the Maestranza Bull Ring, Manuel is at work. The bellows are pumping, and the fires are fanning the puddle iron. On days like this, it is hard for Manuel to distinguish between the heat of the furnace and the heat of the sun. Whereas the fine finishing work can be done at red heat, the heavy forging must be done when the iron is at bright to sparkling white heat, not unlike Sevilla's fervid sun. Before Manuel begins his work with the steam hammer, he hears shooting, or perhaps an explosion. There is a clamoring outside as many start running toward the center.

The shots continue to ring out, rhythmically, menacingly. Manuel calls out to Paco that something is going on. "Watch the furnace. It should be ready soon, and I'll be back before that." And then to Ignacio, "Come on, let's go."

At the civil government building, my grandfather finds a crowd of men, factory workers like himself, demanding the guns and ammunition the *guardia civil* had taken from their homes during the searches. They all know that their confiscated weapons are held here, but the doors are locked and barred shut. The blinds are pulled.

A cry from the crowd goes up calling on people to make for the artillery depot in the Paseo de Colón. "Let's go together! Let's show them our numbers!" cries Ignacio his fist clenched, his arm raised in the Republican salute.

Manuel is buffeted along with the mob, and still the shots are ringing in the air punctuating the Republican chorus, "*¡Viva la República! ¡Viva Democracia!*"

But Queipo de Llano moves faster. An engineer captain with sixty men is ordered to guard the artillery depot where 25,000 rifles are stored. By the time the workers arrive, they are met by gunfire and Queipo's men. Manuel watches, disbelieving, as men fall to the ground, some wounded, others clearly dead. Those not hit, retreat to the shadows.

Queipo's shortage of soldiers is made up for with artillery and bluster. He has no trouble getting a field cannon into the center of Sevilla. After just a few rounds, the guards at the Telephone Exchange in the main square surrender emerging from the building with their hands held high waving white handkerchiefs.

Then the cannon is turned on the Hotel Inglaterra behind which stands the civil government building. Just as quickly, the governor and other authorities slink down the stairs, their hands high over their bowed heads in surrender.

Manuel watches all this as though he is watching a film. There is a surreal quality to seeing an armored tank with an imposing cannon in the center of town slowly turning, gradually advancing, and utterly devastating all in its path. The wake of destruction is complete. And in an equally extraordinary way, the events all seem very expected. As though he knew all along this was going to happen today. As though it were scripted in some universal Passion play.

In a matter of a few hours, Queipo de Llano has taken the center of Spain's fourth largest city. That Sevilla is known for its "Red" predilection is so much the better, Queipo thinks. Franco will be pleased. And that he has conquered Sevilla with only two commandeered majors and some mediocre captains he hasn't yet spoken to, is an extra bonus.

Half an hour later, Queipo takes the radio station and makes his first of many incendiary and propagandistic broadcasts, "*Sevillanos*: To arms! Join me! The Fatherland is in danger and, in order to save it, some men of spirit – some valiant generals – have assumed the responsibility of placing themselves at the forefront of a movement of salvation which is triumphant everywhere."

The radios are blasting from every bar and from the hotel. Queipo's voice is unbelievable: boasting, ribald and brazen in his coup. Manuel is still standing amongst the fallen men in the middle of the street. He pulls some of the wounded into the shade of the hotel as he looks everywhere for Ignacio. There are medics already helping the injured.

The wounded lie like crumpled heaps of clothing, and Manuel sees there is blood running along the cobbles at his feet. Someone's head is opened, and the blood is pouring out. Manuel watches the rivulets forging streams between the cobbles and wonders how so much blood can come from one man. The General's voice is still echoing in the plaza, ricocheting against the stone buildings, the stone streets. Manuel's head is pounding with each guttural syllable grating against his skull. Someone pulls Manuel back to the curb. Falling to his knees, he vomits his breakfast and bile into the gutter until there is nothing left to purge.

Across the plaza the radio rings out, "The Army of Africa is preparing to cross into Spain to take part in our God-sanctioned task of crushing your unworthy government. Your abomination of a government has resolved to destroy traditional Spain in order to convert the country into a colony of Moscow, and it will be overthrown to keep the Fatherland pure ..." Queipo's bawdy and boisterous voice gains bluster.

News spreads fast. Soon there are neighbors and friends from the Macarena quarter roaming the city center looking for each other. Women searching for their men. Mothers seeking their sons. Aurora runs through the crowd looking for her husband. Paco, standing at the roaring bellows, had shrugged his answer when she called out to him over the furnace fires. She zigzags across the street, managing only to look in the faces of the men who are standing. Those lying broken and bloodied on the curb she cannot bear to face. But she can't find Manuel. She doesn't see him sitting on the curb, his head in his hands, Ignacio's bloodied body across his lap, his blond hair matted with blood, his fist clenched still.

And the now hoarse, bibulous voice drones on, "*Sevillanos*: the die is cast, it is useless for you Red scum to resist. Legionaries and Moroccan troops are en route for Sevilla and when they arrive, they will hunt down the troublemakers like wild animals. If you resist the rising, you will be shot like rabid dogs. *¡Viva España!*"

The afternoon sun bleaches the streets where puddles of blood appear black in the harsh glare. The color red is only evident in the spreading roses blossoming on shirts and the crimson petals dripping from wounds. Aurora finds Manuel making his way home. Her breath catches when she sees all the color drained from his face, the blood on his clothes.

"It's not mine," is all Manuel can say to her. His eyes are downcast, focused on the crevices between the chalky cobbles in front of his home, dusty and dirty, but not red.

~

Later, families gather in the streets, seeking the assurance and comfort of one another's company. The fierce sunlight devastates everything it falls on, obliterating all shades of gray. Aurora washes the blood from Manuel's clothes, scrubbing the stain until her fingers are nearly bloodied from the effort. Placing the shirt on branches of the lemon tree to dry, she hopes that the sunlight will bleach away the rust colored stain of Ignacio's blood. She knows Manuel will never not see it.

The neighborhood talk is subdued, still disbelieving the news that is relentlessly trumpeted through the radio. With under 200 men, Queipo de Llano successfully takes control of Sevilla despite a hastily contrived opposition from union militants and some assault guards and hundreds of unarmed workers.

Those who have radios place them in windows so everyone can hear. The talk continues to tease out the truth from the day's events. Everyone has a story to tell. Only Manuel and Aurora seem unable to share. The smell of Ignacio's blood remains pungent in their nostrils.

Later, the radio is still blaring, the rebel general's voice harsh and rasping from overuse. Queipo is now drunk, reveling in his conquest. "Christ has triumphed," he slurs, "through God's army in Spain, of which *Generalissimo* Franco is the sainted leader." With each pronouncement, Queipo reveals more and more of the inner machinations of the coup. "The criminal forces of socialism and communism, which have drawn their slime across our Fatherland, are being vanquished by the soldiers of righteousness. God's soldiers led by Franco and Queipo de Llano and blessed by the Church!" Queipo then speaks directly to the Macarena district, "Your strikes are futile. You are futile without leaders. Return to work. If you do not, you and your families will be shot. God's army is merciful, but Spain will be bled if necessary. *¡Viva España! Viva la Virgen!*"

~

On July 19, 1936, hearing news of the violent uprising in Sevilla and with only hours to prepare, Barcelona defeats Franco's rebel, right-wing insurgency.

~

On July 20, 1936, Madrid also defeats the Franco's generals in their attempt to take over the city and government buildings.

However, that morning, two Fokker bombers carrying legionaries from Morocco, land in Sevilla. In the afternoon, additional mercenaries and Moroccan troops are ferried across the Strait of Gibraltar. It is the beginning of the first major airlift in history.

As soon as the troops arrive, Queipo de Llano orders them driven around the city in flatbed trucks. He makes them sit straight-backed and slightly forward as if they are about to jump off the truck. He shows them how he wants them to hold their rifles, with their trigger finger pointed and poised, the barrel tilted to the sky, the butt pressed to the thigh. The soldiers are paraded through the town all afternoon and into the evening in an effort to make people think far greater numbers had reached Sevilla.

Queipo hears word from an anguished tavern keeper of an ambush planned in the Red *barrio* of la Macarena. "In this heat?"

he bellows, incredulously. "I had promised these men a *bota* after riding around in the heat all day! Hell, even I need a drink!"

On the radio, Queipo issues a warning, "we are carrying on according to the laws of the hot season, and all is tranquil. It is said that the Reds are preparing to attack us violently, but we hope that the heat will prevent it."

But in the Macarena quarter, there are no upraised hands, no white flags waving. And the heat makes no difference to the factory workers accustomed to furnaces and fires. The new moon blankets the night in ideal darkness, just a hint of a halo from the faint reflection off the earth. The absence of light won't hinder the Macarenos in their own neighborhood.

Hidden guns are quickly and quietly rounded up, ammunition is purveyed, and the men and women from the working-class neighborhood meet in prearranged locations. Some on rooftops. Other's behind the city wall. Still others from the frontier of their own homes. A crack in a doorway, a broken pane of glass, these are just enough room for the barrel of a rifle. They wait. When the truck returns filled with Moroccan muscle, they will open fire.

Queipo sends a few of his men to fire off a couple of cannon rounds as a warning from a field piece he had placed near the famous Macarena arch. He thinks this will quiet their misplaced bravery.

But the *barrio* is ready. They are beyond ready. They cock their rusted rifles and steady their aim, ready to defend their lives, livelihood, and their elected government. Others cock their arms, ready to let fly homemade hand grenades that only sometimes explode on target. For too long these men and women have stood by as others profited from their work. For too long they have watched as one Republic failed, as the Monarchy fled, and now another

Republic is threatened. Elections, unions, strikes, rations ... to what end? And when?

Queipo's men advance. The Macarenos start firing, hesitant at first, for their hands are not used to this type of work. Their labor requires a skill with machines, cogs and levers, hammers and bellows – working *with* steel using their arms and hands. This fight requires they use steel against flesh. But it is not long before they acquire all the bloodthirsty contagion like a disease.

The first casualty is a Moroccan legionnaire who is killed by a bullet that miraculously finds its mark, and his fellow soldiers-for-hire jump over him brandishing their rifles, shouting, "Long Live Death! Long Live Death!" as they fire round after round at the Macarenos.

And the Macarenos cry out, "*¡Viva la República! Viva Democracia!*"

The battle rages into the night, but the ambush ultimately fails. The Macarenos are outmatched, outgunned, outmaneuvered. There are dead from both sides that litter the streets, but most are friends, coworkers, and neighbors; fathers and mothers, sons and daughters, brothers and sisters. Before morning, Queipo is informed that the Red *barrio*, the Macarena Quarter, has well and truly fallen. It marks the end of working-class resistance in Sevilla. Before the civil war in Spain fully begins, it is over for Sevilla.

~

Aurora and Manuel are grateful they had had the foresight to take the children over to Manuel's parents. At least they are safe. At least they are safe for now. Several taverns are still smoldering from fires. There is shattered glass, like crystal tears, scattered on the streets. Barefoot children are scurrying about scavenging errant bullets and shell casings.

The next day, when the numbers of dead become the names of the dead, there is anguish like none have ever known. But the keening is kept quiet. The faces on their neighbors remain stony. It is common knowledge that the *guardia civil* has been given carte blanche orders from Queipo to root out any remaining Red and to arrest anyone who is in sympathy with "the feral dogs who fought against the Fatherland."

After helping their neighbors claim their dead, Aurora and Manuel return home. There are bullet holes in the plaster walls of the courtyard, and there are some places where the whitewash has been smeared with blood. They close the shutters to the afternoon sun and fall into each other's arms. Aurora lays close against Manuel. Both are unable to stop shaking. Together they feel the anguished hunting of each other's hands, trembling with their need to feel alive and safe. It is on this sweltering afternoon that my mother is conceived.

~

On July 22, 1936, Queipo de Llano, in another of his radio broadcasts says, "I order and command that anyone caught inciting others to strike, or striking himself, shall be shot immediately. Don't be frightened. If someone tries to compel you, I authorize you to kill him and walk away. I promise you will be free of all responsibility."

But the pamphlets inciting strikes are exchanged, once again, though more stealthily than ever. At the bar, the talk is restrained, reserved. "Did you hear? There was a ceremony. The red, yellow and purple Republican flag was removed, and the red and yellow monarchist flag has been adopted by the Nationalists." Juan is pouring generously today.

"Is that what they call themselves? Nationalists?" asks Paco.

"Queipo says the flag represents 'the blood of our soldiers unstintingly shed and the golden harvests of Andalucía.'" Juan's voice fades as my grandfather looks at his hands and at Ignacio's blood he still sees there.

But in the end, the conversation dies down while Queipo continues his daily radio broadcasts. "If your man is missing a day or two, don't worry. Rest assured he's been shot like the dog he is. And don't forget, these mercenaries haven't had a woman in months – they are ravenous raping beasts." He laughs, "Franco authorizes any and all measures of persuasion to rid Spain of the communist and socialist pigs and their progeny in order to return Spain to her true and rightful place of glory! ¡*Viva España!*"

~

On July 25, 1936, Hitler agrees to support Franco's coup.

~

On July 26, 1936, German and Italian planes, troops, weaponry, and tactical support set course for Spain.

~

"They who go with wolves learn to howl." Aurora tells Manuel of the priests who pander to the people while dining on roasted pork and leg of lamb with the military generals. "It seems they are requesting the General's protection from the 'masses.' The priests have forgotten their mandate from God: that they are here to shepherd and serve us!"

Manuel is washing his face at the sink, the water running dark and gritty from his hands. She passes him a towel, and he sees that Aurora is agitated. He, too, would like to discuss this with her. But she's barely a few months along, and her persistent asthma concerns him.

"I suppose you could say I am protecting the priests from the 'masses' as well," he finally relents.

"What choice do you have? What choice? You have a family to feed. There isn't other work. The Church is the only paying customer." Aurora dips her fingers in the bowl of water and flicks them at the iron resting on the stove. The sudden sputter of droplets dance before disappearing.

"I don't know. I don't want to distract from the artwork and silver and gold relics in the Cathedral, but the commission is clear. The Bishop is demanding *rejas* and gates with bars separated by a certain width, with pointed arrows at the top. They don't say it out loud, but I know that the narrow spacing is so no one can slip through, and the darts at the top are so no one can climb over."

"Your work has always been very beautiful, Manuel. God knows your heart. God knows you." The crease Aurora is ironing into the shirt is a knife's edge.

My *abuelo* knows that God sees his heart, but what about his neighbors? What will those neighbors who also need work think? Will they think he is selling out? He always imagined that it would be easy to be a man of principle and integrity, to know his heart and then follow it.

~

The weather has been dry and hot for over two months. Aurora feels spiritually dry as well. She talks to the picture of la Macarena on her kitchen wall every morning, but more often than not, she feels she is talking to herself. She buries herself in her chores, the relentless tasks at hand that keep her fears from consuming her thoughts. She has just finished washing clothes and is hanging them across the courtyard to dry. "In this heat, these will be dry in no time," she thinks to herself.

"Let's hope they dry before the dust clings!" responds Aurora's neighbor, Conchi.

Aurora is surprised. "Did I speak out loud just now? I must be losing my mind in this heat."

Conchi is emptying a bucket of mop water and is careful not to splash Aurora's wash. "Don't worry. Half the time I don't know if I'm thinking, talking, or praying. Out loud, whisper, or in your head, what difference does it really make. God hears."

In her momentary melancholy, Aurora asks, "do you really think so? Does God hear and see what is happening?"

At just after nine in the morning, the day is already searing. The slant of the sun seems to seek out every darkness and fill it with a light that magnifies every flaw. She thinks she can see the shadows disappearing before her eyes. The river is low from the lack of rain, and the streets are dirty, dry and dusty. Aurora's lungs feel parched and raspy. The dust aggravates her asthma. Esperanza and Manolito are playing beneath the damp laundry a game of hide and seek or tag. Aurora is tired. She doesn't know where they get their energy in this heat.

"Esperanza! Don't pull on the shirts like that! Your hands are dirty."

"*Mamá*, they feel so cool. The arms of the shirts are reaching out to hug me. See? Look, *Mamá*." Esperanza is dancing through Aurora's damp apron hanging on the line, still as a windless day. "Just run past and let the cloth sweep across your face! Pretend you're flying through the clouds!"

"No. Just keep your hands off the clean laundry." At that, Aurora goes inside to shut the shutters against the invading sun. She knows she is being short, but she can't stop herself. She doesn't even want to. She just wants a chance to sit and catch her breath, but she sees the steps need washing, and there is some mending to be done. The shadows are retreating, and the day is at hand.

~

When Franco comes to Sevilla, he finds himself surrounded by his fawning Spanish staff and Queipo who insists on parading around town with the *Generalissimo*. There are impressive displays of military strength in the plazas, but it is clear to everyone that the soldiers are Italian and German men in Spanish uniforms. They perform the stiff-armed fascist salute as Franco passes.

It is impossible for Aurora and Manuel to obey the clergy's exhortations to thank God for Franco and for the economic and political stability he is imposing. She is livid that there is a sermon preached from the high altar in the Cathedral that calls for "the Fatherland, true Spain, to be renewed. That all the evil weed must be uprooted, and all the bad seed completely destroyed so that Spain can be great again." The priest, red-faced, admonishes, "This is not the time for scruples, you must turn in all dissidents – even from within your own family!" Aurora wonders where is God in this? Where is mercy? Charity?

~

No one in my family would ever discuss this time of war, hunger and political oppression. So, in trying to discern a personal truth from the steely silences emanating from everyone, including my mother, I read books. I read histories and novels. I read Hemingway and Orwell and the poets Lorca and Machado. I studied the Spanish philosopher Miguel de Unamuno who was ousted as rector of the University of Salamanca for denouncing Franco. I tried to find a way into this part of my history that is perhaps too unbearable for my family to remember, buried along with the nameless, in the mass graves across Spain.

I learned that by early fall in 1936, at least 25,000 Spaniards had been killed and less than half on any battlefield. Not all were Republicans, not all were Nationalists. Some didn't have a political predisposition at all; they simply tried to eke out a living. By 1957, nearly half of my mother's neighbors from the Macareno *barrio* had been killed, disappeared, or sent to concentration camps. Whereas the atrocities on both sides were incalculable, Franco's regime memorialized the Nationalist coup as a "crusade." Vast monuments were erected, streets were named for Franco's rebel generals, textbooks were rewritten, censorship forbade any mention sympathetic to the Republic. The Republic was persistently vilified and excised from national historic memory while the Nationalists were depicted as the heroic victors.

And as I sit in this church, decades after Franco's death, many of those same monuments honoring Franco's regime remain all across the country. Why is there still so much silence about the fascist dictator? Why haven't the streets been renamed? Why haven't fascist monuments been rededicated or repurposed? Why are the bullet-ridden walls of the cemetery where countless civilians were murdered covered over by meticulously maintained flowering vines as if the bullet holes aren't there if they can't be seen?

~

Most of the killings occur deep in the night. Night after night, in la Macarena *barrio* and all over Spain, men are carved from their weeping families, taken to a cemetery or a nearby field, lined up and shot for supporting their elected government or for expressing political opinions contrary to Franco's fascist agenda. The bodies are then piled into a grave and covered over. There can be no claiming the body, no burial, no service.

The most horrific rumor in the markets and plazas is about how in the Guadarrama mountains north of Madrid, some 80 displaced children and orphans, too young to have any political opinions, are discovered hiding within a church. They are dragged out, lined up along a row of cypresses, and killed by firing squads. Each child shot. And after the guns fall silent, their bodies are left to rot on the ground. It is the first part – the children hiding – that devastates Aurora. That they were hiding in a church, where they should have been safe. That children should have to hide at all. She questions how she can bring a child into this war.

The war rages on north of Sevilla, but in town, things have settled back to the uneasy and hopeless ways of before. The insurgents are able to place nearly 150,000 Moorish troops in Sevilla. The *guardia civil* roam the city in increasing numbers. It seems random the way they take men, and women too, in the middle of the night. Always in the middle of the night. My *abuela* hears the sound of leather scrape across leather as they dismount from their horses, or the squeal and screeching of brakes as they pull up in a truck. These are the sounds that permeate the night and penetrate her nightmares.

It is mid fall, and Aurora takes Esperanza and Manolito for a walk in the rose gardens at the María Luisa Park. Her breath has been somewhat labored, and she worries about having an asthma attack. She hopes that an easy walk in the fresh air will help. Watching her children scamper ahead of her oblivious to all the suffering, she wonders at their future. What will it hold for them? For this little one she carries within?

Aurora wants so many things for her family. Her head aches with all that she wants and cannot have. But at that moment her heart is focused on a single blush rose still in bloom in October. A single, persistent perfection that seems to vibrate with life. She reaches out and touches it. How she would love to cut the stem and take it home. But plucking would be wrong. Instead, she satisfies herself with some spent petals that have fallen. Touching her forehead, she rubs between her brows where the throbbing portends the impending nausea. She knows she should not covet, especially now when she is pregnant, because she believes an unrequited desire will mark the unborn child.

~

On October 11, 1936, la Macarena again comes out of hiding. The Church convinces Her *Hermandad* to bring Her to the Cathedral and celebrate the Nationalist takeover of Sevilla. The Church, as well as General Queipo, want to show the *Sevillanos* that all is the same as before, only better now that the Reds and their leftist government know they cannot penetrate Sevilla's nationalistic pride.

Many thousands of the town's people attempt to crowd into the nave around Her and seem to take comfort from their proximity. The *guardia civil*, with their jackboots and winged black hats, are not allowed to bring their guns and rifles into the Cathedral, yet they remain a conspicuous and prominent presence at the gates. Some they allow in, some others, not.

Just before la Macarena is to egress, Doña Teresa Díaz, a wealthy Sevillana, announces that she will donate some of her houses to the Brotherhood of la Macarena. "This," she proclaims, "is in order to build a new chapel to give la Macarena a new home, a home She deserves after those Red infidels destroyed San Gil."

There is much applause from Sevilla's aristocracy before Doña Teresa Díaz can continue. She reminds everyone that the Catholic Church blesses Franco's crusade against leftist atheists, and she applauds his goal to recuperate and resuscitate traditional Spanish Catholic family values.

~

I know that with his Fascist Italian troops borrowed from Mussolini, and the German forces from Hitler, Franco imposed an authoritarian regime, something he called True Spain. He implemented a return to pre-1931 legislation. And reprisals became commonplace in the Fascist-controlled Sevilla. There was retaliatory action taken against "subversives." For women, it meant a giant step backwards: the loss of public identity; the loss of their vote; a return to submissiveness and restrictive dress codes, to the subservient traditional domestic role of mother and wife.

Franco was adamant in his repeated proclamations, "we must counsel our women that they have no further to look than to our beloved Macarena. Through Her, they can rediscover their natural role in life and how they, too, may reach fulfillment within the glory of the Fatherland – our homeland, our *patria* that will become great once again – and the Church, and traditional Spanish family values."

~

The working class in the Macarena *barrio* is completely terrorized by the repression. There is armed militia on their streets. These armed men drink coffee next to their trucks before - almost as an afterthought - collecting people they will later dispose of. They take some to the cemetery and those who don't come home soon, don't come home at all.

On the way home from work, Manuel sees something that he never imagined even the devil himself could do. A man, his arms roped behind him, is dragged at the tail of a horse that is made to run through the streets.

"Is this what the newspaper *El Debate* meant when it reported the necessity of establishing new disciplines?" At the bar, Manuel reaches for his tobacco pouch – a force of habit – before remembering there is no money for tobacco. There is no tobacco to be found. Just like there is no coffee, no sugar, no bread, no oil. All is being requisitioned for the right-wing Nationalist Army fighting the Republicans in the North.

"There is no debate, no dialogue, in that fascist newspaper! It's all propaganda. Boasting about their exploits. They want us to know their dirty deeds, so we don't try anything," says Juan as he wipes dry the glasses and lines them up behind the bar.

"The Republic didn't change anybody's life. The Republic didn't happen." Everyone within earshot feels Manuel's dejection in the dusky bar.

Manuel, along with every other man at the bar, still works from dawn to dusk for twelve *pesetas* a day. Rations were meager before, but now there is fighting for nothing more than a small roll of bread a day, a quarter of a liter of olive oil, and three ounces of sugar a week. Only scant quantities of garbanzos and rice are allotted and very irregularly distributed. Whatever extra money Manuel brings in allows for black market bread. And on the black market, bread is 12 *pesetas* a kilo, the average daily wage. Now and then – for special occasions – Aurora can purchase a few eggs or some dried cod. Meat is not to be found.

Inside the bar and in the narrow passageways crisscrossing the *barrio*, the Reds still try to pass out their pamphlets. They are the same tracts as before but with a few new choice words that claim that the capitalists and the rich will be traitors to the "Fatherland" if they persist in their incorrigible egoism. Even the Reds are adopting the term "Fatherland." They lean in and whisper their truths, "the refusal to see the trail of hunger, poverty and misery the Nationalists and Capitalist pigs leave in their wake will lead to their own demise. Bread for all, justice for all! Remember, these may be our slogans, but they are not just empty words."

The slogans and battle cries are now nothing more than a slap in the face. A mirror reflecting their failure. A ceramics worker named Arturo pushes his drink away before standing, towering over the young communist, "don't you see that thousands of workers in the city are being systematically executed by the military. Are you going to feed my family if I'm caught with one of your pieces of paper?"

"We can rally! We must for the sake of all workers. The fight is going strong in Madrid and in the north. Don't despair, the fight is ongoing!"

"Don't you understand? We were you just five years ago." Arturo gestures to his neighbors, to Paco and Manuel. "We were you! Full of principles and philosophy. But now ..."

The young man attempting to hand out the pamphlets interrupts, "But now it matters more than ever! What happened here was a warning to those who continue the fight up north. We have to support them now!"

My *abuelo* shakes his head imagining just how long his shadow has grown, "now my pregnant wife is hungry. My two children are hungry. It's no longer just me." He swallows his drink down and turns to leave. "It's no longer about bread for all. This is reality. My children are hungry." He nods to Juan and Arturo, "I'm going home."

~

On the night of November 23, 1936, the abrupt screech of brakes outside their home wakes Aurora and Manuel. They hear the brash singing of *Cara al Sol*, the Spanish fascist anthem, sung by men who don't care whom they awaken. The *Falangista's* song echoes across the stucco walls and turns dreams into nightmares. There is a chirp of leather on leather as one jackboot rakes against the other. Then menacing footsteps marking tempo.

The front door is hammered down. Esperanza and Manolito are terrified as the flashlights scorch across the walls and floor. My *abuelo* is rousted from his bed. Running to her children, my *abuela* places her body between them and the intruders. At the top of her lungs she pleads, "*¡No es communista. No es rojo!* There must be a mistake! *¡Es un hombre bueno!*"

My *abuela's* words fall like shattered glass to the tiled floor. She is kicked aside to clear a path for my *abuelo* as he is dragged out into the street and loaded onto the truck. Her eyes are wide, animal-like. The whites gleaming in the dark. Her hands clutching the children. Hurting them. The kick inside of another child.

Just like that, he is gone. All the air has been sucked out of the house. The room is without any warmth. There is only sound and silence. The children crying, her own rasping breath, her heartbeat pounding in her ears. The absence of Manuel's voice.

On her knees, she huddles her terrified children around her, rocking and repeating, "*no te preocupes,* don't worry. It's a mistake. It's a mistake," over and over until morning.

~

Earlier that night, before my *abuelo* was taken, Queipo de Llano during his nightly radio broadcast had said, "there are those who think that taking a large city is like taking a cup of chocolate. But the task is not easy. It takes constant vigilance, and I am vigilant. I will not rest until every threat to our beloved Fatherland is shot."

As they listened on the patio surrounded by their neighbors, Aurora described to Manuel what she saw in the marketplace: "They shaved her head! They stripped her nearly naked! She was forced to drink castor oil and then led by a rope in her underclothes through the streets. This is what he calls 'constant vigilance?'"

"More like terrorism," answered Manuel.

"That poor woman, half-naked, soiling herself in front of everyone, even children, and then what?"

"Most likely she'll be shot later tonight, in the cemetery," replied my *abuelo* wearily.

Aurora and Manuel returned to their apartment, leaving their neighbors on the patio listening to the radio. There would be music now. Music approved by Franco. Music sanctioned by the Church.

~

Twenty men are rounded up from the Macarena quarter the night my *abuelo* is taken. They are offered a cigarette. They are offered the chance to repent, to confess. Each man is told that if he swears allegiance to Franco and to the Nationalist regime, he will be released. They are told this as rifle butts cut gashes across their cheekbones, their temples. Part of Manuel's ear is severed by a blow, and there is blood trickling down his neck. A slash across his shoulder bleeds through his shirt that is slapping cold against his skin.

One after the other, eighteen men cry out "*¡Ni muerto* – not even when I'm dead!" when asked if they wanted to repent. Over and over, and often through tears of anguish, "*¡Ni muerto! ¡Ni muerto!*" as they are shot against the wall of the San Fernando cemetery.

The nineteenth does not join that chorus. In his confession, he pleads on his knees. "It is not us. You have the wrong men!"

"But you're here on my list of traitors. Your names. Right here," says the rifle-toting, jackboot-wearing man. The smoldering Imperiale bobbing up and down between his bulbous wet lips.

"No, no. We work in the foundry. We supply iron for Franco's munitions factories. We are protecting the Cathedral from ..." But before he finishes, he is dragged to the wall.

"Shut up!" one of the executioners says. "Just shut up! *Dios mío*, what they won't say to avoid what they have coming to them." Holding his gun in one hand, he flicks the spent cigarette at the doomed man, and the glowing ember splinters into a thousand tiny sparks that scatter across his chest bloodied from his bashed-in nose. "Do they think we are stupid? That we don't know who we are sent to take care of?"

Manuel can't speak. He has no control over his thoughts. He can't form the words that might save Paco. "It's true," he wants to shout. He moves his lips, but his tongue is dry and thick and stuck to the roof of his mouth. Nothing comes, nothing but a low guttural sound from the depths of his core.

Paco is gunned down as Manuel watches by the light of the truck's headlamps. He cannot turn his eyes away from his friend in the spotlight. His arms opening wide, his body arching and then falling slowly almost gracefully, his descent captured by the round glare of the headlamp.

Manuel wonders why there is no blood. Just a small hole in his forehead, just above his left eyebrow. But when they kick his friend over and roll him into the shallow pit, my *abuelo* sees that the back of Paco's head is gone. There's just a black, matted wound, steaming and glistening in the cold moonlight. Looking back at the wall, he sees blood. He sees viscous matter clinging to the stucco. Swallowing the bile that has surged up into his mouth, Manuel falls to his knees.

A man holding a gun pulls my *abuelo* back to his feet, supporting his arm almost tenderly. "Your turn. I know it's not easy being last. Do you have any words for the priest?"

The tendons in Manuel's throat strain as he leans away from the gun that is now pressed to his bleeding ear. He is next. My *abuelo's* knees keep buckling under the weight of his fear. His humiliation is manifold, smeared for all to see on the wall over the mass grave where they shoved his friend. He truly wishes he could confess everything in his torn and conflicted heart ... his cowardice, his shameful, despicable work, his fear for his family. But he can't imagine God in this place. He can't imagine God anywhere.

"*Oye*, is this true? Do you supply iron for Franco?" shouts one of the *guardia*, the heavy-set one, who had been attending to his friend's broken body.

"It doesn't matter. His name is on the list," shouts the shorter one who is now stroking the side of Manuel's face with his gun.

After he has kicked the dead into the grave, the big one picks at his teeth and walks over to Manuel. "*¿Cómo se llama?*"

Manuel cannot say his name. He cannot move his tongue. His lips are locked, stuck to his teeth. A strange feral sound comes from his throat, but he cannot form the words that could save him: that he pummels iron for the gates that protect the Cathedral from the hungry, others like himself. And worse, so much worse, that he prepares iron for Franco's fascist rebel army?

"Come on! What's your name? Do you make munitions for Franco? Do you?" Practically spitting, the *guardia* is scouring the list. He has orders, and he wants to do his job and go home to his family. He impatiently lays his rifle down and searches my grandfather's pockets for his identity card.

"Is this your name?"

My *abuelo* nods, almost imperceptibly. Clarity is dawning slowly around the edges of his thought. There *is* another with his name in the Macarena. There are probably many with his name in

Sevilla. It's a common enough name. But do these hired assassins care one from the other? Does God? If he is released, will another Manuel die? And did he forge the iron used to make these weapons that killed his friend, that will point and aim, fire and kill him or the other Manuel? The list is checked again. Addresses are compared. Workplaces confirmed.

The murderers discover too late that my *abuelo's* coworker was telling the truth. The shame washes over my *abuelo* like the blood from all their bodies. His responsibility, he thinks, their blood is on his hands. He goes to work, and he helps create the product that is demanded of him. He brings home some pay. And he feeds his family. Isn't it enough that he is creating the grillwork for the Cathedral? Isn't it enough that he is designing additional iron gates to protect the Church's priceless possessions? "*¡Madre de Dios!*" His first and only words uttered that night are halfway between prayer and damnation, a purgatory of perdition.

Now they are slapping Manuel on the back. They offer him a swig from a *bota* one carries slung around his neck, another offers a cigarette from the pack of Imperiales. "Ay, that was close!" They congratulate themselves on catching their mistake before it was too late. "This one may still be useful."

"*Sí,* but too bad about the other. No one has to know though, right *hombre?*"

It takes Manuel a moment to realize that the question was asked of him. But he doesn't have to answer because the other man, the one with the list, replies for him, "Who is he going to tell? And what would he say? That we killed the wrong man, that we shot his friend while he shit his pants and watched?" Turning to Manuel, he says, "You've been given a reprieve, but watch or you'll soon join your comrades in hell."

My grandfather is released, unceremoniously dumped out of the truck in front of his home in the morning, as the sun's rays crept around buildings and painted slivers of light that fractured the streets of his neighborhood. And my *abuelo* vows that he will shape something else from what scraps are left.

The Third Sorrow: Loss

"After three days they found him in the temple, sitting among the teachers, listening to them and asking them questions; and all who heard him were amazed at his understanding and his answers. And when they saw him they were astonished; and his mother said to him, 'Son why have you treated us so? Behold your father and I have been looking for you anxiously.' And he said to them, 'How is it that you sought me? Did you not know that I must be in my Father's house?' And they did not understand the saying which he spoke to them ... and his mother kept all these things in her heart."

Luke 2:46-50

Aurora gives Esperanza a thick slice of bread fried in olive oil and soaked in hot vinegar, but she is still too weak to eat. "Some broth with egg, then? Just a little?"

The pharmacist gave Aurora some syrup on credit to ease Esperanza's cough. But her daughter's fever won't subside, and her stomach spasms with every bite. Aurora knows that any food she succeeds in feeding Esperanza will come right back up, but she has to try. It's all she can do. The flu that has passed through each of them, lingers in her daughter.

Aurora blames the weather. The rain won't relent, and she believes that Esperanza only needs sun to recover. If only the sun would shine, then Esperanza's lungs would clear and her fever wane, the roses would return to her cheeks. But the house is raw and cold. The wood door is swollen from the damp, yet somehow the frigid wind still finds its way into their rooms. There isn't money for fuel. The brazier beneath the table is abysmally empty and there is nothing to chase the chill away. Aurora stuffs rags into the cracks and around the door, but the moisture keeps running down the walls in trailing, glistening tracks.

~

In a grandiose radio announcement, Queipo de Llano proclaims Sevilla the future capital of Spain. He asserts he is speaking for Franco, that the two of them make every important decision together. He says, "each of you owe your allegiance to two *patrias*:

your *patria grande*, *España*, and your *patria chica*, *Andalucía*, Sevilla, and the *barrio* you call home!"

Aurora mumbles to herself as she frets over Esperanza that her *patria grande* and her *patria chica* is and always will be her family. "Spain has become a playground for fools and bullies."

Queipo goes on to explain how the city is full of life, and the factories are working day and night in an effort to keep up with Spain's surging economy. Manuel listens but adds the missing information, "there is work perhaps, but wages have been cut again. Most of the food is going to the Nationalist soldiers fighting the Republican troops and the International Brigades up north."

Aurora replies simply, "We have become a nation of scavengers," as she presses a dampened cloth to Esperanza's forehead.

The Radio General continues to utter extravagant nightly threats over the airwaves with unabashed swagger and bluster. Most evenings, he passes judgment on international politics and advises Great Britain and France to follow the example of Italy and Germany. But sometimes his drunken proclamations are so insidious and perverse that his own engineers cut the power to his transmissions, blaming an external outage or short in the wiring.

The hotels are full of German and Italian diplomats, engineers, journalists and press agents. Hitler and Mussolini have sent their best propagandists to Sevilla. The Fascist emissaries from Berlin and Rome are giving instructions to the Spanish *Falangistas* on the establishment and organization of syndicates. They are also quick to give strong-armed advice on the technique of the conquest of power; this is something Franco is keen to understand. It is clear that Queipo and Franco still hope to recruit those who had fought so tenaciously, though futilely, when they took Sevilla.

~

Despite their early and persistent involvement on the Nationalist side of the Spanish Civil War, I know that history eventually revealed that neither Hitler nor Mussolini was ever fully satisfied with the Spanish Fascist movement. Spain proved an accessible and fitting training ground for German and Italian soldiers before the onset of World War II, but Hitler would later claim that the Spanish *Falangistas* were too violent, too much inclined to the elimination of their political enemies by torture and death.

~

Six-months pregnant, Aurora kneels on the cold marble tiles in her kitchen. She will pray the rosary again today. For weeks, she has been fervently praying the *Mater Dolorosa* specifically because Esperanza is still ill.

As she begins the seven *Dolors*, she makes the sign of the cross, expressing her belief in the trinity and acknowledging Christ's death on the cross. The dimpled bead at the beginning is the first sorrow, and Aurora concentrates on the prophecy of Simeon as she begins with the Lord's Prayer, continues with seven Ave Marias and concludes with "Virgin Most Sorrowful, pray for us."

Aurora continues through the second sorrow, the striated bead, but stops short of the third sorrow. Pressing the third bead between her thumb and forefinger, she attempts to squeeze out the words, the images and meaning of a mother losing her child. What comfort is there in this, she questions. What help is there reflecting on Mary's sorrows, Her losses, Her grief? Aurora loses herself in her own anguish as she cannot bring herself to articulate the third sorrow.

The third sorrow, where Mary searches for and cannot find Her son Jesus, is when a mother can only imagine the worst: the feelings of loss that Mary must feel, the fear coiling in Her gut, gaining a life of its own. A mother's primary responsibility, to assure the safety of her young one can, at times, be a heavy and unmanageable task. But the children are not always in their mother's care. And they are susceptible to illness. There are all manner of accidents one cannot bear to imagine. All these fears permeate her sleepless nights. Those moments when the child's small hand slips away beyond the mother's grasp. Or when a child slips from a tree limb and falls. When the air that sustains us all cannot find its way into a child's lungs. Or when a mother looks away just for a moment. Just a split second.

Aurora does not want to meditate on this sorrow. She doesn't want to know this pain. These nightmares swarm about her bed enough at night. She can't bear them in the light of day. Such sorrow becomes too palpable, too possible in the light of day. Too impossible to shrug off. She rekindles the fading flickering flames within her stove and unashamedly begs la Macarena to restore her daughter's health.

"*Señora, por favor*. Please, please, I beg you."

She weeps with bowed head, imagining the statue of la Macarena coming to her side. She remembers each of the wooden saints within the sanctuary of San Gil. She remembers their elongated, thin hands extended and the shallow valleys of their upturned palms. She looks down into her own upturned hand, the rosary tucked in the palm of her left hand, the fingers of her right hand still pressing upon the third decade.

My *abuela's* kitchen has become her church. Within these walls she hears Manuel's tortured contrition over the work he must do. It is here that she offers each member of her young family a circle of bread as they commune over their modest meals. It is here that she anoints them with drops of the cloudy olive oil for their broth made of onion and discarded bone. And though water does not turn to wine, there is still the vinegar transformed from wine in the crock, and that completes what she has to offer.

After her petition to la Macarena, Aurora kneels in silence upon her kitchen floor. She listens to her daughter's breath, shallow and labored. She clutches the beads her Godmother gave her when she was confirmed. And she grasps at the remaining crumbs of her faith.

Outside a weak fascist rally cry penetrates the thickly plastered walls: "*¡Arriba España!*"

Aurora is used to seeing the parades in her neighborhood. It is Queipo's way of reminding the *barrio* that he is commander in Sevilla, as if the missing family members and neighbors, the splashes of blood on walls and street were not enough. The *guardia civil* monitors on horseback wearing their ridiculous hats and tall leather boots. They watch to see which workers participate in the rally. And they watch to see who suddenly slips away or finds distraction in an errant shoelace. They take note.

"One!" the crowd responds, uninspired.

"*¡España!*" he shouts again.

"Great!" parrots the obedient public.

"*¡España!*" the fascist leader crows.

"Free!" The cowed crowd completes the cheer, and Aurora imagines their right arms stiffly raised in the brittle straight-armed fascist salute, their hearts aching. She knows it is their clenched fists they long to raise in the workers' salute: arm held high, fists clenched, elbow bent as though set to pound hammer upon anvil. A forced duplicity: truth and lies, faith and fact.

Throwing caution to the wind, Aurora cannot help but petition la Macarena. If there is a price to pay later, she'll pay it. But there is nothing, nothing now or ever, that can be as important or as precious as her daughter Esperanza.

"Please," Aurora prays, "don't let me lose this child as You lost Yours. I am not as strong as You. I won't survive. Please."

"Of course, you will survive. There is her younger brother to consider. And don't forget the child you carry. Of course, you will survive. It is what we do."

Aurora looks up, somehow not surprised to see la Macarena de Esperanza walking towards her, arms outstretched, as if ready to embrace her right there in her kitchen. Cascading rose petals, like confetti, tumble from Her gown.

My *abuela* chokes out a sob. She has no words for the desperate fear she feels rising all around her. "I've been praying and praying for weeks now, and she's still so weak." How can Aurora lose this child who sees her so completely. A mother-daughter bond beyond what she could have imagined. "Please, *Señora*."

La Macarena kneels beside my *abuela*, and for a moment Aurora worries that her floor isn't clean enough for the bent knees of the Virgin. *"I, too, know your heart."* Neither move to wipe away the tears that come in a torrent. Together they watch the fire burn the olive stones, crackling pits of fire that suddenly burst in an arsenal of sparks that scatter into nothing.

"God seems so far. I don't know what ... if I can believe." The familiar sisterly feeling envelopes Aurora for just a moment, and she nearly apologizes for her crisis of faith, until she hears Esperanza wheezing.

"God is here. I am here." The light in the kitchen has become softer, golden, as if it is dawn in the warmth of spring and all the flowers are pollinating. *"All I have is yours. All the love and compassion. It is yours."* La Macarena presses the heels of Her hands against

Her eyes.

"It's not enough! Not nearly!" Aurora cries. "I don't want your compassion. I just want Esperanza!" My *abuela's* mouth is wide and misshapen, and she tries to cover it with her hands. A habit she's had since she was little. A gesture meant to protect her from evil spirits when she is too vulnerable.

Pressing Her palms together, la Macarena whispers, "*Aurora ... the Lord is with you ...*" But my *abuela* won't hear. She rises from her knees and begins sweeping up the spent petals from her kitchen floor.

~

Esperanza dies of influenza. She dies of hunger. She dies of cold. She dies in my *abuela's* arms in the raw, mean light just after dawn as Aurora sits near the cold brazier rocking and rocking, humming absently the little song that Esperanza so loved. The sound of rain, relentless these past weeks, subsides. There is a weight upon Aurora's breast like someone has piled something wet and heavy upon her. A constricting cord of asthma tightens around her chest as she rocks her daughter closer and closer, trying to transfer her own warmth to her daughter's body. Damp trails of condensation slide down the plaster walls as if the house itself weeps.

Manuel sifts through the cold ashes in the brazier. The last remnants of the pamphlets, tracts and leaflets he brought home last night delivered nothing more than their empty promises for the workers and their families. Aurora was grateful for their fleeting fire, but she will allow no more into this house.

Aurora wonders aloud how she will live. She knows she will. But she cannot fathom how. Through her tears she looks at the photograph of la Macarena de Esperanza and silently pleads. "How?"

"I know," la Macarena's voice filters into Aurora's ears, yet none of her sadness abates. *"There is nothing that compares. Your first born. My own. The pain does not lessen with time. It is a sorrow the whole world has not been able to soften. I know."*

Before the sun reaches its zenith, Manuel takes Esperanza's cold body out of Aurora's arms. Together they marvel how small she seems now. Nearly weightless and ephemeral, a sparrow's hollow-boned body, an absence so vast. Both are remembering how she could fill up a room with just her laughter. She was abundant and radiant, and she made their lives full beyond anything they ever imagined. Such fearless love. They didn't know they could love so much.

Neighbors enter to cluck and croon. Conchi moves to open a window as is custom after a death, and Aurora nearly jumps out of her seat to stop her. "Leave it shut. Leave it."

"But, Aurora, she belongs to God now."

"Leave it closed. What do I care about God? What does God care about us? God should beg our forgiveness." And at this, the hovering black-cloaked women cross themselves.

Manuel carefully wraps his firstborn in a lace *mantilla* and bestows a last kiss before he carries her from the house.

A low sound from deep within my *abuela* frightens Manolito as he tugs and tugs at her dress. The dark women emerge from their corners and their hands flap and fan at Manolito, sweeping him away from what he does not recognize.

The neighbors hover, collecting Esperanza's clothing, covering mirrors, washing bedding, preparing food from their combined offerings. Their efforts are a comfort to themselves only. Rejecting food, Aurora gnaws on her grief and swallows her tears. Esperanza is safely buried deep within.

~

For days my grandmother remains in the chair sitting in a private reverie that reveals nothing. No epiphanies. No glimmer of understanding. No broader perspective that imparts anything more than utter loss, an emptiness beyond compare. She continues to rock, feeling her weightlessness without the ballast of her daughter. She feels the air sluice through her as though she is nothing more than a mist. Her quiet moans are throaty and gnarled. She forgets to eat, and the little one inside responds with weakened kicks and turns.

Aurora has no thoughts for this little one. A boy or a girl. Dark like her or fair like Manuel. Whatever longing she felt was lost with Esperanza. All potential, all hope - even love - everything lost with Esperanza.

Manolito runs from room to room, looking all over the house for his big sister, and Aurora can't bring herself to acknowledge him until he steps into Esperanza's shoes and starts dancing as if dancing would bring her home.

"Take those off!" she nearly screams, her voice rough and hollow.

Falling to the floor, Manolito flings off the shoes and runs from his mother confused and afraid. He doesn't understand that she believes germs can be transmitted through wearing another's shoes. Sweat, just like saliva, carries disease, she thinks. And there is no one who could ever walk in Esperanza's shoes.

~

No one approaches Aurora for her sorrow has taken such form. It casts an unyielding and expanding shadow that feels cold and contagious. The neighbors fear for their own children and attend my *abuela* without looking directly at her, not daring to meet her eyes. They know this kind of pain can only grow until she can no longer hold it within herself. Then a part of it will break free and seek a new home – like a parasite – because it can no longer be contained by one grief-stricken and frail body.

She believes an afternoon of sun would have pulled some of the raw chill out of the damp air. Aurora imagines the sun lending its luminosity to the wet cobbles on the road. She always loved how the steam would rise in ghostly whorls when the sun's warmth penetrated the wet stone. She thinks of the sun on her face, warming her own asthma-constricted lungs, opening her ribs, and broadening her back so she can breathe. She remembers the sun's glint in Esperanza's hair until the grief overcomes her again.

~

Silently she sobs now; there is no voice for this pain. She dissolves like this until she starts throwing up. She vomits so violently that she thinks she too might die. She wishes it, because she can no longer live. As Aurora's hope diminishes, sorrow grows more potent, more cogent and consuming.

She knows this sorrow has never been known before, not even by la Macarena. And so, she is going to explore every corner of it. It is something she undertakes willingly, compulsively. She seeks out the darkest parts and curls into a ball there. She finds the jagged edges and rakes her naked memories there. In each experience, she is inventing something new, never before felt, never experienced. Nothing like la Macarena's Seven Sorrows. Her grief at losing a full-grown son is hardly worth comparing. He had his destiny, didn't he? He chose it. But Esperanza? This grief is entirely her own, a grief beyond anything that has gone before. She invented this. She created this. And she is cracking this wide for the world to see. There is no word for this.

From the bar on the corner, a man opens his throat in song,

and the haunting wail of *cante jondo* pierces the night.

~

"You know these rations are not enough to keep a dog alive. And you can't afford to buy on the black market. No one can." Miguel, the grocer and family friend, is trying to convince Aurora to continue claiming Esperanza's rations. He has been trying for several weeks, but she won't hear of it.

"I can't claim rations for a child who is dead." Aurora's voice is flat as she traces the braid on the rope of garlic.

Miguel remembers Esperanza's doll and tries a different argument, "pretend the doll is your child. It takes time for a death to be registered and rations to be adjusted. You can still claim Esperanza's portion. No one has to know. It's been done."

That night, after Manolito is in bed, Aurora and Manuel sit at the table with their legs tucked under the heavy cloth though the brazier has long since grown cold. She tells Manuel what the grocer suggested. "He has no shame."

Aurora sees that Manuel is hesitant, his words caught and struggling in his throat like a fish in a net. She can't believe that he is in agreement. She rises from her chair and turns away from her husband.

"Many people are dying because they eat what they shouldn't. Aurora, we can't pretend that things are different than they are." He imagines if they had had enough food – meat and cheese, real sustaining food – perhaps Esperanza would have been strong enough to withstand the illness. Manuel is nearly whispering, "Aurora ..."

Aurora leaves the room and goes to sit on their bed. Manolito is tucked under the blankets in the middle. She hears him grunt as he rolls over onto his stomach.

She cannot bear to cry anymore in front of Manuel, to see his anguish at her tears. But she is unable to stop. She knows he is right. She knows he is just as hungry as she is. She knows he slips Manolito some of his garbanzos when she is not looking.

The baby inside spins and stretches an elbow here, a foot there. Touching her hand to her belly, Aurora feels nothing but the inevitability of this child. Sharp bony protuberances that cut into her flesh. She wonders if this new baby will be malnourished when all she is eating is the weak broth from scavenged vegetables and beans. There has been no milk, no cheese, no eggs or meat for months. Although she feels no connection with this little one, no thread of affection, no affinity, she does want it to live. She doesn't want it to starve.

Manuel comes to sit beside her on the bed. His hands open, empty on his lap. He looks at the blackened lines crisscrossing constellations on his palms and wonders if they really mark the course of life as the gypsies say. And if so, where on his blistered, callused map is this godforsaken place where a man cannot provide for his family. "Aurora," he whispers.

"*Mañana*," she says quietly. "Claim the doll tomorrow."

~

Manuel arrives early at the Cathedral and enters through the Puerta del Perdón. He imagines what forgiveness could be bestowed simply by walking through a door. And what that might be like. But there is no forgiveness for his sin, no pardon. Not being able to keep his family safe, warm, fed; how does one atone for such a sin? A man's duty, and he failed.

He is at the Cathedral to repair some wrought iron gates that had been vandalized by local men, friends probably. He, too, wants to tear at the bars and rush the saints. But instead of defacing or defiling, he wants to fall at their feet and beg forgiveness. He wants to find the strength to walk into his home and not feel Aurora's pain, her sorrow that etches jagged patterns in the plaster walls and creeps into every crevice.

But any coal he brings, any food or money he brings home, is too late to save Esperanza. He senses Aurora's despair when she pushes her portion of bread to Manolito. It is as though simply subsisting is an insult to her memory. She is losing weight. It is not right, but it's as if she cannot eat or feel warmth because they couldn't provide the same for Esperanza.

At the Cathedral, my *abuelo* bears witness to the Dance of the *Seises*. I had read in a guidebook before coming to Sevilla that the delicate minuet-like dance has been performed for Mary at the Cathedral on the feast days of the Immaculate Conception and Her Ascension since 1613. The *Seises* were originally six small boys dressed as pages who danced before the Blessed Sacrament on the High Altar. Dancing in the Cathedral would be a profane act, in itself a defilement of sacred ground. But a special dispensation for this dance for Mary, the mother of God, has survived Pope after Pope.

After kneeling before the altar and seeking permission to begin, the boys, wearing the same type of costume as they wore over 300 years ago, perform their dance. They play castanets and dance their dainty high-stepping dance all upon the High Altar in their ridiculous plumed hats and sashes with gold tassels. To Manuel, they appear flush-faced and well-fed and absurd.

My *abuelo* watches as the boys dance in two pure straight lines mimicking the rows of massive columns holding aloft the arched canopy of the Cathedral. The pillars lose themselves in the dusk overhead, and long shafts of dim light slant down from the high windows. The austere columns rise perpendicular to the vaulted ceiling and the marble floor. Only the flickering candles in their holders beneath the statues lean this way and that, themselves nearly dancing in the flickering light. Aside from these slender wax pillars that were placed by the faltering hands of the faithful and the penitent prayerful, all else appears right and true.

The boys prance in this ancient petrified forest of towering marble trees, and Manuel stands in his dusty workman's uniform. Like a tilting candle, he lists a little to lean upon a column. The marble is cold and unforgiving. He imagines these boys, the sons of the wealthy in Sevilla; do they know anything of the hunger his little boy feels?

What would happen if he danced for Mary, Manuel wonders? In these clothes. His work boots raising clouds of dust as he stamped out his dire rhythm. With his dirty hands clapping at nothing but the air. His ragged and worn voice singing out, plaintively singing for Her, for *esperanza,* hope. Would there be forgiveness? Would hope revive? The boys sing and dance, and in my *abuelo's* hands are the tools he will need to repair the *rejas* alongside the High Altar when they are done. The families of the dancers ring around, proud and pious. Many dressed in finery Manuel has never imagined. Some dressed in the Nationalist uniform he knows all too well.

They don't see my *abuelo* as he suddenly leans away from the column and attempts his own dance, stepping one foot out before raising the other just as he had seen the boys do at the beginning of their dance. And just as the boys had turned in graceful steps, he spins his slow revolution, lifting his arms in an arc. A shhhush sound rises from his dirty shoes as they scrape upon the polished floor. No one notices as he turns, lifting his arms high and then higher, his hands in white-knuckled fists filled with his tools.

As the music ends, he too completes his dance, ending with a deep and self-conscious bow. He feels the collection of scrap iron in his pocket dig into his leg. The juxtaposition of iron bars and dance, of sanctioned and sacred space, sacrilege and worship, overwhelm him, and he cries his first tears since Esperanza's death. Then he quietly adds an inclining wax pillar to the blaze of candles before starting his work.

~

When Malaga, southeast of Sevilla, fell to the Nationalists in February 1937, the only looted item, the only treasure that held any interest to Franco, was a religious relic from a convent near Ronda. The hand of Saint Teresa of Avila was discovered in the baggage of a captured Republican officer who had absconded with it after a raid on the convent. Instead of being returned to the sisters, it was sent to Franco's headquarters in Salamanca, where he kept it at his bedside as a talisman.

There was much joking in the bar about what Franco did with the hand. "Does he scratch his back?"

"No, no. He picks his nose! One hand to scratch his ass as the other feeds his face ... he needed another hand to attend to that bulbous nose of his!"

"Perhaps a hand-job when he can't find a willing whore."

I know from history books that on November 20, 1975, when Franco took his last breath in a hospital in Madrid, the mummified hand was at his bedside.

~

La Macarena is in attendance and stands near, not hovering, but lingering like a scented breeze, cool and sustaining should Aurora ever breathe again. Since Esperanza died, She has been in nearly constant attendance, but Aurora only glances at Her peripherally, a vague outline, a shadow. She won't talk with Her as before.

The Virgin has removed Her crown and mantle and has pushed up Her sleeves. She places Her hand on Aurora's brow that is beaded with sweat. She breathes along with Aurora when the surges wax, and She whispers words in Aurora's ear when the pains wane. *"Estoy aquí, para ti, Aurora. Siempre aquí."*

Aurora hears Her, as one hears the far cry of doves, or church bells calling from the next village.

"Blessed art thou, Aurora."

My *abuela* says nothing. She won't open her eyes. The soft scent of roses lets her know that la Macarena is near, but she doesn't care. Any capacity to care about anything has abandoned her, and she simply goes through the motions, devoid of any emotion save that of grief.

Earlier, when the waves of labor began to wash over Aurora more frequently, she stopped scrubbing the stains in Manolito's pants. She called over to Susana for help with Manolito. She sent word to Manuel at the foundry and went to the bedroom, shutting the door behind her. Aurora brought old rags and towels to bed, stripped off her clothing, leaned into the pushing, counted her breaths in and then out all the while holding the headboard. And after several hours, she pulled the child into the cool and darkened room. There was no keening, no anguished cry at crowning, no sighs, no moaning. Silence. And with that it was finished. My mother arrived late in the evening, an unassisted birth except for la Macarena who prayed through the *Dolorosa* over and over, ending the seventh with the same breath that began the first again. For Aurora, this birthing was a chore, nothing more than washing the floors, cooking the dinner; one more thing that had to be done.

La Macarena swells with love at seeing this new life. Again, she says, "I am here for you, Aurora. You and our daughter." But Aurora doesn't see Her smiling, and she doesn't take comfort from Her soothing voice. Instead, Aurora hears thunder rumble and roll across the distant Sierras. She smells the acrid, flinty aroma of rain on dust. She tastes the metallic stain of blood on her lip. She doesn't hear la Macarena call this new child "our daughter."

Aurora takes the new baby in her arms. A little thing, all eyes and a wide gaping chasm of a mouth. Dark earth like her sister before her. Skinny little arms that flail and flinch as her first cries wrack her tiny body. Balled up fists batting at unknown demons. Mucous matted dark hair, a sticky webbed mantle over her head. And then, as if her eyes suddenly focus on the whole and not just these particulars, Aurora realizes this new child could be a twin of her Esperanza.

My *abuela* hands this new daughter to Conchi as she collapses over her abandoned womb. Cradling the cavern, she mourns anew her Esperanza. Her emptiness takes on the proportions of the room, sucking all the air and blackening the whitewashed walls. Conchi swiftly removes the baby from the monster that is growing beyond what can be restrained in the small room. The pain is behind Aurora's eyes now. Filling her ears. Opening her mouth. Her teeth and tongue ache for a vocabulary. As all remaining light slips under the bedroom door, she stares at Esperanza's vacant shoes still waiting in the corner of the room.

~

The daughter is washed and wrapped in a shawl. La Macarena watches over Conchi's ministrations, brushing a tendril of hair from the child's brow, softly resting Her thumb on the baby's forehead for a moment, adjusting the shawl to cover her ankle.

Inaudible blessings fall from Her lips like anointing oil from fingertips as She guides Conchi and the baby to Manuel's waiting arms.

Manuel peers down at the squinting shrieking face and prays hard. He prays that she be strong, that she survive this place and time in which she is born. He prays that she is able to penetrate the walls that Aurora has erected around her. That she is persistent as she seeks her way into her mother's heart. La Macarena adds one last prayer to his litany; She prays that this tiny one learns that she cannot be a vessel for her mother's tears, nor should any child claim what her mother cannot contain for herself.

When the raging from the bedroom has calmed to a soft whimper, Conchi brings the baby back to Aurora. The baby continues to cry and though Aurora tries to nurse her, the child has trouble latching on. Exhaustion overtakes Aurora, and Conchi carries the child from the bedroom allowing the little one to suck on the tip of her smallest finger. She'll find some sugar water for the time being.

La Macarena is standing at the threshold between the bedroom and the front room. Her hands are clasped to Her forehead, and She is murmuring in a language beyond the scope of their ears. Her tears fall, crystal shards that splinter into stars upon the stone floor.

Aurora lies back, still tangled in bloodied and damp sheets and stares at the stenciled migrating geese that border her bedroom wall. Her dreams are of a deep and placid lake where she swims across without making a wake, a sandy beach where her silent footfall doesn't leave a print. A child calls and calls to her, but though she searches and cries out, she can't follow the voice. It comes to her from everywhere. She wakes when her dreams take her to a pair of empty shoes and a city full of shoeless children.

"Every breath, each heartbeat, even your thoughts and intentions

influence the world." La Macarena is sitting at the foot of the bed and though Her voice is without judgment, Aurora feels she is being admonished.

"I have no influence, no power, no effect on anything or anyone." Aurora speaks into the pillow, not raising her eyes to see that la Macarena is sitting by her side now, Her heavy embroidered robes blanketing them both. She feels the robes holding her down, keeping her from drifting across the sky, flying away with the geese. Muffled and almost incomprehensible, she sobs, "I couldn't save my daughter."

"There is a new life in your hands. Will you give her hope, or will you allow her to languish?" La Macarena takes Aurora's feet into Her lap and massages the soles with rose oil.

The question cuts through Aurora. What does "allow" have to do with anything in their lives? Did she "allow" Esperanza to die? Did she "allow" anything at all? "I will care for her. I will feed her as I am able. I will take her to mass, and she will be christened. I will do all I can for her." Her voice biting through her bitterness.

"She is very small. You will need to be vigilant in her care. And you must remember, she is not your firstborn." La Macarena tenderly places Aurora's feet on the bed and removes Her mantle, placing it over Aurora's shivering body.

But Aurora wrenches off la Macarena's robes sending rose petals fluttering like fallen leaves across the floor, and her voice is menacingly cool, "she could never be."

"You will need to see her for who she is. Blessed is this fruit of your womb."

Later, after another unsuccessful attempt at nursing, Aurora sees her husband's anxiety etched across his brow. "Don't look so concerned, Manuel. She'll be fine."

"I am worried for you, Aurora." He reaches for a ringlet, then retreats.

"Don't be. My milk will come in soon, and she'll know what to do then. I won't let her go hungry."

Aurora leans over and places this new daughter in Manuel's arms as though she is transferring an antique bone china cup, or a whisper thin glass vase no one dares use. And it is into this container that Aurora will pour all her pain and grief in the guise of attending and nurturing and mothering. This new little girl, so like Esperanza, but not her. Not her.

~

"It is the custom. It is what is done. In our family, the eldest daughter has always been named for the father's mother. She will be Esperanza," Manuel's mother is holding the new baby, cooing softly her words that are meant for Aurora.

Tears continue to roll down my *abuela's* face, but she takes no notice, not even bothering to wipe them away. It's as though her face has become la Macarena's, permanently stained with crystalline teardrops. There was *esperanza*. And now there is none. Hope is not so easily replaced. A child even less so. It seems to her that everyone thinks she should stop grieving now that there is a new daughter, as if Esperanza could be exchanged for this baby.

The other day Aurora heard voices filter in from the patio, "Something to distract," they said. "Something to focus on other than her loss." Someone even went so far as to say that Aurora was too enamored of Esperanza anyway; that God sees such things and takes what is his so we remember to place no one above him. But there is no distraction from her pain. There is nothing that can alleviate this sorrow. She cannot see beyond her lost Esperanza.

Her mother-in-law, losing patience says, "you'll go blind crying so many tears over something you cannot change. *No hay mal que por bien no venga*. Something good always comes from bad." She is still rocking the new baby, but her eyes are now on Aurora. "Many have lost children. You are not special. God wants what God wants."

Bristling, Aurora takes the baby from her mother-in-law and hands her to Manuel. "And you think God wanted me to lose Esperanza?" This new baby changes nothing. Everything is lost.

Walking from the room, "That is not what I said, and if you don't stop crying, your milk will dry up. Think of your child!"

But she is. All she can do is think of her child, her Esperanza. The idea of naming this baby after her beloved Esperanza is beyond offensive to Aurora. As if she could be replaced. Aurora is not about to name this baby, who already looks so much like Esperanza, after a hope that is no longer a possibility.

Instead, my mother is named after her maternal grandmother. She is christened Dolores, after Aurora's own mother, as would be the custom had Esperanza lived. But more, she is named for the pain and sorrow and grief palpable in her sister's wake. My *abuela*, dressed in the black of mourning, with black lace *mantilla* shrouding her downcast face, holds my mother close at the christening. The front of her dress is soaked from her leaking breasts and the tears that continue to fall. It's as if every part of her weeps. Rocking and rocking, a low moaning wells deep within and overflows, surrounding my mother with the sounds that swaddle her home.

~

My mother wore a different christening gown than the one Esperanza wore. It is the palest pink and so soft, with just a hint of lace at the hem and delicate pin tucks at the bodice. I still have both dresses: the one Esperanza wore which my sister also wore at her christening, and the one my mother wore.

My daughter Madeleine wore both, not as christening gowns, but as pieces of her history; delicate ephemeral cloth connecting the new with the old. My mother gave me the dresses when she first came to meet Madeleine. For decades the dresses had been wrapped in baby blankets and tucked away in an attic with some of my sister's baby things and a portrait of my sister as a baby. I had never seen them before.

When my mother met my daughter for the first time, Madeleine was nearly three-months old with a head of dark hair and dark eyes that searched for and found your gaze. My mother was sitting next to my sister when I placed Madeleine in her arms. She pulled my daughter in close and stroked her brow and smoothed a curl behind her tiny ear. She was completely silent for a moment before looking up at my sister and softly cooing, "she looks just like *you* when you were a baby." She reached out and touched my sister on the knee, a gesture that ended in several quick pats as she composed herself anew.

Madeleine's eyes moved from face to face and eventually landed on mine. My daughter's name means "witness," the constant companion of Christ.

As my mother held her first grandchild, she kept looking back and forth between my daughter and her daughter – my sister. Almost to herself, my mother murmured, "the same dark curls, the same big eyes, and her chin." When my sister took Madeleine into her arms, I realized I had been holding my breath.

I knew what would happen next. What was said in this next moment was going to erase me from that portrait. I started to speak aloud a distraction, an anecdote that would be Madeleine's and mine alone, but I was invisible, inconsequential in that moment, and my voice was nothing but a slow jagged exhale, an interrupted sigh. Interrupted by the crushing weight of the boulder I could not seem to roll away.

My mother sat upon the arm of the wingback chair and leaned in close pressing one hand along my sister's back, adjusting the blanket around my daughter with her other hand. They were framed exquisitely. Dark-haired beauties all. A golden aura from the table lamp surrounded them, and I recoiled at the inevitability of the coming question. It would be a variation on so many questions that had come before: at coming-of-age moments; at graduations; at my wedding; milestones; benchmarks. My sister glanced up from Madeleine's face toward her mother's as if she, too, sensed the question had formed completely and was slowly overwhelming our mother. And then quietly, as if my mother knew this question should not be uttered aloud but the need for companions and witnesses to her solitary pain prevailed, she asked my sister if she ever wished that she, too, could have a baby. My sister, forever in the present moment, just laughed and smiled her enigmatic smile not understanding the layers of pain and disappointment.

I saw the exchange from the vast distance of the small room, the miles and miles across our coffee table. I saw my mother searching, riveted to her eldest daughter's face, looking for traces of what might have been, looking to see if my sister felt the same sorrow, if there was a hint of her grief mirrored in her firstborn's eyes.

I felt my husband at my right shoulder pulling me from the shadows. And I saw Madeleine who was still looking at me, not allowing me to vanish as I might have, watching my expression as I struggled to hold very still and remain. Madeleine smiled an invitation to return. John, hand on my shoulder, and my daughter, a witness, were beholding a sacrifice.

~

There are times when Aurora looks at Dolores as if she wants to memorize her every feature. There are other times when she cannot bear to look at her at all for the ghost that she encounters there. When she is able to peer into my mother's face, my grandmother concentrates on a faint birthmark, a diminutive rosebud pinked between Dolores' eyebrows, hardly more than a blush. This is different. The only roses on Esperanza were on her cheeks.

"Remember that rose in the María Luisa Park? The one you so wanted?" La Macarena's voice seems to come from deep within Aurora herself. So far away.

"Yes. It was beautiful." A stirring pulls Aurora to that moment, the rose, its perfection and grace. A simple moment in time. A day when everyone was happy and healthy. A sunlit, beautiful afternoon in the midst of so much uncertainty and fear. At that moment she wanted the rose more than anything. But now the memory forges a shudder so deep and violent, an ugly sound rolls out of her throat. She raises her face to la Macarena, "is *this* my rose?"

"I do not make bread, but I will give you yeast."

"What?" Aurora sees Her now, sitting at the edge of the bed, pulling at the blanket swaddling Dolores. "Is this my rose? Is it?"

"Aurora, the world finds a way to give you what you desire. You know this." The Virgin is tickling Dolores' toes which have peeked out from under the blanket.

"I want Esperanza. I want my daughter" And although Aurora mouths these words, no sound escapes. The cords are tightening around her chest, her breath is rising under her collarbones.

"I know." La Macarena softly pulls the blanket over my mother's feet after She bends low to kiss them.

"The rose was nothing," Aurora's voice is low, visceral. Her eyes are daggers.

"Hope will come again. And our daughter is with you. Attend this moment now."

At that moment, Manolito scurries in and throws up his arms as if he has just discovered the coveted treasure in a game of hide and seek. He had been searching for his big sister and believes he has found her again in Dolores. His big sister has become his little sister. It's the newest incarnation of a game he has been playing these past weeks.

"Her name is Dolores. Call her Dolores." Aurora once again, and with a patience she does not feel, corrects her young son who doesn't understand. "She is not Esperanza."

Aurora looks down at Dolores. She is so skinny, a tiny dark thing. Her ebony hair curling around her shell ears, her dark lashes fringing a delicate border around her sleepy eyes. A small rose in the beginning of bloom, elegant between two perfectly parenthetical brows.

~

I, too, am a second daughter, born after the beloved first. But the firstborn daughter holds so much for the new mother: possibility, potential, purpose all projected into such a small package. With our daughters there is the chance to love as we would like to have been loved, to mother as we wished we were mothered, and to nurture, not only these precious little daughters, but also ourselves. We are witnesses to each other.

I know this is true for Madeleine and myself. I can only imagine it was true of my grandmother and my mother with their firstborn daughters: Esperanza and Aurora; my sister and Dolores. As well as Madeleine and me. Full and complicated, eternal and unconditional love. This is the love that redeems the world.

However, the second daughter, one who is born after the loss of the beloved first, is a distorted mirror. A warped trick mirror that hurls contorted images, hollow-eyed reflections of pain and despair that are difficult, if not impossible, to claim.

Sitting in this pew at the foot of la Macarena, I imagine how life must have been for my mother. A ghost child like myself, born in the shadow of my grandmother's devastating and consuming grief, not unlike the pool of despair and sorrow in which I was born. Neither of us viable distractions for our mothers, neither of us salve, much less salvation, from their losses. Neither of us sufficiently tangible to detract from the overwhelming evidence of absence. Our mother's sorrow separates us, like a shroud, a veil of sadness. Both of us vessels filled with impossible expectations and misplaced hopes and irrepressible grief. Both of us loved in that we were protected; we were fed and clothed and sheltered. But between our mothers and ourselves, a distance, a distraction, because we are the embodiment of a repressed memory at once alluring and devastating. These are some things my mother and I have in common.

I attempt to connect these threads, weave them, as I stumble into the third sorrow. The beads in my hand now warmed by my constant fumbling. Jesus is lost and then three days later he is found in the temple. The fear and anxiety his mother must feel. The impotence of not being able to do anything. His casual reply that he is in his Father's house. Lost and found again but changed. Each of them changed. And the pain from that deformed growth. Even my mother and I, as daughters lost in the shadows, twist and grow, searching for our mothers' light.

~

Easter week in 1937 is simpler and more modest than in years past.

Some Brotherhoods are able to process with only a simple wooden crucifix this year. So many effigies have been ruined in fires and will need vast restoration before coming out in procession again. And many others are tucked away still in hiding. Aurora reminds herself that they are lucky that la Macarena has returned to them. Her presence does so much for the morale of the people, and She brings the city together – if only for this one night – even if she herself cannot bear to look at Her.

During the afternoon of Maundy Thursday in 1937, Cardinal Illudain y Esteban washes the feet of some of the poorest of Sevilla's workers. He purposefully attends the workers in the Macarena quarter where most of the hostilities toward the Church have been encountered and because it is the city's poorest. It is in this *"rojo" barrio* where most of the churches have burned. These are the workers, the Reds, who have led strikes, who failed at the uprising against Queipo de Llano, who persist in their surreptitious and clandestine antifascist, anti-Church activities. He feels magnanimous in his outreach, benevolent in his sacrifice at attending even these. And he is surprised by the vast numbers of faithful who arrive for Maundy Thursday and the celebration of mass. He did not expect such devotion from this faithless quarter. He judges them by their deeds, not by their hearts.

Some of the same hard and callused feet Cardinal Illundain y Esteban washed on Thursday are bloodied and bruised by the end of Friday's processions. Torn around the ankles where shackles have cut close to the bone, scraped and sore from the rough cobbles of the streets, the *costaleros* are nearly hobbled by their pilgrimage through the city. The smeared drops of blood left on the stones are evidence of penitent and faithful hearts. The Church knows nothing about these people of the Macarena.

For four hours in the early morning darkness of Good Friday, in his own effort to appeal to the Red *barrio*, General Gonzalo Queipo de Llano carries a four-foot tall ivory candle in procession behind la Macarena de Esperanza. He wears his dress uniform, and his chest is adorned with a multitude of medals and ribbons. Even still, not many recognize him. Most know him only by his outlandish and ostentatious radio broadcasts. In his silence, he could be anyone. But Aurora sees. His swagger speaks volumes.

"*Sin vergüenza.* The shameless pig. Trying to win our hearts by claiming affinity with our Virgin!" Aurora crosses herself at the incongruous sight of such a blasphemous ass beside the most holy Virgin.

"Just as they don't know your heart, you cannot know theirs." La Macarena is glancing back at Aurora who is holding their Dolores in her arms. Aurora's arms are constantly filled with Dolores as if holding her she can keep her safe from the same fate that took Esperanza, or as though she can contain her pain in this small bundle.

The main streets and Cathedral routes are slippery with hardened puddles of wax from the tens of thousands of candles. Queipo's patent leather boots slip, and he suffers an awkward indignity before quickly righting himself. Aurora laughs out loud as he glances around to see if anyone was watching.

Manuel turns to Aurora. She tries to divert his attention away from her though, "there isn't a humble, penitent bone in his body. I don't know who he thinks he's fooling."

La Macarena has moved on, whispering as She glides as if upon the waters, towards the Cathedral. "*... Aurora, pray for us sinners now and at the hour of our death ...*"

~

In my research, I learned that Queipo was walking a portion of the processional route because he had been made a life member of the *Hermandad*. La Macarena's Brotherhood had presented the Virgin's golden crown to the General for the Nationalist cause, but also because they were afraid of the looting and fires and wanted Queipo's protection. Since the general refused to sell the crown and instead returned it to the Brotherhood, they felt even more obliged to admit him into the Brotherhood. They invited him to process alongside them – they in their hooded penitent cloaks, and he in general's regalia. In reading this history, I wondered what might have been had they instead offered to sell the crown to feed La Macarena's starving devotees.

~

Posters of Franco are being slathered hurriedly over the highly stylized Communist propaganda that had only recently been plastered on walls. Giant banners of Franco with his tiny mustache and the slogan "One State! One Country! One Chief! Franco! Franco!" are hung in shop windows and across city walls. With the help and support of German and Italian troops, Franco gradually begins to take control of the rest of Spain.

Aurora mutters to herself as she prepares the family supper, "Franco, Franco, he's forgotten who puts food on his table. Walking around with that ridiculous little mustache, perhaps he should go eat in Germany with his brother Adolf." And then aloud to whomever will hear, "*dime con quien andas y te diré quien eres.*" She knows we are judged by the company we keep.

She and Manuel know these fascists will win. They will win because they possess more than enough brute force. Bullies have the power to take what they want, but they will never convince.

~

On July 1, 1937, the bishops put forth a letter to be read over Radio Sevilla. It is a collective epistle unequivocally supporting Franco and his generals. "Whereas the Church would forgive the people who murdered priests and nuns, burned churches and convents, looted sacred artifacts, attacked religious education and tradition, it would no longer bless them as long as they did not support *Generalissimo* Francisco Franco."

The letter is read with authority and urgency, and it tears in two the hearts of *Sevillanos* who love their Virgin and had put faith in their vote for the Republic of Spain.

The radio address continues, "This war is an armed plebiscite. On one side spiritual values are defended by the insurgents who rose to defend law and order, social peace, traditional civilization, and religion. On the other side, the worship of materialism – call it Marxist, communist, or anarchist – which wants to abolish Spain's ancient civilization through fraudulent elections. Traditional Spain must be defended."

Almost immediately the Church reaps its reward in a rigidly enforced restoration of religious teaching in the schools, where classrooms are adorned with portraits of Franco with the words *el Caudillo* emblazoned beneath his pouchy face. Images of the Virgin Mary are plastered right alongside him as if they are brother and sister, king and queen. School textbooks are rewritten and warn against stimulants like coffee, tobacco, alcohol, newspapers, politics, cinema, and other "indulgences" that would undermine the Spanish people and lay waste to their bodies and minds.

Women are once again relegated to second-class citizens as the schoolbooks declare that "women have never discovered anything. They lack the creative talent which God has reserved for men." The quickly contrived law further asserts that "a wife has no rights over her own body and that upon marriage she gives up those rights to her husband. He is the only one who can use those rights and only for reproduction." The women of Spain revolt, having only recently learned the sound and power of their voices. Their uproar is deafening. Across Spain more and more women join the Republican fight against Franco. They will fight alongside. They will kill and be killed alongside their brothers.

Church attendance becomes obligatory for all military and civilian officials. Soon Pope Pius XI will bless Franco's "crusade" with his denunciation of what he calls the Republican government's "truly satanic hatred of God." The message is clear: to love God, to adore la Macarena, you must also support Franco's Spain.

~

My grandparents did not know that across the world people were horrified by what was happening in Spain. Men and women who had never set foot in Spain came in legion to fight against the fascist takeover. On their lips, the foretelling words, "we must fight this injustice against others, for who will fight for us when our time comes?"

This sentiment was prevalent at the World Exhibition in Paris. So many people from so many countries anxiously awaited the attractions and the first and only national pavilion that Republican Spain ever had in a World Fair. On July 12, after a seven-week delay, the prefabricated pavilion designed by José Luis Sert was ready for the world. The assigned location for the three-story Spanish pavilion was the topic of much reporting; it was a tragic glimpse into the fight being waged in Spain as well as a foreshadowing of what would soon erupt across Europe.

Spain's unpretentious pavilion was installed beneath the conflicting shadows of the towering and politically posturing edifices from Nazi Germany and Soviet Russia. Contrasting dramatically with the overpowering, monumental Nazi and Soviet structures that soared over all other pavilions, Sert's design was modest and necessarily inexpensive. But the delicate glass and steel construction was also open and elegant, a transparent Modernist revelation of the fragility and the strength of the Spanish Republic. And for many, it was the quiet resolute strength of the Spanish pavilion that beckoned instead of the neighboring behemoths.

The Spanish exposition drew hordes of people clamoring to witness for themselves all the contributions from the great Spanish artists and writers currently in exile in Paris. And there was no questioning the statement the Republic was making. In the front courtyard stood the spare and sinewy sculpture from Alberto Sanchez; beneath it the inscription, "The Spanish people have a path, it leads to a star."

At the entrance, before one was fully inside, there was an immense photographic mural of Republican Soldiers standing with their arms bent at the elbow, raised, ready fists clenched, staring off into a distant horizon. Beneath the mural, their slogan, bold and speaking to the hearts of everyone: "We are fighting for the essential unity of Spain. We are fighting for the integrity of Spanish soil. We are fighting for the independence of our country and for the right of Spanish people to determine their own destiny."

These words conveyed an ideal that was nothing more than what so many consider a birthright, a freedom beyond reproach. And the proclamation echoed a sentiment held dear throughout the world.

Spain proved to be an early battleground in the great clash between the fascist tenets being promoted by Hitler and Mussolini and the communism of Stalin's Soviet Russia. Hitler's Luftwaffe first tested the broad sweeping carpet-bombing of civilian populations with alarming precision upon Spanish soil. Mussolini provided abundant troops and supplies to further Franco's aim. Stalin backed the International Brigades but eventually ended up stealing much of Spain's gold. The Spanish Civil War exposed a much greater global war of ideologies.

Emboldened by the sentiment of the mural, with the words of the slogan still ringing in their ears, many visitors to the pavilion then felt assaulted by Picasso's contribution. His painting, *Guernica*, confronted visitors with the brutal atrocities that were being perpetrated in his beloved Spain. His offering was a warning against complacency. *Guernica* would not allow the observer to keep what was happening on Spanish soil merely in the ideological realm. It was real. It was visceral and mangled and bloody. And his painting forced everyone to experience the raw, weeping wound.

Walking through the Spanish Pavilion there were images of dead children. There was Joan Miró's large panel entitled "The Reaper" depicting an upraised arm and resolute fist. There was Alexander Calder's "Mercury Fountain" that was a memorial to the siege of Almadén, which at that time supplied 60% of the world's mercury. Above it, his bloody red mobile hung in the balance. There were photographs of dismembered limbs and bloodied torsos amidst the ruin of rubble-strewn streets. There were dramatic and graphic films by Luis Buñuel and Joris Ivens and Ernest Hemingway about the brutality of Franco's troops. There were looped sound recordings of families recounting their loss, their hunger, their suffering. And there were postcards made of Picasso's series of drawings, "The Dream and Lie of Franco," on sale to raise funds for relief work.

Many visitors to the Spanish Pavilion were offended by the

images and graphic descriptions of the war in Spain. They did not appreciate being challenged to witness the horrors and implored to speak out for justice. Many would not understand that what was on display in the poetry, photographs, and paintings was something to celebrate. Here for anyone to see was Spain's persevering spirit, Spain's tenacious will to live life fully, with integrity and purpose, and free. Spain's heart, bloodied and bruised, was on display in the pavilion. It was all Spain had left. It was what they were still fighting for.

Picasso's *Guernica*, dismissed as "the dream of a madman," proved to be a prophetic vision when Europe was plunged into a war that eventually engulfed the world. When I first saw the painting, the confusing structure and figures were assaulting. I couldn't clearly point out the heroes and the villains amidst the black, white and predominantly gray devastation and chaos. I could only try to imagine how it might have been for those who lived through this, to have survived it.

And whereas my *abuelo* could only whisper his loathing quietly in the patios and bars of Franco's conquered Sevilla, the famed artist would declare his to the world: "I clearly express my abhorrence of the military caste that has sunk Spain in an ocean of pain and death." I now know that Picasso's words echoed the sentiment of many in Sevilla.

~

No one could imagine the ocean of pain and death growing any more vast or deep, but each day reality would prove their imaginations insufficient to the suffering they could endure. My *abuela* is able to find less and less to eat at the market stalls. The stores are all but barren. All around Andalucía, fields are lying barren. Many farmers are standing impotent with idle hands, the first time in centuries, because there is no seed. Because the crops that are being produced on Spanish soil are being sent to the Nationalist troops, there are fewer rations to go around. But still she visits the market in case there is something they can afford, something that may satisfy for today.

Aurora marches ahead with her basket hanging loosely from her hand. In her pocket are a few *centimos* that she hopes will go further than she knows they will. She imagines what might be at an affordable price. What might be about to rot and sold at discount? And sometimes, what might be discarded as no longer salable, though this seems to happen less and less.

Manolito stumbles along after her grasping at her skirt. Dolores is tucked in the pram, fingers reaching and grasping at air. Manolito hopes that maybe he'll find some *madroños* growing wild alongside the road today, or if he's lucky, some discarded cactus fruit at the market. And it is possible that Dolores will drop the crust of bread she is teething on.

It is still early, and so Aurora is not surprised when she sees two young men, best friends and new apprentices to Manuel at the foundry, are also scrounging for food. It is not an unfamiliar sight. Often it is children who search while those able to work look for work. But on this day, these two young men are looking for food as they cross the plaza on their way to the foundry. As everyone says, "*a quien madrugá, Dios le ayuda*." And Aurora prays that God does indeed help those who rise early.

The events transpire so slowly that Aurora feels that she could have stopped them. She thinks she could have called their names and reminded them that they are *amigos*, friends who have grown up together; she could have thrown her meager coins at their feet. But then, things are happening so slowly that she can hardly believe that her mind isn't playing a trick on her.

Lately there are bright stars that dance in her periphery. Dazzling and head spinning, bright golden stars play across the edges of her world. Sometimes life spins very slowly and she has to sit down for a moment so that the revolutions will stop. She blinks deliberately and gives her head a small shake wondering if she is going to have to sit down there in the middle of the street. And in the middle of that same blink of an eye, halfway into her labored breath, she sees the cart's wheel fall into a deep rut. She sees a small loaf of bread balance precariously and then tumble. She sees, as does everyone in the market square, the bread fall gracelessly off the cart and into the dirty gutter. She sees both boys lunge. She sees the fight, the hunger, their desperate need and the not enough. And before she sees it, she hears it. The sunken sound of a head split against the cobbled stones, the gaped opening, the slackened mouth, the stillness. The bread soaked with blood.

Of that day, Aurora will remember the market women crossing themselves hurriedly, as if there were more to that swift flurry of motion than a habit long devoid of meaning. She will remember the bread vendor attempting, almost in vain, to give away all his bread to anyone who would take it. His words echoing against the buildings in the plaza, "Take, take ... take this bread. Eat."

~

The French Prime Minister Daladier is threatening to freeze the left-wing Republican gold deposited in France at the beginning of the war. This would cut off Spain from all financial resources because the other Spanish gold is in Russia, impossible to obtain now. Franco is negotiating with Hitler and Mussolini about credit and how he might repay his enormous debt. The Fascist army continues their numerous air raids on Spanish cities to the north.

Everyone wonders how much longer the Republic can resist.

International supplies of food and medications are being purchased, yet the supply ships bringing the provisions are constantly bombed and the food sinks, wasted in the straits of Gibraltar. Even when the supply ships aren't hit, the incessant raids delay unloading, sometimes for weeks, and the food spoils. Trucks carrying supplies inland are raided and looted. The lack of vitamins and food is causing eruptions of boils on necks and armpits. So many people are suffering from chilblains and open oozing sores from exposure to the cold and damp.

The black market enables Aurora to obtain additional food, but Manuel can hardly eat what he feels is tainted by Franco's blood money. His choice feels impossible to him. Could he be like Abraham, willing to sacrifice his family for his convictions? Would the knife be spared at the last minute? How could he join forces with the Republican Army when that would mean certain death for his family? Defeated and demoralized, my grandfather's collection of small bits of scrap iron is sometimes the only thing that keeps him from falling under the weight of his cross. Because there is a war and the appointed Fascist army overseer in the foundry is ever vigilant, scavenging is dangerous. But he continues to collect. Not much, but every day. Enough to weigh his pockets. He tightens his belt another notch.

~

The early morning hours are dark and full of expectation. Another year, another Holy Week. Despite fatigue, many are out for the processions, the women wrapped in shawls and *mantóns* against the soft cool night, the men with their shoulders up around their ears. Only the children, hanging from trees and climbing the city wall, seem unaffected by the damp night air.

As the Virgin emerges in procession from the Macarena Arch, a gasp and then a hush ripple through the crowd. Then, from a balcony above, a lone pain-stricken voice pierces the silence. The song, a heartfelt *saeta*, is sung to la Macarena. It is a throaty and earthy *sotto voce*, twisting and plunging, soaring into the night air like an arrow. It dives deep into the hearts of everyone listening. Penetrating and vibrant and resonant with an understanding of Her sorrow as well as Her enduring hope, the song balances the impossible feelings of Good Friday. Like life, the *saeta* is a type of *cante jondo*, a deep song about both death and renewal.

After the salute to la Macarena, Her *costaleros* carry Her one-and-a-half-ton *paso* – strong enough to support the roof, but tender enough to quiver in the soft night breeze. She appears to sway as the drums roll out their thunder and the trumpets wail the sentimental marches that will accompany Her through the streets to the Cathedral.

It has been over a year since Aurora and la Macarena have knelt together. Over a year since they have shared the contents of their hearts. And though she still cannot bring herself to talk with the Virgin – despite Her being ever present around the house and in the courtyard – Aurora is angry about something else entirely. Aurora cannot abide how Queipo de Llano has claimed Her as his own.

This year his involvement has created quite a stir. Not only is he present for the *Madrugá*, he also pulled strings to have the processional times rearranged to suit his schedule. Despite his austere appearance and silent reverence as he walks behind the beloved Macarena, Aurora is furious. She glowers at him as he walks alongside the exhausted, overworked and underfed men of her *barrio*. She sees the buttons pulling across Queipo's belly, and she stares at the bare ankles of the men carrying la Macarena. She sees the torn flesh and the smears of blood left on the streets. As the processions recede, the crowds remain breathlessly silent except for the whisper of prayers as they watch the passing sacred figure, brightly illuminated with the golden light of hundreds of candles. She reaches for Manuel's hand, his reassuring presence, but his hands are thrust deep inside his pockets feeling the rough edges of today's collected scrap.

There is a great rivalry between the neighborhoods of la Macarena and Triana, the neighborhood just across the river. Both *barrios* have beautiful and revered Virgins who process on Good Friday during the *Madrugá*. Both Virgins are Dolorosas, depicting the sorrowing Virgin after the death of Her son. And both are named Esperanza, expressing the hope we must maintain in the face of overwhelming grief. But despite this kinship, or perhaps because of it, the two inspire fierce rivalries. The Macarena *barrio* upholds la Macarena as the most beautiful and beloved of all Virgins, and across the Guadalquivir, the neighborhood of Triana embraces their own Esperanza.

Both processions have an extensive following of worshipful devotees, and the times and processional routes for each Virgin are carefully charted for simple crowd control. But this year, because the Radio General Queipo de Llano couldn't mesh his schedule with the ages old and carefully orchestrated times of the many processions, he deigned to rearrange the established rule and la Macarena's march through the pre-dawn hours. For this, the fiercely proud devotees of the two Virgins are in the same place at the same time.

"*¡La de Triana!*" shouts one group from across the river.

"*!La Macarena es mas guapa, mas hermosa!*" shouts the Macarenos.

Two distinct crowds pressing up and against each other, the Virgins wedged between.

"The streets belong to *la de Triana*!"

"Sevilla belongs to our beautiful Macarena!"

This is the first time the two Virgins meet, and they are face to face in the middle of an intersection. The *pasos* are jostled by the pressing crowds, and it appears that both *la de Triana* and *la Macarena* might fall, faces first, onto the street. Aurora crosses herself and locks eyes with la Macarena. Her worry overcomes her residual anger.

The crowd rushes in, and the *costaleros* are jostled so much that the delicate balance they carry tips precariously to one side and then the other as they compensate. Both Esperanzas appear at first to be dancing together. It seems a familiar Sevillana and for a moment Aurora thinks she hears the crowd begin *tocando palmas*, clapping and shouting *olé*. But then the scene changes and it is not a dance but an awkward sideways shuffling, as if two strangers needing to pass each other keep stepping the same way.

Suddenly Aurora sees la Macarena in Her youthful stance and vigilance as She stamps Her foot to rouse Her *costaleros* who are slumped over with the weight of Her. The *capitaz* immediately calls a halt. The abruptness causes la Macarena to pitch forward toward the other Virgin in such a way that Aurora could swear She is now challenging the Virgin from Triana, as if the two Virgins are children playing at *toreador* and *toro*, rushing forward and then retreating. All around Aurora, the crowd sucks in their breath; all jostling is suspended as their hands prepare to catch a falling Virgin. But then Aurora sees la Macarena glance over at the other Virgin and give a quick wink as well as the softest, almost apologetic, smile. Aurora sees a slight shrug from la Esperanza of Triana, a shift in Her weight.

The most striking thing Aurora notices about la Macarena is Her youthfulness. Aurora is suddenly feeling older than la Macarena. It is as though for the first time she notices Her oval face that is exquisitely proportioned. Her brow that is short and smooth with Her profound sadness appearing only in Her eyes and brows which are knit together in grief. There are no lines mapping Her sorrow like the ones Aurora is beginning to see around her own eyes and across her forehead. La Macarena's eyes are big and dark, shadowed yet flashing in the flickering candlelight. They seem to be searching for understanding, compassion, reconciliation. Teardrops stain Her cheek, and Her mouth is slightly open in that eternal still moment between breathing in and breathing out. Expectant, knowing, and full of grace. And She is reaching out, always reaching. Perhaps even toward my *abuela*.

Both Virgins exemplify grace and beauty despite being racked by suffering. They are "*Dolorosas*," Queens of Grief crowned in gold, regally robed in richly embroidered gowns and cloaks. Their jewels sparkling under the night sky. But a striking difference reveals itself to Aurora as quick as the wink and shrug that passed between the Virgins: la Macarena's suffering reveals a key paradox. There is a smile behind Her tears. She has somehow found consolation. It is as though la Macarena is in that moment of accepting Her martyrdom and now welcomes the chance to suffer along with all the world. And she is showing the world how our anguish can be soothed. With that realization, Aurora forgives la Macarena.

~

After the processions of Good Friday, Aurora is accustomed to spending Holy Saturday with la Macarena in solemn observance. Yet now it is also the day Aurora feels closer to la Macarena. It is the day when Her son Jesus is truly dead, like Aurora's own Esperanza. For my *abuela*, it is not disconcerting that Jesus should be dead, or that he is in the realm of the dead. She knows the dead hasten toward Jesus and cry out: "Son of God, have mercy on us; deal with us according to your kindness and lead us from the chains of darkness. Let us also be redeemed with You."

As they sit in silence, la Macarena and Aurora reflect on what Jesus then says of those souls in the land of the dead, "and I heard their voice, and placed their faith in my heart. And I placed my name upon their head, because they are free and they are mine." Aurora believes that with those few words he redeems those locked in death, he takes them as his own. Even her Esperanza.

"You know Aurora, your despair could provoke a desire to understand life fully." La Macarena picks at a snagged thread on Her robes.

"It is still hard to imagine life without her." Aurora's eyes are shut. She places her palms over her eyelids and presses there until stars prick.

"You have been living in a purgatory, a Holy Saturday, made up of two distinct types of pain." The thread is getting longer as la Macarena teases it from the embroidered border.

The stars are stabbing at her eyelids, and Aurora focuses on the one, the largest, that doesn't spin. "No. It is just one: sorrow."

"Aurora, there are two. You have been wishing for a miracle that you can have your Esperanza again. And the other sorrow is manifest in the loss of hope when you see your Dolores and recognize that it is impossible. These two arise in you one after the other. Over and over." La Macarena has pulled the gold thread and it is puckering the heavy brocade. *"I want you to know there is another way, Aurora."*

"I am trying."

"Today is Holy Saturday – the day the world knows my son to be

dead – yet he is doing his most important work. He is claiming you for his own. He claims each of us by name, Aurora." Holding Her sleeve up to Aurora, la Macarena beckons her help with the snag.

Aurora takes up the heavy silk between her fingers and gently tugs until the thread is pulled back into the weave and the pucker disappears. "He claims the dead. I am not dead. Esperanza is."

"Each person, by name. He is freeing you from the in-between where you are stuck. He is freeing you from the despair of wanting what can never be." La Macarena holds out Her arm and examines Aurora's handiwork. She compares it to Her other sleeve and smiles.

"But *Señora,* I still ache for her," Aurora chokes out her broken words between sobs. "My arms ache for her."

Taking Aurora into Her arms, the Virgin tries to pull her over the threshold. She is so close. *"But do you see how this despair is different? It's not wanting what you cannot have. It is grieving what is lost. This sorrow can point you to a deeper faith and a new life."*

"New life?"

"Everyone you hold dear, Aurora, is vulnerable. Your grief can help you recognize that everything and everyone is fresh and new, created in every moment. New life, Aurora. Fragile yet eternal." She wipes their tears and cradles Aurora's face, bringing their foreheads together.

The light has turned liquid. Aurora feels she is swimming in warm golden water. "New life." The beads are turning again in my *abuela's* hands.

~

In 1938, Sevilla along with two-thirds of Spain is under Fascist control. The last vestiges of Republican Spain are facing an army of more than 100,000 armed Italian soldiers. The Condor Legion, comprised of volunteers from the German Air Force and Army, is the most technically advanced in the world, and German ground troops, a strong tank unit, and German artillery units support it. There are also over 60,000 Moorish mercenaries and Franco's own troops, close to a million well-armed soldiers. Republican Spain fights on despite Franco's coordinated and unrelenting campaign supported by Mussolini and Hitler.

Newspapers around the world cannot fathom how the spirit among Republican soldiers and the Loyalist Spanish citizens is still high enough not only to resist, but to attack. The persistence of the Spanish human spirit toward freedom baffles a world that sees only a beaten underdog growling at inevitable annihilation.

As the war in Spain is dominating the world news, there are some internationally famous papers reporting favorably towards Franco, claiming that he is attempting to restore cherished family values in keeping with Catholic faith and Spanish tradition. These family values extol keeping families together, keeping wives and mothers at home, forbidding women from working once they become married: first obey the Church, then obey the man of the house. These are the laws that govern traditional Spain and Franco's plan for the future. By extension, Hitler and Mussolini are praised as well for their aide to Franco's mission, his "crusade." Queipo brings this growing world interest to his radio broadcast as if the accolades are for him alone.

"One of the world's most prominent periodicals is praising me and Franco as we attempt to tame the savagery that has come over our glorious Spain. LIFE Magazine from America supports Fascist politics in Spain and all of Europe." Everyone can hear as Queipo turns the pages of the magazine.

That night my grandparents hear Queipo claim that despite the thousands of men and women from all over the world coming to Spain to help, the LIFE reporters in Spain are maintaining a propagandistic campaign against the Republic. The reporters are unabashedly pro-Franco while referring to the Republican army as a "Spanish Mob" and a "Spanish Horde." The publication goes so far as to call the legal and democratically elected Spanish government the "real rebels and mutineers."

Queipo relays all this to the *Sevillanos* listening. "Everyone in the world can read how I, Queipo de Llano, and Franco along with our troops, are presented as noble and honest soldiers. Listen to this! America is praising us as the rescuers of Spain who will bring peace and justice for all Spaniards. You Red dogs should lay down your guns and be grateful for our benevolence! We are doing God's work!"

In other radio broadcasts, my grandparents will learn that France and Britain now officially recognize Franco's Nationalist government. They will listen as President Azana resigns. They will cringe as Queipo delivers the news that the United States of America now recognizes Franco's fascist regime.

~

It is officially, finally finished in April of 1939. The remaining Republican army surrenders. In the bar, Manuel listens to a new and imposed silence, an emptiness that belies the hope that was once voiced. He pulls from his pocket a scrap of iron, like a piece of shrapnel, and says almost to himself, "there are no records. No accounting for the names."

Someone hears him and says, "not only that, we're not allowed to remember."

~

By July 1939, three months after the official cease-fire, there are still an estimated 80 executions a day in Sevilla. These are deemed legal executions after summary trials wherein the accused has roughly one minute to defend himself. The bodies are laid in the sprawling common grave at the cemetery. There is no court except for Queipo de Llano, and he rules on his whim. A local peasant is shot for refusing to sell his mule to the chief of the *guardia civil*. A pregnant widow, along with her two children under five years of age, are killed because she sought aid, extra rations, but her husband had fought for the Republic. This is when Aurora stops claiming the rations for Esperanza's doll. It is too close, too similar to the widow's situation. She'll find another way.

Out of desperation, people are finding unlikely things to eat. Neighbors in the *barrio* have discovered there are some weeds that have a little hooded berry, and these are okay to eat though bitter and leave a sharp edge to the teeth. Small flowers called *conejitos* grow on a broad-limbed tree on the grounds of the municipal building. My mother and her brother learn to scamper up the trees in search of *conejitos*, sometimes just because the climbing is exhilarating. More often because they are hungry.

Manolito and Dolores learn to suck honeysuckle blossoms that grow over the gates and fences. The burst of fragranced flavor is fleeting. Someone in the neighborhood discovers that striking the hard apricot stone between the pavement and a rock reveals a meaty inside. Aurora says it is indigestible, but others, perhaps hungrier, eat the dense core. The truly desperate eat the little yellowish berries hidden in bushes at the side of the roads, but Manolito and Dolores discover that those berries will make you have diarrhea for days.

Many mornings Aurora hustles Manolito and Dolores out the door so she doesn't have to see their hunger. If they play, they'll forget, she thinks as she stands in the rations line that snakes around the market square. Some days a sweet potato, more rarely a segment of bone, today a handful of lentils. The conversation in line is always about food: how to flavor the lentils with boiled onion skin; how cat tastes like rabbit; how dog tastes like lamb. Maybe that is why the usual strays haven't been around, Aurora imagines. A recipe for a soup made from a couple of spoons of flour fried in olive oil with a crushed clove of garlic and added water becomes a staple in the Macarena *barrio*.

When Manolito and Dolores are lucky, they find discarded scraps behind houses in the more affluent areas, where the government officials live. Aurora always gives whatever she's kept aside to Dolores because she is so skinny. "Eat *hija*, or the wind will carry you away like a kite." Manolito knows there is no extra crust for him. He knows that whatever is left after his mother rations out portions will be saved and passed to Dolores. She is small for her age, wiry and taut. However, Dolores keeps up with Manolito, running through the neighborhood and scavenging through the wreckage of gutted stores. She's strong and fast, almost as fast as Manolito. But Aurora doesn't see this – she sees only the thin spindly arms and the knobby knees sticking out below.

~

In late autumn of 1939, another daughter is born, and she is named Esperanza because she looks nothing like the first Esperanza and nothing like Dolores, and because Aurora's mother-in-law is still waiting for her namesake. This daughter is golden and blue-eye with roses on her cheeks, "where they belong," thinks Aurora.

La Macarena again sits with Aurora. She places her hand gently above Aurora's heart to slow the beating and calm the breathing. *"I know, I know,"* is all She says, over and over.

"She looks nothing like her. Nothing. Night and Day." Aurora's words sputter between gasps and coughs.

"Do you think you will not have to worry, Aurora? Do you think she will be immune to the fate of her sister because she is blond instead of dark?" La Macarena places drops of ointment made from eucalyptus leaves on Aurora's breasts and gently rubs circles, a pattern that Aurora feels but cannot trace.

Aurora breathes as deeply as she is able and knows that la Macarena understands her answer before she speaks. "With Dolores, I live constantly in remembrance. And sometimes I imagine that any minute she could ..."

"But don't you see the gift in that, Aurora?" La Macarena's eyebrows lift in question, pulling Aurora into the question.

"Gift? No. This is no gift, to imagine that at any moment she may be taken again. What possible gift could be in that?" Aurora tries to lift herself onto her elbows but the room spins in shadows and stars.

"Shhh, Aurora. Hush now." La Macarena leans down to plump the pillow behind Aurora. *"What I mean is that Esperanza was taken home. That is past. This is a new moment where you have two healthy daughters. Two beautiful, healthy daughters and a strong son. And they live."*

"But Dolores could be taken ..." my *abuela's* despair so deep and so close to the surface, she shakes her head unable to bear the thoughts that spin with the room.

"So could Manuel or Manolito or this little one." La Macarena is whispering, *"so could this rosy Esperanza."* She rubs her tiny circles up to the base of Aurora's neck and behind her ears.

Aurora shoves la Macarena's hand aside and attempts to move away.

"Stay here, Aurora. Stay here with me now," and She grasps Aurora's hands rubbing the oil now into her callused palms. *"What will happen will happen. There is nothing we can do to change that, and*

worry doesn't help."

Lifting her hand to her face, Aurora breathes in the delicate perfume that somehow slows the dancing stars and spinning shadows. "So then, what do You mean by 'gift?'"

"Each moment, new and precious, is a gift. If you live this way, each moment is as full and round as eternity. But each moment is also fleeting as though a shroud of death is ever present. The gift endures when we carry on in the knowledge that this moment is fleeting and full at once. Eternal and transient. Do you understand, Aurora?"

Manuel enters before Aurora can answer. He stands hesitant at the threshold, "did you call for me?"

"No, no. I must have been dreaming," Aurora stammers and shifts slightly making room for him to sit.

Manuel can tell Aurora is distracted but doesn't know what to do. He arranges the coverlet and wipes at her brow. "Do you want to talk about the dream?"

With both Manuel's and la Macarena's hands attending her, Aurora's flustered thoughts cannot focus.

La Macarena buttons Aurora's nightgown and leans over and whispers, *"I'll leave you two to finish our talk."*

Aurora watches la Macarena move toward the corner of the room and slip away before she turns attention to Manuel's question. "No. It's just the same ... babies come and then they ... there is not enough ... I'm sorry. I'm just so tired."

Manuel is often exasperated by Aurora's superstitions, but her being able to name this daughter Esperanza only because she looks nothing like the first is beyond him. "We can't live in fear of God as well as the fascists!"

"I don't live in fear of God. I just don't want to tempt him, that is all." She is twisting the sheet around her wrist, pulling tightly.

"Tempt him how?" Manuel pulls Aurora into his arms, but she can feel his frustration.

Manuel leans in and pulls his fingers through the damp curls at her nape. Aurora sucks in her breath and holds it trying to find the words he might understand. "*I* don't want to forget her. My Esperanza. My firstborn, *mi hija*. I don't want to replace her. I don't want her ever to feel replaced. This new daughter, with her blond curls and blue eyes won't remind anyone of Esperanza. She won't remind *me* of my lost Esperanza." Aurora is stumbling over her words. Her breath is catching in her throat, and her eyes are glassy as they dart this way and that looking for something, anything on which to focus. Anything other than Manuel's eyes.

The room suddenly feels chilled. Aurora catches his hand and makes herself look into his eyes, silently imploring him to understand.

"Dolores? She reminds you?" Manuel asks as understanding washes over him.

The answer comes immediately to Aurora, but she hesitates before speaking aloud because she knows he will feel helpless in the face of her pain. But she answers anyway because they have always been honest with each other. "Every day," she breathes.

Manuel reaches over to hold Aurora, but she shrinks away, turning her face into the pillow.

~

In 1941, Cardinal Segura lays the cornerstone of the new Macareno Temple that will be built just inside the Macarena Gate. In attendance are the hardworking people of the Macarena *barrio* as well as civilian and military authorities. For this auspicious occasion, la Macarena is brought out in procession. When completed, this will be Her new home.

Despite the fact that jails are now filled beyond capacity, the authorities are arresting more and more of whom they call anarchists. The bullring is transformed into a temporary holding pen detaining as many as 20,000 anti-fascists that will be either transferred to other prisons or killed behind the wall at the cemetery. Midnight raids continue to be a nightly occurrence, and the lists of anyone ever associated with the anarchists, communists, socialists or republicans are growing more lengthy as more names are betrayed when rifles are hoisted against the foreheads or pressed into the backs of the men and women taken in the night.

Sugar is selling for 50 to 70 *centimos* a kilo on the black market, although it is legally priced at 10 *centimos*. Fishermen are no longer allowed to fish at night because too many are attempting escape across the straits into Africa. The wheat harvest is less than half its pre-war crop. Mines and steel mills in Northern Spain that were captured early in the war are working overtime because of the rise in exports to Germany. And Spain's foreign trade that once flowed with exports of olive oil, oranges, and lemons has diminished radically as Franco is sending most goods to Germany. This is debt repayment; Franco had already reaped whatever compensation was due in the form of bombs and military support during the war.

~

I learned that during that same time, Spain was also exporting arms, munitions, citrus, wool, cotton, and textiles to Germany. And despite the desperate lack of food in Spain, nearly 250,000 tons of foodstuffs were sent annually to Germany. Tungsten ore, used for armaments, was exported to Germany at the rate of about 200 tons a month despite a promised embargo. The world saw that though professed neutral, Spain increased deliveries of raw materials to Germany by one-third.

Hitler's demand for repayment from Franco starved my grand-parents, their children, and all of Sevilla's working families. In Spain, between 1940 and 1944, close to 20,000 people died of starvation, a level of hunger unknown since the Middle Ages.

The Fourth Sorrow: Grieved

The meeting of Jesus and Mary on the way to the cross: "And there followed him a great multitude of the people, and of women who bewailed and lamented him. But Jesus turning to them said, 'Daughters of Jerusalem, do not weep for me, but weep for yourselves and for your children.'"

Luke 23:27-28

My mother was born into the Spanish Civil War and its subsequent wake. She knows nothing of the carefree days others speak about, those times when there may not have been much, but there was enough. Enough food, enough work, enough warmth, enough love to go around.

My mother instead learns how to scavenge for food along roadsides, in treetops, scrambling along after carts destined for a market. She learns to beg in the plazas and at the Cathedral. She learns all this, and because she is so young and has never known anything other, it can be a game sometimes. When the shadow's slant reaches across the street, my mother and her brother return home, faces turned toward the setting sun, running barefoot, tiptoeing through broken glass, watchful of the dark men on horseback with patent leather tricorn hats like folded black paper boats. They see how their neighbors look down at their feet whenever the dark men approach. They see how fear is transcribed onto every motion, how voices can change in timbre and tone. They learn that their many questions are met with only profound silence. And they too will become silent. This is an early imprint. These observations instill a strong intuitive and guarded nature that will stay with my mother forever.

One night, Aurora and Manuel stand in the doorway of the children's bedroom holding their breath so not to pass the cough that is rampant this spring and has found its way into their home.

Forevermore vigilant over sickbeds, Aurora frets over clammy brows, tucks in tightly against drafts, steams, bathes, and anoints. Manuel seeing her inability to stop worrying attempts to pull her away from the door.

"Let them sleep. They are fine."

"I know they are fine." snaps Aurora.

Manuel tries a diversion, touching her elbow and pulling her close, "Manolito is growing too big for his name."

"He loves her so much. I don't think he is confused any longer." Aurora smiles. "I've been watching them together, and he seems to know now."

"It is a hard thing to lose his older sister and then meet her twin in his younger sister. It is a hard thing for us all." This last part he whispers softly, hesitantly.

"You know, Dolores has passed the age when ..." Aurora stops short.

"It's amazing how much she looks like her. But they are so different." Manuel quickly interjects. He presses his palm into the small of Aurora's back and holds her from turning away.

"Yes. Esperanza was always so full of questions. Always pestering me with this and that, showing me a bug or a new clapping game. Maybe that child had too much life for this world."

"And Dolores is?" Manuel asks hoping Aurora will come forth with some insight that shows she is just as attuned to her as she is to the others.

"I don't know." Aurora wrings her hands in her apron. "Dolores is an easy child. She follows direction. She does as she's told, but ..."

"What?" He pulls her away from the door so he can see her face.

"She can seem so afraid of her own shadow. I don't know, she seems more fearful than joyful. She imagines there is only one right and true way, when in fact there are many paths. She is guarded, protective of her thoughts and feelings. She keeps everything to herself. But when she's with her brother, she shines."

"She is young, and this is a difficult time for all of us. Perhaps it is best to be guarded. To live in the shadows."

~

A son is born to Aurora and Manuel. He is dark with hazel eyes that remind Aurora of her lost Esperanza. But he is a boy with a ferocious kick and a healthy wail, so the family is happy. Manuel lifts his newborn son and claims a new beginning that is "worthy of praise and gratitude" despite, or perhaps in spite, of Franco's reign. For this he is named Antonio.

La Macarena whispers gently into Aurora's ear, "His name suits him. He will make you proud. A good man with a fine heart."

Aurora is lying across the bed trying to gain control of her breathing. Each inhalation seems to require every muscle in her chest. She pulls deeply at the air as if her body is reluctant to be filled again now that it is emptied. But when la Macarena leans in closer, the scent of roses opening, releasing perfume, opens also my *abuela's* lungs. Once again, la Macarena's heavy robes drape across Aurora, providing a warmth and weight that calms her shivering and gasping. Together they exchange breaths, accepting and releasing the softly scented air surrounding them.

With Aurora so busy taking care of Antonio and Esperanza, Manolito and Dolores are let loose on their own for much of the day, and Aurora hardly notices that they've been elsewhere. However anytime my *abuela* sees Manolito, she admonishes him to "*cuide a su hermana.*"

But Manolito is always careful of his sister. He doesn't need to be reminded because to him, she is his Esperanza. He sees it every day. Dolores becoming more and more like his sister – at least physically. She has returned to him, and he doesn't want her to leave again. Though this is his secret. He is always careful to call her Dolores.

When Dolores and Manolito find Francisco José in a trunk tucked away with some little shoes, she pulls the doll out, and Manolito watches Dolores for any signs of recognition. He tries to sing the little song Esperanza taught him: "T*engo una muñeca vestida de azul; Con su camisita y su canesú ...*"

Dolores doesn't like the song, and she doesn't like the way Manolito is trying to get her to sing along as if she should know it. Why is he always doing that? Making her feel like she should be smarter? Bigger? Older?

Manolito lifts a pair of shoes out of the trunk and hands them to Dolores, "*ponerlos*. Put them on."

Dolores lays the doll down and starts to unfasten the button and slip the shoes on, but the shoes are just a bit too big for her feet. She steps into them anyway and stands holding her arms akimbo.

"*Baile.*" If she can dance in these shoes, Manuel knows she is his sister come back to stay.

She sets one foot out at an angle and raises her arms just like she's seen women do all over the neighborhood when there is music and the sun is setting. She turns her head toward Manolito who has started singing a song, a *seguidilla*. Chin up and challenging, she steps out in the shoes, but something changes in Manolito's expression, and it stops her. It's as if he is looking at a ghost.

Angry and somehow ashamed, she throws the doll back into the trunk and they both hear the doll's head crack against the lid. She kicks the shoes off and throws these into the trunk as well.

"What is it? What happened?" Manolito is grabbing at Dolores' arms, trying to stop her.

But whatever enchantment had been conjured is vanquished now. Dolores runs from the room, and Manolito follows. They run out the door and up to the roof. Dolores flings open the door to the pigeon coop and watches them fly up, but not away. Not as far away as she would like. They circle and circle overhead, staying close despite the pebbles Dolores throws. But then she catches herself and calls nervously, cooing them back to their home.

With Aurora always watching and worrying, slipping extra food into her pockets, and Manolito dragging her everywhere, Dolores learns that the care her family feels for her is somehow tempered with fear. But she doesn't know of what or why. Dolores doesn't like the way her mother sometimes seems to look into the core of her as if she is searching for something or someone; or other times when her mother looks right through her as though she were nothing more than a shadow. Sometimes Dolores feels her mother watching her, but as soon as she turns to meet the gaze, her mother looks away, glancing over the room as though she wasn't really searching out something in her second daughter or as though what she was looking for can't be found. At other times, Dolores tries to catch and hold her mother's eyes, but what mirror she finds there is cloudy, a faulty reflection. And no matter how much she eats, her mother is always trying to get her to eat more, more. It is confusing and disconcerting, this invisibility and attention.

~

No one ever talked about her older sister, the Esperanza who died. What my mother knew, she learned from listening to the neighbors whispering in the courtyard or her parents late at night. My mother learned about her sister the same way I discovered what happened to my sister: surreptitiously and in the shadows. These are not conversations we could have with our mothers because their pain and grief flashed furiously, immediately. We could even see it when they tried to hide. It was too close to the bone and so close to the surface, always, even still. As children, my mother and I felt somehow responsible because we were here and healthy, in this moment. So we quieted our questions. My mother and I listened to the silences. We tiptoed. We intuited. We discovered bits and pieces by gleaning scraps of overheard conversations, by connecting the few facts we understood, and by interpreting the elliptical orbits of silence.

~

Of these early years, my *abuela* will have little memory. She rose with the sun, she attended to the children so they were fed and clothed, but her movements felt as though she were covered by a wet woolen blanket, sodden and heavy. Often her thoughts were drawn inward where there is no language. She was not lost in thought. She was not reciting the prayers. The slow incantation of the Virgin's Seven Sorrows could not reach this place.

Aurora placed one foot in front of the other and progressed through the quotidian of her days as though through a bog, mired down by a weight within her very bones, a preponderance of heaviness. And emerging from this suffocating cocoon could be nothing more effortful than a shift in light, or a voice calling out, a tug on her skirts and the ever-awaiting Manolito who always seemed to know his mother would return. There might be something in the way he darted into the room, expectant, forgiving, though he would say there was nothing to forgive. And suddenly she would see him, hear his step on the floor, the weight of him somehow different, as though she were seeing him afresh, anew, after a very long time. In that instant, it would seem to her that he had grown.

His boyish embrace now nearly knocking her over. And though he was so different, so much bigger, he was still the same sweet boy who used to follow Esperanza everywhere. She recognized him immediately.

Not so the daughter who now trailed him. Now it was Dolores, not Esperanza, who was Manolito's constant companion, and there was always a moment of wondering how this little one came to be. A moment of no memory. A moment of looking past Dolores for Esperanza to enter laughing in her bright singsong voice. There would be, just for that moment, no recognition, no memory of the child tucked behind Manolito's shadow. Just for a breath, there was no feeling of "I know you. I remember you."

Here was this daughter, Dolores, a complete mystery, somehow still just beyond reach through a dense fog of grief or through vibrant memories of a time Dolores had no part in. Time had become fractured with Esperanza's death. There was Esperanza time and it included all those who had known her: Manuel, Manolito, the neighbors, the *barrio*, la Macarena. And then there was after Esperanza, in which time folded in upon itself. It was harder to hold onto those who came after. There was no thread stitching them all together into one garment. It was as though they had not taken root in her being so that she could carry them with her. She was no longer earth enough to hold their roots. She was no longer earth. She was this labored breath in and that breath out.

My breath catches in my throat as I imagine my mother, a vessel for her mother's grief, a warped mirror of what might have been, a ghost. And I imagine myself, too. The fourth sorrow pulls me under. "Do not weep for me, but weep for yourselves and for your children." My hands are clenched and sweating, and the rosary beads slip in my grasp. We are all just children. We are all just our mother's children.

~

Aurora begins taking in more washing, and the laundry piles up in corners and drapes across furniture. As an old man, my *tío* Manolo – no longer Manolito for he is a big man – will remember his mother with the front of her dress always wet as she stood over a pot of boiling water or as she scrubbed the stains from other's clothing. He will remember how she said the steam helps her breathing. He will remember her strong hand at his back gently pushing him out the door to school. He will remember the extra portions she saved for Dolores while she herself ate very little always saying, "I'll eat later when all you children play." Or "How can I enjoy my meal with all you clamoring about?" He will remember the flower beneath her left ear. Always a flower plucked from the iron gates in the patio, a begonia, a rose, a spray of jasmine.

Aurora's work brings in a little money that enables her to purchase food on the black market. This adds a little bulk to their rations that have been cut once again as Franco requisitions more monuments and tributes to his glory. Many sell the bulk of their sugar ration tickets for more black-market bread because bread is filling. But my *abuela* keeps a bit of sugar in the house to help make the gritty bread more palatable. She will sprinkle a bit of sugar on the children's bread in the morning. A bit extra for Dolores who never seems to have an appetite, who seems to be disappearing before her eyes.

Deaths from malnutrition are rising alarmingly across Spain, and Aurora worries that she doesn't have enough. *"Aurora, she is not ill."* La Macarena's voice in the kitchen is no longer a surprise. It seems that She often comes when Esperanza is leaning against the washboard or scrubbing the floor. Their work together is a choreographed *sevillana* as their chins are set firm and their arms are rising and falling with their task. Their steps advance and retreat in a syncopated staccato.

"She is skinny. And she will not eat." Aurora scrubs at a stubborn stain.

"Let her be. See her for who she is. She is healthy and strong. Do you see how fast she runs? Do you see how she has grown?"

"Yes, she is fast and slippery. Always disappearing," she says, snapping the wet shirt and lifting it overhead to the clothesline stretching from the kitchen window.

"*I don't think she is running from you.*" The Virgin steps closer, handing Aurora a pin.

Aurora turns away; she knows what Dolores runs from. She herself would run if she could escape the ghosts of Sevilla. "She runs and runs, but she doesn't eat."

"*Face your fear, Aurora.*" La Macarena takes a turn scrubbing a stain that will not release. "*You cannot love fully when you have so much fear. She is not Esperanza.*"

"No. She's not. But sometimes it feels as though she doesn't eat to spite me. She'll be eating and then stop when I offer her more."

"Did it ever occur to you that she sees you holding back? Maybe it is an act of love. Children show their love in many ways, Aurora."

"I can't eat with all those children around me. I eat when it's quiet, she knows this. I eat when there is a bit of peace." Aurora reaches for more of the lye soap to rub into the stain.

"Aurora, do not give me the same excuses you give your family."

"I eat what I can."

La Macarena pours the rinse water over the shirt. "*Are you keeping your grief alive through Dolores? Are you pushing her away for those same reasons?*"

Aurora flinches and turns away. It's true. At every age she sees the ghost of her Esperanza in the ever-changing Dolores who is growing up and beyond her older sister. Sometimes it is all she can see – what might have been. "No. She just needs to eat."

~

I think my mother understood that death was a presence for her mother just as I know the grief of what-might-have-been is a constant companion for my mother. There is another child we can't see, but our mothers do. My mother and I sense them. Their forms outlined in the gaze of our mothers.

Maybe my mother thought perhaps there was some loathsome promise Aurora made to God or *la Señora* or some far off deity that she would hold her pain always, just as la Macarena with her diamond tears. As if that would ward off further death. But I don't believe my grandmother or my mother made any promises to God. Instead, I think they could not forgive themselves for what happened. Mothers are supposed to protect their children; they are supposed to nurture them, keep them from harm, support and love them. And this is what neither of them could do for their first-born daughters. That guilt, that shame and grief, continued to seep into every new moment, each new day. Eventually they came to embrace the guilt because even it was a form of remembrance. Dolores did not remind my grandmother of Esperanza herself, but instead she reminded her that Esperanza was no longer alive. Dolores reminded Aurora of her sorrow and loss, of how she could not save Esperanza. I remind my mother of what will never be; a glimpse into a forfeited future of what might have been for my sister. My mother and I are reminders of sorrow so vast, yet not enough to fill the void.

~

More children are born. Francisco comes first. He is named for Esperanza's doll. It is an act of gratitude for those extra rations during the war. And his name Francisco means "God's promise of free land." Someday, for her children if not for herself, free land, freedom, enough. Aurora prays.

Then arrives José. He, too, is named for the doll. And he is named José because the sound of his name is a prayer that "God will increase and bless." And this is Aurora's prayer since she can think of little else but how she will feed these children.

José's birth is difficult and nearly kills Aurora. Not only does she lose a lot of blood, but her asthma has worsened to the point that every breath is a trial. Mustard packs helped at first, after Francisco's birth. But then the fumes made it nearly as difficult to exhale as to inhale. Steam from water steeped with eucalyptus leaves soothes somewhat, but nothing relieves her as before.

Manuel opens the door to the bedroom and watches his wife's chest rise and fall. She clutches at her *camiseta* pulling it away from her neck. What he does not see is la Macarena smoothing the oil all along Aurora's collarbone to her breastbone and up her neck to her jaw. She gently rubs the small circles that is the only relief Aurora knows. He doesn't hear what isn't meant for his ears.

"Tranquila, easy now, easy. Estoy aquí, contigo. I am here with you."

Aurora concentrates on the circles, the pulse and pattern of la Macarena's hand. She tries to match her breath, an inhale, an exhale. But her thoughts return again to her seven children, and the six who remain. "How?" Her question coming as silent as thought.

"Vamos a ver. We don't know what will come, Aurora. We don't know how God will strengthen us. Let's wait and see."

"I have no strength left. I have nothing to give my children."

"Of course, you do, Aurora. You have love. You have tenderness and understanding. You have the only gift children ever really want: the gift of yourself. You will continue to give them yourself."

"They need food and fire and ..."

"You are tired, Aurora. Now you must think of yourself. Only yourself. But in time, you will grow strong again and you will be what your children need you to be."

Aurora drifts in and out of the conversation, but she hears la Macarena as though in a dream: *"Be their true reflection, a mirror for them so they know their beauty. Encourage and support them so they realize their dreams. Be constant and forgiving so they learn to forgive themselves and know redemption through you."*

Manuel watches his wife struggle with the air around her, her fight to receive it and her struggle to release it. The new baby in Conchi's arms cries out, and he turns toward this newest member of their household, the red-faced José. He will want to eat soon. So will Manolito, Dolores, Antonio, Esperanza, and Francisco.

~

In the early morning sunlight of March 19, 1949, la Macarena is brought to her new church. The candles burn dimly, but the faces of those who have come for this homecoming shine brilliantly. Aurora, Manuel, Manolito, Dolores, Esperanza, Antonio, Francisco, and the swaddled baby José are all in attendance as is more than half of Sevilla. It is the moment Aurora has been awaiting. La Macarena is coming home to Her new church just inside the city gate.

In a few years the church will be granted the title of Minor Basilica Macarena, but on the day the Virgin returned, it is the humble, simple *iglesia* de la Macarena next to the Macarena gate and a stone's throw from Aurora's home. Everyone has waited all these many years as wars were fought, as plans were drawn, and money allocated, for the day that la Macarena would be given Her own church. And today is that day. La Macarena is finally home.

"*¡Guapa, guapa!*" the crowd exclaims as She is paraded past the city's walls and through the Macarena Gate. "*¡Guapísima!*"

The return of la Macarena is breathtaking. Although Aurora sees Her often in her very own kitchen, to see Her out in the streets and in broad daylight is something to behold. No matter where, in a street or square, during the day or night, at sunrise or at sunset, the appearance of la Macarena's float surging through the undulating sea of humanity cannot fail to fascinate Aurora. But Dolores finds her mother's adoration tedious and impossible to reconcile with her simultaneous frustration with the Church. Regardless, she is glad for this opportunity to gather all together. Manolito, Dolores, Esperanza and Antonio spy friends and start weaving through the crushing throng.

When the *saeta* begins, everyone, even the children, stops. Part prayer, part commentary, part song, the soulful *saeta* is an act of devotion cried out loud. Its music is individual, no rules govern it, no norms. It is the *cante jondo* that emerges from the singer and the collective Andalucían consciousness. The singer's throat opens to the intimately profound torrent, subject only to individual emotion. The lament is a plaintive passionate response to the elegance, sorrows, frustrations, dreams, loves and losses of the people. As la Macarena is borne through the gates like an apparition from heaven, the *cantaor* sings, expressing modulations so intricate that it is impossible to distinguish between the spiritual and the earthly components, they are so interwoven.

More than 4000 tons of candles are burned each year to the saints in Sevilla, and the day after la Macarena first processes to

Her new church, nearly all the yearly allotment will be shoveled off the streets. In that light, the sun's brilliance and the candles' faint glow, Aurora saw, as if for the first time, the faces of her neighbors. Still solemn, their faces had the crude beauty of the landscape, of la Macarena herself. War-ravaged, scarred, tear-stained, but nonetheless beautiful.

~

When I watched yesterday's Good Friday processions, as la Macarena passed through the gates, it was a woman who sang the *saeta* from a balcony just above the heads of the crowd. She wore a black *mantón*, heavily fringed and embroidered with an intricate design that mimicked the stitching on la Macarena's cape. She kept her right hand just below her breasts at her diaphragm, and her left hand reached out toward la Macarena. It was as if the *cantaora* was surrendering her own heart to the song. Her voice, deep and powerful and resonant with a thousand nuances that nearly escaped my inexperienced ear, pierced through the suddenly silent night.

I stood there, shoulder to shoulder with thousands of people. A crowd so still, so quiet, I felt I could hear my heart beating. The woman next to me closed her fan and held it to her breast. The man with her supported her elbow with his hand. The smell of carnations and marigolds and candles burning filled my throat and seemed to choke me from within. And as I stood there, suddenly still after following procession after procession through serpentine streets of countless cobblestones, I could still feel the stones shifting beneath my feet. I could still feel the current of bodies pressing in and pulling me along. I felt drunk and unsteady. Unmoored and unable to breathe. But the *saeta* had me pinned in place.

I read that *saeta* means arrow, and it is a choice metaphor because its aim is to pierce the heart; its musical lament is meant to reopen and examine the wound that binds us together. It draws from the deep well of emotion that so often remains untapped because there is little room left for such unbridled feeling. The *saeta* singer sings to la Macarena, yes, but also for all the people and on behalf of all the people. And as I looked at the upturned faces surrounding la Macarena listening to the *saeta*, I wondered, is it the war's enduring and silenced legacy that binds us? And is my personal wound bound by this inheritance of silence?

~

On the night my *abuela* watches la Macarena come home, the *cantaor's* voice – the raw, open, achingly open-throat sound – grabs hold of my *abuela's* viscera. The sharp intake of breath causes Manuel to study her complexion, and he takes her elbow. Is she having another asthma attack? No. She is lost in the *saeta* and the voice that lays bare our vulnerability in four eight-syllable verses. The *cantaor's* voice remains defiant and gallant and brutally honest.

Las Lagrimas de la Virgen
Iban cayendo en la tierra.
Y de cada una brotaba
Una rosa y una perla.

The tears of the Virgin
Were falling to the ground.
And sprouting from each one of them
Were a rose and a pearl.

A rose and a pearl. From Her tears, a rose and a pearl. Aurora is awash in images from not so long ago, a lifetime ago: the petals being tossed by a skipping Esperanza in the María Luisa Park; the beautiful rose that she wanted more than anything, but just for a moment; the rose, again, blooming on Dolores' forehead; and a pearl, lustrous and glowing with an inner light despite being born from the pain of an abrasive grit within the shell of an oyster. The opening vulnerability of a rose and the polished hard pearl born of suffering. Aurora's Esperanza and Dolores. Hope and Sorrow.

Then all at once, the *paso* holding la Macarena jumps. She shudders almost imperceptibly. Her candles spill wax, and the smoldering aroma hangs heavy along with the sweet scent of carnations while the *costaleros* begin their steady shuffling steps toward Her new church. The crowd parts, hands darting forward as if to touch the silver *paso*, the hem of Her train.

~

At the Feria this year, Dolores and Manolito take the younger kids and wander through the stalls that are set up along the riverbank. They admire the horses on display. The beautiful carriages decorated with flowers and ribbons. They try their hands at the games of chance, the shooting gallery, and the ring-toss. Each one wins a prize, a piece of candy. They run through streets festooned with paper and balloons. Festive colored bulbs swaying on strings between trees light their way until deep into the night. They bounce into and out of the thick crowd in their traditional costumes, looking for friends.

When they stop to catch their breath, they join in the singing. When they find a group dancing, they join in dancing the *sevillana*, stomping their feet and calling out to each other. They dance with their whole bodies to these songs they've heard their entire lives: the head erect, the arched back, the agile movements of the arms, the graceful turn of the wrists and the rhythm of the feet, beating their untold secrets into the earth. The dance is more a varied formation of sculptural poses. They dance because they watched their mothers, fathers, aunts, uncles, cousins, and neighbors dance in courtyards, kitchens, and at the fair. I have never seen my mother dance, but my *tío* Manolo told me she was the best, she danced like no one else.

The beauty of the Feria is that it has something for everyone. For the children it is a made-to-order heaven of color and sound. They are dressed especially for the fair by their parents: the girls in their bright dotted gypsy dresses, the boys in the traditional short black Andalucían jacket. By the time the fair begins, there is not a scrap of spotted fabric to be found in the shops, not a colored comb, not a festive *mantilla*, nor a broad-brimmed hat.

Parents exhibit their little *gitanas* and *flamencos* who are miniature replicas of their elders. Not a detail is lacking. There are some that go to the fair in normal clothes instead of the Andalucían costume. But they wear their best clothes, probably new for the occasion.

That morning, Aurora had curled Dolores' and Esperanza's hair with an iron she had held close to the fire. They are both in beautiful dresses Aurora made from cutting a couple of old dresses from her own youth. Dolores is proud in her dress with tiered ruffles that dance of their own accord as she merely walks. She and her younger sister Esperanza complete the look with a dab of rouge on their cheeks and silver rings in their ears.

Both girls dance the *sevillana* with one group of children and then run off to find other groups. Their feet kick up the yellow dust into soft billowy saffron clouds that swirl as the girls twirl their full flounced skirts. Dolores has draped her fringed shawl over the shoulders of her gypsy dress and watches outside a private pavilion – a *caseta* – with her siblings. She watches this different class of people as they dance. She marvels at how their faces are not as dark, as if they had not faced the sun in the heat of an afternoon.

She watches as the wine is poured freely and the plates heaped high with food are passed. *Botas* filled with wine vie for place on the tables, and *patas negra* hang from the *caseta's* bracing. Just looking at the hanging hams and the bowls of sweets is intoxicating.

While Dolores watches the party, music begins again, and there is more dancing. There are children, too. And one girl, about the same age as Dolores, pulls her into the tent to dance along with her. Dolores hesitates, looking around for permission, for an excuse to run away. But Esperanza pushes her forward, "*¡anda, anda!*"

Together, these two young girls from such different backgrounds, dance shoulder to shoulder. First the guitar and then the clapping. Soon the men and women start calling out encouragement. Esperanza stands outside and watches her older sister with this other girl. She calls her brothers over to watch, and they all stand watching Dolores and the rich girl stamp at the carpeted packed earth as they turn their chins to the heavens.

The *caseta* is grand, and Dolores is enamored of the beautiful woman this other girl calls mother. She is tall and pretty, dressed in a draped white fabric with a shawl of embroidered red silk. The temporary pavilion set up for the Feria is better appointed than anything Dolores has ever seen. There are gilt framed paintings of mustachioed dons on the canvas walls and real satin-upholstered furniture with fringed trim. There are braided silken drapes gathered at the entrance, and dividing the room is an elegantly painted silk screen of flowers in full bloom. There are so many vases overflowing with flowers – flowers like none Dolores has ever seen. These are not the roses or gardenias of the market or the twisting jasmine that climbs the iron fences. And in the center of one gleaming chestnut table there is a cut-glass bowl that sends rainbows of light across the canvas walls of the *caseta*. The bowl is bigger than the iron pot in which Aurora makes her stews, and it is filled with *dulces*. Sweet candies like the almond nougat *turon*, candied oranges, and crumbly cookies called *polvorones*. It is a feast for her eyes and as she dances, she takes it all in indiscriminately.

No one can dance like Dolores, and as she spins and stamps the carpeted ground within this *caseta*, she memorizes each detail, each shining surface and every neglected indulgence. When she is finished with her dance, the mother offers her a few items from the crystal bowl. These Dolores takes outside to her brothers and sister and divides the lot between them. Later, Dolores will be haunted by a dream of all that food covering a dining room table – the *pata negra*, the *queso*, the great rounds of bread, the barrels of olives, the bowl full of tiny quail eggs, the bottles and bottles of sparkling amber liquid – while she stands watching from the shadows as her mother and her older ghostly sister Esperanza take turns filling each other's plates until they overflow.

~

Once it is summer again, the outdoor *cine* unrolls the canvas screen and sets up the projector. Families pull out chairs and blankets, children race around cracking *pipas* between their teeth and spitting the husks at the pigeons.

Before the film begins, there is music played. Handclapping and castanets articulate a beat to which all the young, and many of the older *vecinos*, dance the *seguidilla*. Other types of *cante jondo* are being sung: the *soledades* revealing the solitude of an anguished lover; the *soleares* expressing a more existential ache; the *bularías* detailing the sorrows of our daily existence. The songs' inspiration and rhythm is instinctive. At the denouement, a final *soleares* subdues the crowd into an anticipatory stillness.

Rita Hayworth is a favorite in the *barrio* because her father was from Sevilla, and her name is really Margarita Carmen Dolores Cansino. And today it is a Rita Hayworth movie called "The Loves of Carmen." As soon as she comes on screen, everyone jumps up and cheers. Here is a neighborhood girl making it big in Hollywood. And this time, Rita is playing a young and beautiful woman from Spain. She will show the world Spain's enduring glory. She will redeem Spain from the realms of ugly and unmentionable war.

The much-anticipated evening is spent bombarding the sinister shadows with stones and shouting advice or warning to their beloved heroine who just happens to be the villain in this film. How could their beloved Rita be a character so heartless? How could she take advantage of the young man who loves her? Everyone waits for her to redeem herself, to separate from the young innocent soldier, to feel remorse over the life of crime into which she has led him. But when she fails at an opportunity to sacrifice herself to save the ruined soldier, the audience is audibly exasperated.

While Dolores enjoys the film, she can hardly abide how the audience attempts to change the course of the characters' lives by shouting out stage direction and advice when it is clear that the characters are predestined to the lives they will lead on screen. The exuberant participation of her friends and family is nearly an embarrassment. Everything is completely predictable. Nothing will change. But what captures my mother's attention is that this time Rita Hayworth is playing a gypsy – *una gitana* – who dances the *sevillana* just like she does. Dolores sees that in this American film, the gypsy is a wanton whore, *una putana*, who will stop at nothing to ruin the lives around her and whose dance is vulgar and shameful. She wonders if this is how America sees Spain. How an

American would see her.

~

Dolores overhears her parents talking one night as she is preparing for bed. She stops brushing her short dark curls to listen to their hushed voices. "The boys must go to school because they will need to support a family. They must learn to read and write and do their figures," whispers her father. "Even for work in the factories."

Aurora knows he is right, but she dreads telling her girls, Dolores first and then Esperanza, that they will need to stop school and work. And she wanted more for her boys; more than the hard living a trade would provide.

"They will work to live, Aurora, not live to work. It's useless to wish more than that for them." Dolores sees her father's looming shadow move from high on the wall to something dark and small on the floor.

Aurora is pacing now, holding closed the collar of her house-dress. "Dolores is old enough. I suppose she can get work at the candle factory. At least I know the woman in charge of the girls. Or perhaps we can find her a post with a seamstress. I've taught her well. She can cut a true pattern and sew a straight seam."

Manuel sits on the bed, and Dolores can no longer see his shadow. "How will she take it?"

"I don't know. *Cara vemos, corazon no sabemos.* With Dolores, we see only her face, we can't know her heart." Aurora sits beside her husband, and their shadows merge.

And so it is decided. Dolores quits school and begins working as an unpaid assistant to a seamstress with the hope of earning after a trial period. She won't make a living sewing shirtwaists or blouses, but she certainly can help afford an education for her three younger brothers by eliminating the cost of her own schooling. My mother is just barely twelve years old.

~

Dolores apprentices under a notable local seamstress who shows her how to thread the needle on a machine, how to replace the bobbin, and adjust the tension. She learns how to cut, pin and sew pieces of fabric into shirtwaists. And soon she learns that to do one quickly, she has to put the fabric pieces in the machine without pinning it, instead aligning the pieces with her fingertips as she guides the fabric under the stabbing needle.

She cuts the fabric shapes and then slips them under the needle of the machine. She makes the collars first, then sews them onto the neckbands. The sleeves come next, attaching the cuffs before sewing the sleeves to the body. Then, she hems and places the buttons, her needle flashing as she sits in the window of the shop. The buttonholes are made last, by hand. And even in this tedious task, Dolores enjoys discovering ways to keep her needle moving. She cuts loose threads at the end and all at once. She will be paid by the completed piece once she is officially hired, and she becomes efficient and precise in her efforts.

The machine has its good and bad days. Like anyone, Dolores supposes. On the bad days, the thread might get tangled in the seams and make loose loops. When she trims the loops, the entire seam comes apart as if the fabric has never been stitched at all. Sometimes the thread pulls too tight and puckers the fabric or breaks the needle. Needles are expensive and will come out of her pay if she earns the job. It is very important to check the tension often, and Dolores is very good at sensing the balance of pull and give before it slows her work.

My mother discovers she likes the routine, the day in and day out of her work. She likes the constancy and predictability. She likes knowing what is expected of her, and she likes being good at her job. She thrives within the safety of repetition, the narrow boundaries of measured patterns. Here, there are rules and direction, a right way and a wrong way.

Aurora was afraid that Dolores would be upset or feel shortchanged since, as a girl, her education is less important than her brothers' schooling. She tells her maybe she can be a famous designer one day and reminds Dolores that la Macarena was sculpted by a woman, Luisa Ignacia Roldán over two hundred years ago. "La Roldána was the first female sculptor to the Spanish Court. So perhaps you can be something amazing as well. Perhaps a famous dress designer." Aurora's voice is light and hopeful, still with an edge of searching or perhaps consolation as she pulls laundry in from the line.

Dolores is simply grateful that she doesn't have to go to work in the candle factory like her friend Ana. It is hot work, sweaty work, and her friend has been burned. Dolores knows that Ana hopes to someday be one of the girls who molds the delicate flowers and little bells out of wax for the processional candles. This she could do sitting down instead of working over hot cauldrons of molten wax. Dolores nods at her mother as she snaps the sun-dried sheets her mother hands her.

"Some will tell you that She is of unknown origin, but I think, no, I *know* la Roldána created her." As Aurora continues to reveal all the secrets of la Macarena's creation, Dolores feels her mother begin to slip away into a private reverie imagining the "birth" of her Macarena. "Of course, a woman made Her. Who else but a woman knows how we feel, the depth of our feeling? You need to know that I am here for you, too, Dolores." But her daughter has already slipped away.

Aurora knows her grief eclipsed so much that might have allowed Dolores to grow, to thrive, and to connect. She knows her grief choked her of sharing an early language of love and tenderness. The only language Aurora spoke those early years was one of sorrow. And she knows that grief stands between them, even now, all these years later. She did not bond early with this child, and she knows that between mothers and daughters, it must happen early. It is a guilt she shares with la Macarena often.

Manuel's effort to console his daughter for having to leave school is an attempt at giving her something to love, a focus other than the daily toil she will be faced with every day. He brings home a stray kitten he found in the Cathedral where he was working. A kitten, he thinks, will bring laughter to her eyes. He, too, doesn't understand that the shop brings Dolores a freedom within the confines of her time clock.

He brings the kitten home mid-day the day before Dolores is to officially start earning a wage at her job. Manuel sits at the table; his hands are busy tucking and rolling tobacco into a cigarette he will enjoy after his meal. There's a glint of mischief in his eyes, and he calls Dolores to the table to sit with him. "Tomorrow's the big day, eh?" Concentrating on rolling his cigarette, "You'll start making some money. This will help."

Before Dolores can answer, the kitten is mewling loud enough for all the children to come racing to the table. Manuel sighs and pulls the smallest black kitten from his pocket. The tiny thing is all teeth and eyes, with little knife-tipped paws spread wide. Manuel holds it out to Dolores by the scruff of its neck and looks expectantly into Dolores' eyes. His daughter has such a capacity for intensity and vulnerability. Always reliably responsible, she's also always dividing the world and all its particulars into friends and enemies. He sees now, this kitten is not a friend, and she doesn't want a distraction.

Still, he tries. Manuel tells the children how the Cardinal was sitting upon his throne with his robes arranged all around him and with the incense burning, "and just as the priest raises the host to the heavens, three little kittens tumble out from under the Cardinal's scarlet skirts. It was as if His Eminence had given birth himself!"

The children all laugh as Manuel continues the story hoping to pull a smile from Dolores. "The Cardinal quickly kicks the little fur balls aside, and Mass continues as if nothing had happened. But I see that the Cardinal's pock-marked face is as red as his robes. Of course, I pretend not to see a thing."

Manuel manages to rescue the tiny things and waits for the mother to return to her brooding place. When she doesn't, he releases two of the kittens in the tree-filled Patio de Naranjos where the old ladies will surely feed them, and he tucks the smallest in his pocket. The family names the kitten Canonico for his auspicious birth under the Cardinal's chair on the main altar at the Cathedral and for the tiny patch of white, like a clerical collar, beneath his chin amidst all the black fur.

The kitten chooses where to sleep each night, and it always picks the void made by the bend in Dolores' legs, behind her knees. When Dolores is home, it follows her around, tripping her and rubbing its length around and through her ankles all the while purring in an unnerving way. She doesn't like its unpredictability. She doesn't like its rough kisses and constant kneading and needing. She doesn't like the additional responsibility as though she doesn't help out enough with her little brothers. Though she knows the younger boys are too rough with the kitten, my mother doesn't understand why it chooses her over her sister. But Canonico will have nothing to do with Esperanza despite her being much more maternally inclined, always playing with cats and children as if they were her own babies. Before long, the little tom is escaping into the night. He always returns home battered and torn, often bringing home little birds and mice, placing them delicately at Dolores' feet before dawn.

~

Now that she is older and is developing in the way girls do, the priest at the Macareno church wants to hear confessions from Dolores. "Tell me," he insists after Dolores has entered the confessional booth and recited her requisite lines. He pressures Dolores, now 14, to tell him her thoughts, what she allows the neighborhood boys, what she does for herself.

When Aurora questions my mother why she is no longer going to confession, she reluctantly expresses her confusion to her mother. Aurora shrugs it away, "everyone knows the difference between what the priests preach and their personal conduct. *Para muestra, basta un botón.* You may know the entire sack by a single handful."

Dolores doesn't want to talk about these things with her mother. She doesn't want to know "what everyone knows," and she doesn't want her mother to attempt this intimacy that neither of them feel. But Aurora tries again, "you do not have to tell him anything. You be a good girl, and then you will know that you are right with God. And always remember that you can tell la Macarena anything. She will listen. She will not judge."

My mother begins going with my *abuela* to sit with la Macarena in the mornings. She sits in this church counting through her beads just as her mother does. Just as I am doing on this Holy

Saturday. But soon Dolores realizes that this is her mother's time. She feels she is intruding on something private or interrupting a conversation. My mother begins rising earlier and earlier, leaving for work before Aurora's daily visits to the church.

And when Queipo de Llano – the general who captured Sevilla for Franco and then ordered a murderous repression of Republican supporters in all of Andalucía – dies in 1951 and is laid to rest in a tomb within the plastered walls of the Macarena church, there are many more who stop attending mass. The *barrio* remains ever faithful and loyal to la Macarena, but they will not abide in the Church's decision to honor such a bloodthirsty man within the sacred stones of la Macarena's church.

The Fifth Sorrow: Crucified

But standing by the cross of Jesus were his mother and his mother's sister, Mary the wife of Clopus, and Mary Mag'dalene. When Jesus saw his mother and the disciple whom he loved standing near, he said to his mother, 'Woman, behold, your son!' Then he said to the disciple, 'Behold, your mother!' And from that hour, the disciple took her to his own home."

John 19:25-27

In 1953, when my mother is 16 and years after the civil war has ended, Franco signs a defense agreement with the United States that allows the establishment of U.S. military bases on its territory. However, Franco suspects that the liberty-loving and liberty-taking habits of the servicemen might prove contagious, and he wants as little fraternizing as possible. He enlists the Church in a massive propaganda campaign to drive a wedge of fear and suspicion between the Americans and Spaniards.

Spain's bishops, fearing that the U.S. servicemen might entice good Catholics into Protestant proselytism, demand legal protections for Catholic *señoritas* who might fall for the Americans. The bishops point out that Roman Catholicism is the state religion in Spain and that canon law is the law of the land so far as marriage is concerned. A hastily drawn Administrative Covenant between the Spanish Church and state authorities forbids U.S. servicemen or women to enter into "mixed marriages" with Spanish nationals, unless the Spanish Catholic Church approves.

Dolores continues to work sewing shirtwaists and blouses, and her employer finds her reliable and hardworking. Her sense of responsibility and trustworthiness has earned her several promotions, and she is now meeting with individuals to tailor their purchases to fit. She has watched carefully and has become quite accomplished.

After four years of daily labor, my mother can now fly across a seam keeping the edges of the fabric together, maintaining the even stitches required just by touch, allowing her eyes to locate the next piece and its position. Soon, Dolores can make the turns and reinforce corners without stopping the machine to raise or lower the foot, guiding with her fingers as the needle races along stabbing, looping, collecting, lifting.

The day the needle plunges into her thumb, piercing through her nail and narrowly missing the bone, she had been distracted by something at the window. Upon feeling the sharp pain, she lifts her foot off the pedal, and the needle stops still deeply embedded. After taking a full breath, she turns the wheel slowly, raising the needle. Her thumb raises a fraction too before she realizes that she will have to press her thumb down, pull against the lift of the needle. She braces her knees against the sewing cabinet and tries again. Slowly turning the wheel, she forces her left hand to remain flat against the machine. The needle tugs at her thumb, but she holds it firm, biting her lip. The tip finally emerges, and she darts her thumb into her mouth, feeling with her tongue the pinhole puncture on her nail, tasting the blood that oozes. She checks the needle for breakage and the garment she was sewing for blood.

Taking a scrap of cutaway and wrapping it around her thumb, she creates a bandage by winding thread around the cloth before finishing the garment. From her machine in the window, she sees the American GIs walking along the streets as if they own the ground beneath their feet.

~

For the first time in recent memory there is snow during the winter of 1955, and the whole of southern Spain is covered with a white dusting like a lacy shroud. It is terribly cold, and coal is still as scarce as ever.

My mother is nearly 18, and this is the first time she sees snow. Before anyone else is awake, she senses the early morning quiet. The warming stone at the foot of her and her sister's bed has long grown cold and she hesitates to move. There is a difference to this quiet. The cat is draped across her ankle, and she kicks Canonico away hoping once again that her dislike for the animal will encourage it to find other sleeping arrangements.

Slipping out of bed and shivering as she tiptoes to the window, my mother opens the shutter and peers out onto the snow-covered streets. The hush is nearly reverent, and it is astounding how the thin blanket of snow transforms her *barrio*. Everything appears clean and new. The most ordinary things – the neighbor's bicycle leaning against the gate, the fountain, the lamppost still alight with the thin gas flame nearly transparent in the blue tint of morning – are now sculptures in the sparkling white. The tiled roofs of all the houses are dusted with a fine powder. A layer of what looks like icing sugar lays atop the gates, outlining and articulating the intricate designs in such a way that everything is seen with new eyes.

Within minutes, the family is wide awake, and the spell is broken. Their clamor is all the more disrupting for their intrusion into her private moment. A moment that she is still trying to capture. Antonio, Francisco, and even little José, all race to the window to see what has happened. Esperanza peeks out from behind Dolores. It is all Aurora can do to get them all to put on their espadrilles before running out the door to collect handfuls of snow and toss them to the gray sky, making it snow again and again.

That snow-crusted day, Dolores takes dinner to her father at the foundry in the Maestranza neighborhood. This he will eat with the point of his knife next to his fires. These past months he has been working late into the evenings, and Aurora doesn't want him to miss any more meals. She wishes he would give some of the work to his coworkers or his apprentice, but he says that this is something he has to do himself. Aurora is simultaneously proud and frustrated that her husband's artistry is so highly regarded.

Dolores is mesmerized by the open fires of the foundry as soon as she enters. The roof of the building drips melted snow in a steady rhythm. Her father is standing near the furnace in his shirtsleeves, and soon Dolores is peeling away the layers she had put on to protect herself from the biting cold. She watches her father wield the enormous tongs that clamp onto the molten iron. He works the small pieces with a steam hammer, bending, turning. Dolores knows this is called "red heat work." And she recognizes the delicate flowers and twining vines that adorn so much of his *reja* work. She thinks of her mother's complaint, "*En casa de herrero, cuchara de palo*." But they don't use wooden spoons at home, just like the shoemaker's children don't go barefoot. She can see his more complex handiwork all over town and in the churches. It would be nice to have some of this delicate, flowery, filigreed work at home instead of the utilitarian grid work that covers their windows. But what they have serves just as well.

When he sees her, he nods a greeting. Dolores knows that her father enjoys this creative work more than the forge welding, riveting, and collaring work that he often has to do. She spreads a cloth on a table away from the furnaces and lays out his food. When she asks him what he is working on, he simply says it's a private commission. "No, it won't pay. But it is something I have to do. It's for a project close to my heart."

~

My mother has grown into a very beautiful young woman whose smile, though elusive, is brilliant and lights up her dark eyes with an *alegria* more infectious for the shadow that precedes it. And when she sings and dances, all the boys shout their encouragement and admiration. Dolores tucks her chin in embarrassment. She pretends that she doesn't like the attention, but she loves the dance, and she loves that others watch her. She loves the near unselfconsciousness of the dance.

Aurora worries that Dolores doesn't seem grounded and confident in her own choices, that she goes along with her friends without any inner guidance. She doesn't have la Macarena, and she certainly doesn't confide in her. When she approaches her daughter telling her that she should trust in her heart and know when her companions do not have her best interest in mind, Dolores seems baffled. Aurora explains, "*Muchos componedones descomponen la novia*," warning that too many cooks spoil the broth. Dolores just shakes her head at her mother's clichés and superstitions. "Remember, your reputation is not up to you. It is up to what others say about you." Aurora pushes Manolo, now too big to be called Manolito, out the door to watch over his sister.

But it is a mistake for Aurora to imagine that Dolores would yield easily to love. Dolores does not want to appear *sin vergüenza*. She wants to hold her head high, do her work, and wait. But she also knows the boys like to look at her. She knows that they want to walk with her during *paseo*. But she has no trouble saying no when the suggestions go too far. She has had plenty of practice avoiding appraising and appreciative eyes at the second job she found at the neighborhood bar across the street from la Macarena's church. Here she washes glasses and the small dishes for *tapas*. She wipes down the tables and bar always keeping her eyes downcast.

My mother is careful with her feelings, arranging them just so to stay out of the unpredictable waters of emotion. Though she is not a tease and makes no promises, she is not unaware of how her downcast eyes or her hand brushing a wisp of hair across her brow affects the boys watching. She keeps her dark curls trimmed just above her long-arched brows; this accentuates her changeable hazel eyes, sometimes gray, sometimes green. This also hides her mother's unrequited rose.

~

In 1956, southern Spain experiences incessant rains from October through April. The banks of the river rise beyond the flood walls. The last time unrelenting rains came was the winter of 1936-37, the winter Esperanza died.

Aurora's breathing is eased some by a new medication that she inhales but still, the constricting ropes around her ribs tighten as the rain persists. Flooding causes the construction to be suspended on the military base outside of Sevilla, and the American GIs help sandbag the river against the rising tide. Their effort to protect the city goes a long way toward changing how they are perceived by the *Sevillanos*. But the Church continues to cast a wary eye and warn the *señoritas* about falling from grace.

My father has been stationed at the supply base in San Pablo near Sevilla for just over a year. He has taken the requisite Spanish course from the Air Force and invests in the Berlitz Spanish language records. He is just 25 years old and although he was in Korea, he counts this experience as his first real travel abroad. Korea was war, this is Europe.

His overall first impressions of the city are subdued. He opens his senses and takes in as much as his body allows. All the smells and sights and sounds, the tastes and touch; indiscriminately he allows the city to wash over him and through him. He notes how Sevilla is situated on flat ground, with no mountains, slopes or hills. In fact, the city itself is the only summit. A glance at the horizon takes in tortuous and sinuous streets, lacking any symmetry, as if easy rules of grid and line, pattern and plan, had purposely been avoided to deliver a surprise around every corner. The asymmetry and irregularity delight my father. His sense of wonder heightens as he meanders at once confounded and captivated. He is always entranced and often lost.

He learns to find a landmark, something by which he can navigate the serpentine streets of Sevilla. In his sights, he keeps the Giralda as his point of reference, his beacon above all the other buildings. In the balmy air and almost warm sunshine, the Giralda joins in the city's gaiety with the music box cacophony of its bell tower. It becomes a melody in itself, sending forth harmonious sounds in a wealth of rhythm. Other times, the Giralda is the conductor of a great orchestra, towering over a city that is, in itself, a symphony of reflection and color.

Beneath the Giralda, Bill knows the Cathedral lays sprawling and prostrate as it hugs the earth, and from there he can find his way almost anywhere. The Giralda and the beautiful woman with her bow and arrow on top, are all he needs to find the Cathedral, his point of reference, his point of way and return. From every angle, the offered panorama of the city is dominated by this tower, this architectural emblem of varied origin, my father's compass rose. He is lost only until he looks up.

My father is bewitched, mesmerized by the Cathedral – the world's largest Gothic cathedral. All accounts spoke of its grandeur and the architectural splendors it had to offer. He read of the *reredos* – largest in all Christendom – of the silver and bronze tombs, the great store of Goya and Murillo masterpieces, the 47 silver monstrances carried in the Corpus Christi procession. And possibly the most curious to my father is the much-admired gift of a stuffed crocodile presented by the Sultan of Egypt. The candles and the chanting and the sudden gusts of incense ignite a synesthetic and overwhelming effect. The columns and sculptures of the great gold *retablos* spreading behind the high altar are nothing at all like the small whitewashed clapboard Methodist church back home.

He takes notice of another outstanding feature of the city: the river. It slices the city in a tipsy lopsided smile as if there is some private joke it might share. To my father, the river hints at the *alegria* so many talk about, that he himself has experienced in Sevilla. In the sunshine, the river glistens, radiant surface reflecting infinite lights. Its Arab name, Guadalquivir, feels awkward in his mouth, and though he works at the colliding consonants, it remains unpronounceable for his American tongue.

Water is evident everywhere despite the arid climate of southern Spain. The Moorish legacy of water fountains and canals, around which so many houses were built, are enclosed with tiny gardens of Eden, like a small oasis, seen through wrought iron grills, ornate ironwork, and heavily gated doorways that shut the houses off from the outside world. It appears almost a mirage, the twilit moss-green world of the patio, as seen from the street. He loves the cafes where vines grow over the patio, where he can sip Jerez, listen to guitars, and watch the beautiful women pass. Myrtle, jasmine, and a lemon tree give scented shade, a respite from the heat. Everywhere his eye rests, it finds movement and color. He loves the tawny colors of its streets beneath a sky, blue even by slimmest moonlight.

Bill doesn't pay visits to *las casas de niñas,* the brothels that some of his friends frequent. But he listens to their advice about how in Spain there are only three types of women: married, virgins, and those you can find in *las casas*. And while there is no stigma attached to getting what you need, you should stay away from the virgins. "Unless you want to get married." But the women draped in the windows and doorways of *las casas* are more intimidating than enticing to Bill. They beckon, but he remains unmoved. He is more comfortable in the bars where there is a mixture of young and old, men and women, conversation, and *cerverza* to quench his thirst.

My father finds a tavern in one of the *barrios* to the north that has a highly polished bar with a wrought iron footrest where men rest one leg and then the other, shifting their weight as they stand and sip their drinks. The wood bar has taken on the weight and worry of generations and is worn with slight depressions along the surface where an arm might rest. The footrest, too, is worn down thinner in places where countless men have leaned.

My father is watchful, and he takes note of the unhurried dignity and noblesse with which the men handle their drinks. It is so different from the way he and his fellow Air Force buddies take a drink. It dawns on him, in fact, that this is the difference. He and his friends *take* their drinks, just as they would *take* communion if they were so inclined, or perhaps *take* a wife. But the Spaniards with whom he is becoming acquainted seem to *receive* their drink, never gulping down, panicked and pleading with the barman for just one more. He imagines it is just how they would *receive* the sacrament or *receive* the tender charms of a woman. Drinking here in Sevilla seems to be one of the inherent privileges of living rather than the temporary sedation or sip-by-sip suicide it so often is for others.

He likes how the barmaid brings a little something to eat with his beer, "*una tapa*," he hears her say. The waitress is gracious but always cool and reserved. She is serene, confident, and self-possessed, as if she sees him fully and has already considered and dismissed him as a possible lover.

The tapas are small dishes of the most extraordinary delicacies. He eats *pulpo* and *boquerones*, craggy oysters, crabs, *calamares* heaped in golden rings, olives nestled in palm leaves, bowls of mussels, plump pink shrimp. Also, on offer might be the little sizzling saucers of kidney or roasted sparrow, snails, sautéed squid, hot prawns in garlic, or stewed pork. Nobody drinks without also eating, and neither does he despite being leery of the curled creature or the fish eye looking back at him. He doesn't want to embarrass himself or seem ungrateful to the friendly people he is meeting. Later, back in the barracks, he checks his pocket Spanish-to-English dictionary and is amused to learn he's eaten octopus, squid and fried whole sardines. He imagines the letter he'll write home.

Bill returns to this small bar just inside the Macarena Gate on his days off because he likes that he can recognize some of the regulars and that they raise their chin to him as he removes his hat and nods to them. He comes and sits at the bar or at a small table in the back and watches. Listening to the conversations and soaking in the sense of belonging these people seem to have, he imagines what it might be like to be from such a place as this instead of his hometown in Oklahoma. These folks seem just as small town and provincial, but they don't seem at all despairing, not at all depressed like many in his dustbowl home.

On certain nights there might be music as someone picks up a guitar and begins playing. Someone else will start singing or clapping along. It all seems so spontaneous and improvised, but he isn't sure. He wonders who in the crowd of people are the performers and who comprise the audience. Perhaps this is a band hired for the evening, but it seems more like a gathering of friends who all just happen to be in the same place at the same time. And my father especially loves the evenings when there is dancing.

When the women jump up from their seats and start the whole dance with a furious stamp of their feet, he knows he is in for something special, something extraordinary. The first time he saw this, he wondered if the woman was a jilted lover or a wife done wrong, but as soon as the clapping started and the dancer whipped her shawl in an arc through the crackling summer air, throwing it around her shoulders, he realized there is a story being told in each step. It is here, in this bar, that Dolores and Bill first meet.

Though she has served him his beer and he's seen her dance while the older men clap and shout what they shout, he has never seen her eyes. Not until the one day she allows the dark fringe of her lashes to flicker up and reveal the hazel flash with hints of golden sun, like the sparkle off the green gray Guadalquivir in the Andalucían sunlight, does he realize he's just seen a glimpse of his future.

That evening there is dancing, and he watches this dark-haired beauty dance with a blond girl who can't stop laughing. The two seem to know each other and look as though they've danced together before. The blond is giggling and calling out to friends as she dances, and the dark one is serious, and her face doesn't move as her arms, bent at the elbow, twist and turn. Her mouth is a straight line, and her brow remains smooth though her eyes fling daggers as the music becomes more and more furious. He is nearly breathless as the crescendo of clapping and strumming envelopes the dancers in a blur of color and motion. He wants to clap along, but the rhythm is too syncopated, a mixture of tempo and signature he cannot follow. Just as he begins to anticipate the changes and curious confluence of chords, the music stops in a sudden crack of thunder, and the dancers still as if frozen in the fierce fire of lightning. There is no denouement, no gradual fall to the end of the dance, just an increasingly tumultuous torrent that ends in a gasp. He feels himself tremble in the wake.

The blond girl crumples over in a heap of self-conscious laughter as the darker one holds her expression and pose just a moment longer. Her only movement is in the unconscious rising and falling of her breast as her heart continues to dance to the beat of the now silent music. The crowd calls for more song, more dance.

"*¡La Morena y la Rubia! ¡Dolores y Esperanza, las hermanas mas guapas!*" This is how Bill learns the dancers are sisters, one dark named Dolores and the other blond called Esperanza. He knows from his language courses their names mean sorrow and hope.

"*¡Anda, anda, híja!*"

At that, Dolores shushes them all and picks up her dishrag flicking it at her younger sister, a move so familiar and intimate Bill almost looks away. He notes how her voice laughs when she asks the crowd if they want to fetch their own drinks. And it becomes clear to my father that they all know each other. The girls are sisters. They have brothers in the crowd, perhaps even parents. Family and friends and neighbors. He is probably the only one who doesn't belong.

Only a few days pass before Bill brings his buddy Euin to the bar. Even though Bill has worked at Morón USAF Base since 1955 and has immersed himself in the Spanish language, he needs someone there to help him break the ice with this beautiful girl. Bill is shy and needs someone like Euin, with his unabashed way of working through the music of their language, someone with nothing to lose.

"Buenas tardes, señorita." Euin pulls his cap off and runs his hand through his sandy cropped hair.

She nods at the Americans in their beige uniforms and good-natured smiles. She smiles back just enough.

Euin laughs at himself and scratches at his crew cut, "*¿cómo se llama?*"

Glancing quickly at Bill before allowing her gaze to fall on Euin, she answers quietly, succinctly. This is how Bill confirms that this dark-haired beauty's name is Dolores. He sounds it out again and again in his head and falls into her name as though down a deep well.

~

I walk out into the bright sunlight. My back is sore from sitting so long on the wooden pew, my eyes unaccustomed to the midday sun. The thought of food propels me to a bar across the street. I'm suddenly starving. There's a small round table by the front window. Pointing to it, I ask the bartender if it's okay. It's too early in the afternoon for locals to be eating, but my stomach has been reluctant to change from its distinctly American mealtimes.

I am self-conscious as I order a sandwich – *un bocadillo con jamón serrano* – and a Fanta, but the bartender smiles. I think I got it right. Out the window, I can see the ochre-stuccoed church where I've been sitting for hours. I also see part of the bank's facade where my mother's home once stood. But still, the places are mere thumbtacks in a map. Not even my own map.

The waiter brings my order and asks if I'm a *turista* here for Holy Week. He sets my sandwich down in front of me as well as my orange drink. Yes, I say. I am a tourist, feeling all at once certain that I am a foreigner here. I tell him I'm visiting from America. That I wanted to see la Macarena. His eyes light up.

"She is the most beautiful."

Yes, I say. *Muy hermosa*. Beautiful.

"America is far away, *tan lejos*." He kneads the rag in his hand as he pronounces the English words. He is young, perhaps 20, and his eagerness is sweet.

I nod. Yes, *muy lejos*. My mouth twists around the pronunciation.

I wonder, was this the bar where my mother worked after her shift with the dressmaker? Is this the bar where my grandfather rolled his cigarettes? Is this where my parents met? Maybe this is all a wild and florid dream drawn rashly and haphazardly across generations to find some comfort, some understanding, some meaning. Maybe. I don't know. Like so much of this story – a fiction from few facts – I don't know if it will be true, or even true enough.

The *bocadillo* is good. The bread is dense and chewy, drizzled with a peppery olive oil and stuffed with layers and layers of translucent cured ham. The crust scrapes the roof of my mouth as I wrestle to claim a bite. But it is wonderful. I eat it slowly, savoring the flavors. The waiter asks if I want another Fanta, but I change to red wine. A *vino tinto* just because.

There are fewer people out now. The midday rest away from the full force of the sun pulls people home. A pause. Like today, like Holy Saturday. Another respite between the impassioned press and pageantry of Good Friday and the celebration of Easter. I seem to feel most comfortable in this moment between exhale and inhale, far from the crowds.

At one point near the gates yesterday, the crush of the crowds for la Macarena's procession overwhelmed me. The push and pull of so many people all clamoring to get closer pressed. And the smell of the spilled wax coated my throat. I couldn't breathe. I needed air. But as I tried to stand still to allow the crowds to pass me, I was lifted and buffeted along, carried aloft in the procession. The rising panic reminded me of a time I was caught in a rip current in Galveston and couldn't make my way back to the beach. Growing increasingly more exhausted and anxious, I finally remembered I needed to swim parallel to the shore. This same technique allowed me to find an edge to the masses and duck down a side street. Leaning my full weight against a building, I broke out in sobs. Everything felt so surreal and strange. The hooded *nazarenos*, the songs, the solemn mixed with the hopeful – all my senses were engulfed.

After catching my breath, I tried to follow the sounds of the la Macarena's band as they played their funereal marches, but the narrow twisting streets and close buildings echoed the trumpets. I couldn't tell which direction I should go. The streets all turn into each other, and I didn't know my way. I found myself going in circles. I was lost. It was well past midnight, and it would be hours before I saw la Macarena again, just outside the Cathedral, making Her way back home.

When the wine arrives, I nod my gratitude. He asks me if everything is okay, gesturing to the sandwich. I wish I had the words to tell him that this sunny spot by the window, this meal, this moment here in his bar is true nourishment. I feel nourished through and through. But instead, I nod and smile.

Nodding and smiling has been my passport this entire week. It's my own fault. I could have taken more classes in college. Four years in high school was not enough. And it's true: you use it or you lose it. There are adult programs. Tutors. But there's also this disconnect I feel. Disenfranchised. Disinherited. Without an inheritance, a *patria*.

Once, in high school, my teacher asked why I didn't already

speak Spanish. After all, my mother is from Spain. She could help me with these tenses and vocabulary. The teacher went on to tell me I had wonderful pronunciation, a native's beautiful accent. She thought I must have gleaned my accent when my mother spoke Spanish to me because the trilled R and the lisped S, the rhythm and open-mouthed vowels, seemed to come naturally to me. Yet these complicated tenses and conjugations were like calculus to me. It seemed I didn't know the structure and brace of the language, only the music. The next year, I didn't mention my heritage to my teacher.

We never spoke Spanish at home. Doctors had explained that two languages would be far too confusing for my sister. By the time I was born, my mother had a rudimentary and heavily accented grasp of English, enough for the day-to-day: food, chores, clothing, exercises, bath, yard, hairbrush, laundry, car. Simple sentences, direct and unambiguous. We had plenty of words but little of the story that connects words into meaning.

We didn't have the vocabulary for the ephemeral and the intangible: how to frame my crippling feelings of shame and guilt because I was healthy, strong, and capable yet always so afraid; or how to describe the devastating dreams that held me paralyzed so I couldn't call out, or the recurring dream of a voice speaking in a language I didn't recognize telling me something I needed to remember. We didn't have the fluency for wonder and curiosity, or why only one connect-the-dot pattern of stars makes the true constellation, while the infinite other variations are only imagined and therefore untrue.

Deeper meanings, answers to my questions, exploring curiosity and story, these were sacrificed in order to become linguistically assimilated into American life. What I missed are the soothing sounds of my mother's melodic fluency to fill the gaps and spaces between the words. I missed the clapping games, the endearments, the nursery rhyme and lullaby. I missed the small musings and whispered secrets between mother and daughter. As we both learned to speak and formulate thoughts in the English language, my mother's native language was eroded alongside my own inheritance. I never heard my mother's original voice speaking just to me.

It is a loss I couldn't begin to understand until I heard it echoed in the laments of a country brought to its knees by its own. Historians have estimated about 500,000 people from both sides were killed in the Spanish Civil War, the war that was sparked by Franco's insurgency against the democratically elected left-wing "Republican Loyalist" government. A further 50,000 opponents of Franco are thought to have been executed in the years following his victory – though some claim that number of "disappeared" is closer to 114,000. Between 1939 and 1947, 400,000 Spaniards were imprisoned in concentration camps. And over 500,000 others managed to flee Spain during Franco's heavy-handed rule, leaving behind family, language, history, and story buried beneath the rubble.

Those who did not side with the rebel general Francisco Franco's "Nationalists" were considered traitors to Spain. Laws were passed to suppress their voices and under these laws, my family – my mother, her parents, all her brothers and her sister – were considered traitors. Their fear and humiliation kept them silent, and their silence kept them safe under Franco's fascist campaign of terror. While those who fought for the nationalist cause were glorified by Franco's regime and the Roman Catholic Church, the bodies of those who opposed Franco are buried in countless unmarked shallow graves all over Spain. From 1936 until Franco's death in 1975, the defeated in Spain's civil war lived in silence imposed by his brutal dictatorship. In silence they suppressed the memory of their hard-won and short-lived democracy and its bloody succession. In silence they mourned their losses and endured the oppressive reality imposed by the dictator.

In 1977, two years after Franco died, the newly formed Spanish Parliament founded the Law of Amnesty – known as the Pact of Forgetting – to ensure continued suppression of all memory of Franco's decades in power. Not only did the law seek to erase the memory of injustices perpetrated by Franco and his government, it sought a future that rendered those injustices invisible. But forgetting has a price. For without knowing what we are obliged to forget, there can be no understanding, no acceptance, and no forgiveness. I know this silence as my inheritance too tender to touch, too heartbreaking. Because over time, the legislated and enforced amnesty atrophied into the brain-damage of amnesia. Words and names that might have been fashioned into story could no longer be recalled, and my family history was lost to me.

For years, the Pact of Forgetting mandated what was written and spoken, but it could not legislate time. Eventually everything hidden away is brought out into the open. The new generation - the grandchildren, others like myself who, detached by distance and time - were breaking the pact of silence. And in 2007, Spain finally enacted the Law of Historical Memory, a law which explicitly condemned the acts of violence committed during the Franco era and gave descendants the right to locate and identify and claim the remains of the victims. Emboldened by the new law, some of the grandchildren become part of a Truth Commission founded to uncover the abuses that occurred during Franco's fascist rule. Some want to find out where their relatives are buried in hopes of providing, at long last, a proper grave with the family name carved on the stone. Still others want to recover the dignity of their ancestors' names. I want to roll away the stone that has weighed so heavily and for so long.

The wine is full and throaty. I imagine if it had a voice, it would sing a *saeta* like those I heard yesterday. It's perfect accompaniment to the *bocadillo*. I open my phone to look at the pictures my son Ben texted earlier. He had taken pictures of our brown house, the two cats, and a silly selfie of him with his sister. And there's another shot of my husband John drinking his coffee and reading the paper. Ben strung all these images together captioned with lyrics from a Crosby, Stills and Nash song. He knows it's a favorite. It seems this "son of my right hand" – my Ben – who encouraged me to take this trip is now feeling the need to remind me where my heart is.

For a moment, I wonder whether or not to go back to the church and finish the *Dolorosa* prayers. My back is aching, I'm tired from last night, and tomorrow I am returning home. I think of calling it a day when I realize I don't have the rosary. It's not in my pockets, my bag. I don't have it.

Motioning to the waiter for the tab, I finish the rest of my meal, pay the bill, and race back across the street. How could I have left my *abuela's* rosary?

The doors are still open, and the coolness envelopes me as I step into the still and empty basilica. My shoes click a crisp staccato against the marble floor as I find my pew and sidestep to my place. At first, I don't see them, and a rising panic takes my breath. But then, as my eyes adjust to the lower light. I see them, curled in the corner, deep in shadow.

~

Dolores notices a scar on my father's lip, and it reveals a story that hearkens to his birth. Her mother would want to weave a fabled story saying he was caught up in the great fisherman's hook and line, that he struggled against the taut line tugging him upward as he fought to remain here to complete his noble journey. But that is what her mother would say. Dolores knows that his triangulated upper lip reveals only that he had the reparative surgeries on his lip and perhaps his palate that so many here cannot afford. But it is his eyes that pull at her attentions. They are animated and blue like shallow water over river stones, and they sparkle up at her expectantly, hopeful.

She leaves Bill and Euin to their American talk filled with words that end before they are finished and continues to work her way around the bar, wiping up rings and rinsing her rag. It is his face that she returns to again and again throughout the evening. He is a head taller than she is, his hair is dark and wavy over a high forehead, and he carries himself slow and easy. There is a kindness in his smile, a perceived strength along his jaw. He catches her eye more than once. Both look away as soon as their eyes meet.

Over the next weeks, Dolores slowly learns more and more about Bill. His cautious and earnest way of working through the words of her language. His embarrassment when he fails. His and Euin's attempts to teach her some of their words: glass, beer, wine, beautiful. At first the words all seem to end abruptly in consonants instead of flowing seamlessly. But eventually, she discovers she likes the clipped percussive cadence. There is something more definitive about this language where words don't cascade one into the other. Whereas she doesn't want to speak it, she loves to listen.

When she introduces Bill to her family, she studies their faces for reactions. Her hazel eyes, closer to green today, restlessly glance from face to face. As her gaze alights on each person in her family, she summons her history, their history together full of losses and struggle. But when she looks at Bill's face, she sees a future less shadowed, filled with light and hope. One she imagines without ghosts and grief. Not knowing when or how, Bill becomes her "valiant protector" – just like his name suggests – he who might free her to a new world. The new world.

Aurora is concerned though, as mothers are. In their bed, after the city has become quiet, she confides in Manuel, *"la cabra de mi vecina da más leche que la mía."* Aurora nudges Manuel's arm from around her shoulder so she can turn to him. "She has always imagined that others live a better life. Remember that family she met during Feria?"

"How could I forget. She talked about them incessantly: the candies, food, the paintings! Everyone in that *caseta* was happy and in comparison, we had nothing. It's always been all or nothing." He shifts closer, "do you think she imagines the American is an escape?"

"Not just for her, but for all of us. She wants to pull us all out of our history. We remind her." Aurora, herself, slipping into memory. "And the American has no history."

"Ah, don't you mean she reminds you?"

"Yes, maybe. She and I remind each other."

Manuel pulls Aurora close and tickles her ear with his fingertips. "Yes, it's been hard. It still is sometimes. But we've made a beautiful family."

Aurora is playful as she bats Manuel away, but her voice betrays her, "Yes, a beautiful family."

~

Bill tells Dolores all the stories he can of where he's from in his halting and endearing Spanish. She wants to know all about America, but he's been only to his home in Oklahoma and to San Antonio, Texas, where he was stationed.

Texas is especially interesting to Dolores as she's seen some Westerns and is curious about cowboys and ranches. She asks questions about whether guns really hang from the slim hips of young men on horseback. If there are gunfights, stampedes, oil wells. If everyone really is so rich.

"Those are just movies. I don't think they even represent what once was. The city where I've spent most of my time in Texas is San Antonio, and it's a city on a river. Very much like Sevilla."

Dolores can't imagine that. Those people are in America. She's seen the movies. She knows that everyone is happy with houses of their own and land that stretches out to the horizon. She knows that there is plenty of food and money, fast cars, and beautiful clothing. Plenty. More than enough.

My father shakes his head, "you know, the town I come from is small and dusty. There's not much there but peanut farms and dirt." Yet Bill finds himself, surprisingly, feeling some pride in her vision of his homeland as she asks more and more questions.

He starts talking about Oklahoma and the vast fields of corn and peanuts and wheat. He talks about the cotton he picked as a boy during the summer to earn money for his family. He talks about the fishing hole he would go to instead of school. He tells her of his family: his strong mother, his father recently passed, his brothers and his sister. As he talks about his small town, Dolores and Bill bond over the similar feelings of provincial life, of big dreams, of wanting change. He can't understand how she can feel the same being from this cosmopolitan city full of light and music and movement, but he can see in her the same desire for more and better.

Bill asks her questions about Sevilla. She takes him to the Thursday Market called El Jueves, where a cluttered assortment of diverse wares is displayed on the street. Bill takes in the immense flea market where there is everything from antique treasures to mundane housewares. Dolores sees junk and people selling everything they own for a few *pesetas*. Bill sees riches, history, and so much of what was always missing in his scrappy and hardscrabble life. Everything is so inexpensive, and he feels flush as he contemplates the possibilities. Of special interest are the philatelists who gather at Santa Marta square. The old stamps are particularly provocative, showing tiny glimpses of exotic places he's never been, images of where his life might take him.

On the narrow, curving street, Bill and Dolores walk, taking in all the local artisans. The delicate lacework for the *mantillas* and shawls; the fine leatherwork saddles, shoes and boots; the wide variety of ceramics, the glazed tiles and painted pots; the multicolored mosaics; the silver jewelry; and the Cartuja porcelain in all its myriad of colors. It is all dazzling. There are the beautifully crafted combs of ivory, tortoise shell, and ebony, the delicate manufacture of guitars and filigree castanets. The entire day is awash in color. And it is only a Thursday. Sevilla is nothing like his dry and dusty Oklahoma, and he feels perpetually parched for this beauty.

For him, Sevilla is the home of romance and elegance, but for Dolores it is everything she would escape. She does not make her disdain known to Bill, and she sees his enamored rapture of her city as his falling in love with her. He tries to pull her into his affection for the flower-banked houses that fan out and up from each bank of the river, but she is blind to what she has always seen.

That night Aurora makes a special dinner of shrimp and clams with peppers, onions, and garlic stewed in tomatoes. The *cazuela de mariscos* is all prepared in a large earthenware crock, and it is delicious. The aroma is almost as intoxicating as the wine that is poured. Bill doesn't know that the family doesn't eat and drink this way every night. He just knows that the warmth and generosity of Aurora and Manuel presents a type of beacon, something he's been longing for his whole life.

After everyone has eaten, Manuel leans back in his chair and begins rolling tobacco into a small creased paper. Bill pulls out his pack of Kent cigarettes and offers them to Dolores' father. Manuel takes the white, perfectly cylindrical cigarette and pinches the filter off and lights it. He finishes rolling his cigarette and puts it away with his pouch of tobacco. The small bottle of whiskey Bill bought at the base commissary is opened and poured into small tumblers.

It seems almost everyone likes Bill immediately. He manages to speak their language unlike many of the American servicemen and is humble and respectful of their customs. Bill is sincere. He is funny, charismatic and extremely generous, providing gifts of commissary goods from the base exchange. His gift of a jar of peanut butter and grape jelly with a loaf of Wonder Bread for Dolores' youngest brothers is met with a curious hesitancy. But as soon as Francisco and José taste the roasted peanut spread on the fluffy white bread, they devour so much that their mouths are tacky with the taste of it. Everyone is laughing, and Bill is pleased to be bringing a bit of American plenty to their table.

~

Spring is a flurry of activity as if the sun's warmth and the soft breezes off the river bring a list of chores to the inhabitants of Sevilla. My father imagines it is the same anywhere: spring cleaning, spring blossoming, spring birds and bees. Bill watches as women whitewash the fronts of their houses, shaking out rugs and hanging out bedding in the clear sunlight. In the park, the quality of rippling light dappling the cobbles through the branches of orange trees is dizzying, especially when accompanied by the sound of water flowing in marble fountains. The shops in town are all displaying row upon row of bright dotted flamenco dresses for little girls. This is more than spring cleaning he thinks. This is preparation for something big.

Dolores' family invite him to participate in Holy Week activities with them, and though he cannot take time off from work during the day, he is able to watch the late-night processions through the streets of Sevilla alongside this family that is so kind to him. He learns of the brotherhoods, the confraternities that carry the Macarena and other statues in the processions through the streets during Holy Week. He learns how membership in a confraternity depends on a man's parish or his class or even his color. The city's upper classes have traditionally gravitated towards the statue of Jesús del Gran Poder. The Esperanza Macarena draws Her followers from the poorer, working class *barrios* of the north – from Dolores' neighborhood. But la Macarena's brotherhood has also included some of Spain's bullfighters, some giving Her their magnificent bejeweled coats – *traje de luces* – or presenting Her with radiant jewels.

As the more austere confraternities pass carrying their effigies of Jesus – El Silencio and the Gran Poder – the crowds seem cowed by the heavy incense, the funereal music, the lines of gowned *Nazarenos*. For Bill, the mystery of the evening takes on an ominous feel that he cannot quite place and that does not seem to be a part of Dolores' and Manolo's experience.

"Remember the time when the Gran Poder and la Sentencia crossed paths?" Manolo and Dolores are talking so fast that Bill isn't sure he understood correctly.

Dolores laughs a liquid silvery sound behind her tapered fingers. She shakes her head and nods to Manolo to continue. Manolo takes Bill by the arm and whispers almost conspiratorially, "the matter became so heated that it was settled just barely before going to the courts. Even though la Sentencia has precedence over the Gran Poder, He gave way and allowed the Gran Poder to process first. But even today, the Gran Poder must seek la Sentencia's consent. And each year, la Sentencia gives his permission."

Manolo is laughing so hard Bill believes he is pulling his leg. But Dolores explains that it is true. The two figures of Jesus meet on the street, just as the Virgins from Macarena and Triana once met. Bill imagines the two statues meeting, one petitioning the other to go first. What emerges from his imagination is comical, especially considering the severe visages of these two statues. He imagines the austere Jesús del Gran Poder who is bent and ragged under the weight of his cross, seeing clearly a pivotal moment from his past as he meets and seeks permission from the austere Jesús de la Sentencia who is still standing erect before his accusers. The two locked in the moment foretold by their naming.

To Bill, this celebration is unlike anything from his small-town Methodist upbringing where this season is marked by colorful Easter outfits and pastel-dyed eggs. Here the intensity of the colors, the sounds, the emotions, the pushing and pulling of the crowds around him, the lessening of boundaries, and the embrace of complete strangers, it is all nearly more than he can manage. He finds everything intensely personal and communal as the entire pageant of Easter week is played out on the streets among the people. But this story of Jesús del Gran Poder and Jesús de la Sentencia shows Bill just how very real and ordinary this surreal and extraordinary event is to the people all around him. The very public joining of material and spiritual satisfies something deep within him.

Checking his pocket dictionary, Bill learns that Gran Poder means Great Power: Jesus, the Great Power. Defeat and victory, humility and power: it is all there in Jesús del Gran Poder. Everyone's gaze is fixed on the statue whose head is bent and inclined as he nearly buckles under the weight of his cross. His hair is falling forward and not at all contained by the fourfold ring of thorns. His eyes are something like a pale gray that change color in the flickering candlelight, and his gaze seems to be fixed on the spiritual, far from the violence all around, as if he is concentrating on the interior vision of his redeeming mission. This is nothing like the bare wooden cross that hangs behind the altar in Bill's church.

My father can't help but stare at the suffering face of the statue when a voice rises up in the night. A *saeta*, Manolo explains. The song is chilling and grips Bill across the throat as he listens to the singer's voice so raw and exposed. And just as the song commands that we all look at the hollowed face, angular cheekbones, and tortured brow of Jesús del Gran Poder, Bill discovers he is simultaneously revolted and riveted by the *paso*. The blackness of the night is broken by the dancing glow of the candles which throw reflections on the shoulders and arms of all in attendance. It is as if Jesus were walking past just now. In this moment, Bill is witness to the march toward Calvary.

Just when Bill thinks he can manage no more, Manolo and Dolores are pulling him toward another *paso* coming through an arched ochre gate. They find the rest of Dolores' family here, waiting. It would seem the entire crowd that was just recently struck silent and immobile is now pressing forward along with them. They are being carried, and Bill knows that if he should stop, he would be carried along by the crowd or crushed.

It is a huge thing, looming – all velvet and lace and ablaze with so many candles – wobbling on the shoulders of the barefoot *costaleros*. Through the thick forest of blazing candles, Bill sees a sooty but beautiful face under a halo of gold and silver. Glistening on the finely featured face are tears like diamonds. Bill learns that the Virgin Esperanza of the Macarena leaves Her church at midnight and after a 13-hour journey returns to Her church. During that time, She, Her hundreds of hooded brothers, and Her escort of young men dressed up in costumes and armor to represent Roman Legionaries, will snake slowly through the city along a set route to the Cathedral. Bill, along with Dolores' family, follow this procession.

Bill is trying to understand. He asks Dolores about Her name, what does it mean. But she can't hear him. Instead Aurora leans in, "Yes, she is a *Dolorosa* because She depicts the Virgin after the crucifixion. She is full of sorrow because Her son is dead, but that is not Her purpose." Though Aurora speaks to my father, her eyes do not leave la Macarena. "She teaches us more than the resignation of sorrow, more than defeat. She shows us how we can surrender to our pain and be resurrected anew in hope. Her purpose is in Her name, Esperanza. She is *la Virgen de la Esperanza Macarena.*"

Bill senses that there is something definitely different about this statue. She is utterly beautiful with Her dirty, tear-tracked face, enrobed in a heavy velvet gown and cape with lavish embroidery and lace. The roof of the *paso* shimmies and shakes to a halt, and a woman's voice cries out, another *saeta* of praise and adoration rings out into the cool, clear night. "This lighthouse of our lives," sings the *cantaora* in the style of the muezzin's plaintive cry that summons the faithful to prayer. Bill hears how the lilt of the melody sounds somewhat Arabic, how it is bewailing the bereavement of the Virgin. The singer's face shines brilliantly as she leans from her balcony toward la Macarena. Her voice is fractured but forceful. It is at first ugly to Bill, without melody or structure, but soon he feels caught up and finds himself quite moved by the song that is somewhere between wailing and praying.

Manolo leans close to Bill and explains how one year She was decked out in mourning for the death of Her *hermano mayor*, her "big brother" the *matador* Joselito, "who was killed in the bullring at Talavera. She still wears the five emerald broaches he gave Her! Those jewels were supposed to bring him protection, and I guess they did, but only for eight years! La Macarena wore the widow's black when he died, and they say Her tears fell like rain."

All at once the *paso* jumps and begins its slow shuffle across the square, and Bill is startled by a solitary call: "*¡La Macarena!*"

In unison, the crowd cries, "*¡Guapa!*"

"*¡La Macarena!*" again.

"*¡Guapa!*"

From the early morning hours of Good Friday, until the sun reaches its zenith that afternoon, Bill follows the *paso* with Dolores's family. For my father, it is a homecoming of sorts. A spiritual one, at least. A tremendous catharsis wrought from sorrow and joy. Aurora pats his arm and laughs at the utterly unselfconscious look across Bill's broad forehead, "it is both, just like in life: death and renewal always come together."

And as my father watches the processions and how Sevilla becomes an open-air temple, my mother watches him. Dolores feels she is seeing *Semana Santa* for the first time through his eyes. As he marvels over the *costaleros*, *nazarenos*, and *pasos*, she watches him.

His face is awash in wonder and amazement. When he glimpses the *nazarenos* with their long-pointed white hoods, cloaks and sandals, she doesn't know he is conjuring horrifying images of Ku Klux Klan members, but she sees a shadow pass over his brow. When he leans down to see the hobbled and bloodied feet of the *costaleros* – some with shackles – she doesn't know he remembers the chain-gangs working along highways, but she sees the lingering question at the corner of his crooked mouth. She takes note of the quizzical expressions and open-mouthed awe that sit with her in an uncomfortable way. She doesn't know the stark quality of his protestant upbringing or how this merging of color, sound, light is pressing upon him like a fever dream.

~

Dolores looks forward to taking Bill to the April Fair but she is also apprehensive. She knows he will appreciate the music and dancing, the costumes. But she is worried that he will see her and her friends like the gypsies who travel into town for the Feria – the dirty, begging, stealing, fortune-telling gypsies who would just as soon sell their bodies as sell a carnation. Just as the rich Sevillanos look down on the poor and working classes of la Macarena, her neighborhood denigrates the traveling gypsies. She wants Bill to understand the difference between her barrio and those who have no *patria*, no homeland at all.

She dresses meticulously in her *vestida de flamenco* with the big white dots on a red background and the layers and layers of ruffles. She drapes the black fringed silk shawl across her shoulders and knots the ends just below her breasts. Her short dark hair is slicked back with combs. She has fashioned small curls across her forehead and has fastened a red carnation behind her ear.

When Bill arrives, Manolo explains that the Feria used to be held in the Prado de San Sebastián where the Inquisition once burned people, but it outgrew the space and has recently been moved. "We go about mid-afternoon, have lunch at about seven in the evening, dinner at two in the morning, and go to bed at six. Just as the sun is rising."

Bill finds out that in between these established mealtimes, everyone parades up and down long lines of striped tents called *casetas*, greeting each other and drinking a lot of sherry. Everyone offers drinks to everyone else. The air is full of "*¡hola!*" and "*¿cómo está?*" Some of the young men in the Andalucían costumes worn by their fathers and grandfathers prance by on their meticulously groomed steeds. Some very beautiful women, wearing brightly colored ruffled dresses that look like confections, are riding side-saddle or in antique horse drawn carriages. Meaningful glances are darting back and forth from behind splayed fans. And these fans flutter open and snap shut in a precise and time-honored language. But none of the women are as beautiful as Dolores. None begin to compare.

Dolores attempts to explain the subtle language of fans to Bill. They laugh and laugh as she feigns flirting behind her fan. Her words are so quick and fiery, sounding like an insult or perhaps like she's angry, but said with a smile, with laughter in her voice. He cannot translate. His courses in Spanish did not prepare him for this, for her.

Before long, the guitars in one *caseta* begin a race; the tambourines - played in a way Bill has never seen - join in; and the castanets - like the clattering heels of the dancers - lend their beat. He tries clumsily to clap his hands in time, and Dolores gives him a lesson on just how to bring the cupped palm of one hand down to the palm of his other hand as if attempting to trap the air. But it is hopeless.

Dolores takes him to the *caseta* of the Hermandad of la Macarena which overflows with bottles and sherry glasses. Passersby are asked in for a drink of the best *Finos* and the most select *Olorosos*. The man pouring confides, "It is the best cure for your ills and will give you a new lease on life. Without this, life is not worth living." And Dolores is proud that she is accompanied by her handsome brother and Bill, an American. She is aware that behind their fans, some girls are talking.

It is as though everything is new for her as well. Walking through the gates, she sees that everything shimmers and glows as if by magic. And when the guitars start their driving rhythms, she dances along with most of the other girls. Each holding her shawl so the embroidered flowers become a colorful garden swaying with the undulating rhythm of the guitars. Dolores keeps her eyes transfixed on Bill, and her dance is all the more intoxicating for the focus. She sees that he can't take his eyes off her, and the intricate designs of the garlands of colored lights create distorted halos above their heads.

~

My parents fall in love during the Feria de Abril. On *paseo* – the evening promenade along the treelined river – they join other couples strolling along, stopping now and then to taste the savory *tortillas* being cooked on most street corners. Bill tries to tell her the *tortillas* are very much like an egg dish called an omelet in the U.S. She tries but can't pronounce the word. Bill laughs and tells her not to bother because he prefers the Spanish words for everything now.

Dolores and Bill are escorted by Manolo, and sometimes the younger brothers as well. My parents don't mind because more often than not the boys are too distracted by the games at the booths to see the brush of his fingers on her arm or how her eyes linger a little too long on his face: the cleft in his chin, the blue glass of his eyes.

Dolores doesn't mind when her little brothers pull out an old photograph of her taken when she was only about three. She has always hated the photo because she remembers the day it was taken. She was dressed in a ruffled dress, the traditional gypsy costume her older sister had worn the year before she died, and her mother had taken great care in dressing her and fixing her hair just so. The photographer had given her a guitar to hold so she would look like a little *gitana*. But the instrument had a broken string. The photo shows Dolores scowling. Bill is enchanted by the photograph and teases her about her grimace. When he asks her why she was so upset, she explains about the string and how it felt all wrong like she was supposed to be something or someone she wasn't. Dolores doesn't divulge how she complained to her mother about the string. She doesn't tell Bill how puzzled she was that her mother wouldn't say anything no matter how she protested. She doesn't confess how frightened she was when slowly, as if the light shifted, she saw her mother's gaze look right through her as if to her shadow behind, a look she had seen many times before and since. It wasn't until the flash of the camera that Aurora returned, breathing shallowly and forcing a laugh at her angry little gypsy. Dolores puts the photo in her purse and shoos her brothers away along with the memory of that day.

I have seen this picture of my mother as a little girl many times. I have seen how angry she was, how hard she was trying to express her frustration, to be seen and heard in that moment. And I know how painful it is to feel invisible and to see that haunted look pass across your mother's face. I know how frightening and confusing those ghosts can be.

Manolo has been courting a girl named Isabel and starts looking for her amid the groups of young women. So, Dolores and Bill continue their walk around the fairgrounds alone, aware that the jangling current of electricity that flows between them is lost on those who could reveal their secret. This perhaps emboldens them, and they risk letting their fingertips touch.

In the early morning hours, after a night of sherry and stolen touches, after he has escorted Dolores home, the smells and smoke from the various stalls selling *churros* waft sickly, and Bill quickly dives into an alley heaving. He has never felt this full to overflowing. It overpowers him. The debris of chairs and tables and colored paper streamers are scattered pell-mell, and those still awake are singing somewhat more quietly. Dawn is breaking, and he sees people weary from perhaps too much *alegria*. He, too, is weary and somewhat bleary-eyed, but he is sure he sees Dolores' father pushing a large handcart a block away. Bill calls out, but the man abruptly turns a corner and is gone.

~

"Ah, Dolores, civilization is good and progress is necessary for all people. But civilization and progress mean much more than an unquenchable thirst for new things or a race toward what others have." Manuel looks into his daughter's eyes and longs to reach her.

She just shakes her head at him as she cuts a slice from the tortilla made from eggs, onion and potato. Placing it on Bill's plate next to the goat cheese and torn bread, she hums her indifference.

The María Luisa Park is verdant with trees leafing and flowers budding. Even Aurora's favorite roses are unclenching their tightly fisted buds. Manuel looks away from Dolores and picks at blades of grass, "whatever economic lessons *España* can learn from other countries, those countries could learn a thing or two about the art of living from us."

Everyone slowly eats from the picnic as Manuel continues, "work is not so much a good in itself as it is a means to a life lived comfortably and with family." My grandfather takes a generous bite of bread and chews slowly, thoughtfully. "I would prefer to limit my wants rather than to increase my labor."

Aurora slices another piece of tortilla for Manuel, "but when wants have been limited to basic needs, you too increase your labor," she says.

"Of course, I do what I can for my family. What man wouldn't?"

Bill is listening hard, trying to understand. He has all but stopped eating for concentrating on how to phrase his questions. "And the strikes? Are these for more money? Better working conditions?"

"Wages are rarely raised and yet there is inflation. Hours increase but pay does not. The only day we don't work is Sunday, and that day they want us to pray." Manuel speaks slowly, simply.

Manolo takes an orange and divides it into sections, "contrary to what the Church and Franco think, the workers have not developed a greater feeling for Christian life as dictated by the Church. Most of us are indifferent to religion."

Dolores starts to roll her eyes heavenward because she knows where this conversation is headed now. And sure enough, Aurora puts down her plate and ventures quietly in, "that is not to say we are indifferent to God. No, to God and la Macarena, we give our hearts. But to those fat priests ..." She throws her hands in the air, "we may be indifferent to religion, but never to la Macarena."

Manuel's knife stabs at an olive swimming in oil, "Franco

blames the Marxists, calling them a virus that rusts the soul, but it's the priests. It is our real hunger and sickness in the face of the opulent wealth the Church flaunts that can't be reconciled."

"Our Macarena is different. She's not like the priests. We know that both the Church and priests listen to the wealthy landowners and not to us. And we see how the Church protects the rich more than the poor. But la Macarena sees us." Aurora crosses herself with a gesture that ends with kissing her thumb.

Bill is nodding, doing his best to understand. He tells them how much he appreciates their slow pace, and they laugh. "But Franco. He has been around some time now. Nearly 20 years ..."

Antonio interrupts, "Yes, yes, it has lasted 20 years, and perhaps when Franco dies ... *todo esto es una cosa politica*. It is simply politics and politics change."

"But do our lives change?" Finishes Manuel, nodding at his second son.

The confusion across Bill's face shows in his brows pinching in the middle and his eyes squinting. "I heard so much about the poor and the homeless, the maimed and deformed, but I haven't seen any. Franco must be helping with aid?"

"As a result of the many articles that were written about the unfortunates in your American papers and magazines, the authorities have had to take measures. But it is not what you think." Manuel puts his plate down.

"You just don't know where to go. I could show you." Manolo offers.

"Was this what the war was about? Between fascism and communism?" The McCarthy hearings are still fresh in Bill's mind, and he imagines communism is just as ugly as fascism.

"No. Never. It was a fight for bread, for fair wages, for a chance to vote your conscience and have it count. Democracy! To have a voice. To have a name." Manuel pushes his plate away.

Bill looks up at the blinding white sky until his eyes start to water. "Then it was about differing ideologies."

"Take your philosophies and political treatises and ..." Aurora slaps at Manuel's arm before he can finish. He takes a deep breath, "these are not worth any man's spilled blood, no child's empty stomach. These are not worth fighting for. To feed your family, *that* is worth fighting for."

Bill, knowing that he is in Spain because the U.S. supports Franco's vision for the country, asks, "and Franco? He says he stands up for all of Spain."

Manuel nods because he knows this subject is confusing to even those who've lived in Spain all their lives. "Franco may say he was fighting for traditional Spain, but even that is an ideal not worth fighting for, if you ask me. No idea is worth fighting for, the idea of Spain no less. Only people are worth fighting for. The Church, the generals and the bishops betrayed the heart ..." Manuel's voice catches, "they betrayed my heart, our Esperanza."

Suddenly everything becomes very still. Dolores appears to visibly shrink, and her brothers and sister stop eating and look between their parents. Bill feels he has overstepped as Manuel reaches his hand across Aurora's lap to her balled fist. "What I'm saying is that Spanish tradition also demands peasants remain poor. It requires workers to continue working for next to nothing and farmers to hand over their meager harvests because the land they have nurtured is not their own. Traditional Spain, this romantic idea that you have, that so many have, demands that the landlords remain lords over the tenant farmers, using them as one would an ox or a plow horse. And the traditional Spain that Franco so upholds, obliges the Church impose its ..."

Aurora rubs Manuel's knuckles and interrupts, "... it is like the difference between religion and faith. Spain is a country of tremendous faith, though we are not all tremendously religious. Without faith, how could we have survived?" My *abuela's* eyes are wet, and Dolores quickly pulls out a bar of almond *turrón* and offers it around.

Bill is aware that some great wall has been raised and is about to offer his apology, but Manuel tries once more, "did you know that even when there was looting of the shops and factories during the war, no one stole the goods for profit? When we were forced to steal food to feed our children, we never took more than we needed for that day. Only that day, Bill."

Aurora finishes when Manuel's voice falters, "because tomorrow always holds God's promise. Tomorrow's need belongs to God, and there was always something like hope."

Manuel looks at the palms of his callused hands, at the constellations made from the etched stars. Nothing is written there. There are so many paths between those stars. He looks up at Aurora and sees her careful balance. "What would you do, Bill? What wouldn't you do for your children? Perhaps I should have done more. Perhaps I could have ... but we are not thieves."

~

What my *abuelo* could not tell anyone while Franco still lived, what I didn't learn until many years after Franco died, is that from the small scraps of iron he collected over those war-torn years, he forged a bit of redemption for himself and a poignant homage to the thousands who were assassinated in Sevilla.

In 1980, as my grandfather lay close to death, he told only his eldest son, my *tío* Manolo. He swore him to secrecy despite the decades that had passed. He did not want to endanger his family because even though Franco was dead, those years of war and hunger were still buried under a nation's enforced silence. The Pact of Forgetting, a law of great silence, still prevailed, enforcing this brain-injury, this vast national amnesia. So many secrets were dying with my *abuelo's* generation, and he wanted to share his before it, too, was lost forever.

For another 25 years, the truth stayed a secret my *tío* Manolo would not divulge because that is what he promised on his father's deathbed. Manolo kept the secret until he learned that stories were beginning to emerge like damp-winged moths seeking the light.

From the *barrio*, from all over Sevilla, from every region of Spain, people were coming out of the shadows to say out loud the names of their loved ones who disappeared during the Franco years. Websites were created for people to post pictures and ask questions; sites where people could list the names of their loved ones and tell the fragmented stories they had pieced together, such as this story I tell from the names and scraps of history I know.

Articles were written even in the most prominent periodicals, and no one was being taken in the night. No one was disappearing. No one was being shot against the cemetery walls. It was nearly 30 years after Franco had died, 25 after my grandfather died, and finally, finally it was safe to talk about this national trauma.

Eventually, thanks to the Law of Historical Memory that in 2007 permitted and encouraged open discussion of the Franco era, even some of the mass graves would be opened so family members could search for and claim their dead. It wasn't without fear and some trepidation, but as more and more stories came to light, my *tío* Manolo decided it was time. These atrocities *had* happened. No one had forgotten. The pain and devastation was still raw and weeping, an open wound unable to heal in the shadows. Manolo didn't want his father's story to remain unheard because leaving it a secret did not help the healing that was finally beginning all over Spain.

In 2007, my uncle contacted the journalist, Eva Ruiz, and explained the whole history over several cups of coffee and one bittersweet trip to the San Fernando cemetery. Manolo tried to tell Eva the story just as his father told it to him. His attempts were broken and splintered, filled with stops and starts as he fashioned the words into a story that had had no voice for so long. No voice and no ear until then. "There is an eight-foot iron cross in the far section of the San Fernando cemetery," he began.

Eva put her cup of coffee down and took out her notepad, "do you mean the 'cross without a name.'"

"Yes. That is it." My uncle raised his cup of coffee to his lips but returned it to the table without taking a sip. The day was still cool, but the sun was gaining strength. My uncle was grateful for the shade under the awning. "The cross marks one of the mass-graves where there are buried thousands of men, women, and even children who were shot during the coup against the elected government."

"I know the one you are talking about. It has wrought iron ivy and flowers? It's draped with the tri-colored flag?" The reporter scribbled notes and nodded as my uncle told the story.

"Yes, the Republican flag." Manolo nodded and smiled just a little. "My father was a blacksmith by trade. That is what he did his whole life. His hands were blackened by the fires. He was a craftsman, an artist, forced to do the unthinkable." Manolo stopped, stared at his hands, at the cup of coffee wishing it were something stronger. "Franco made him forge munitions. But that is not a story for today. My father was an artist, but he saw too much blood, too much hunger and death during all those years of war ... and after, too. It tormented him that so many had been killed and left in those shallow graves with no marker. No names." Manolo choked on his words and his eyes filled.

Eva had seen so many grown men cry these past months as she collected stories and names. As each one revealed the secret in his heart – the lost loved ones, the betrayals, the fears, the hopes and sorrows of that time – a tremendous burden was lifted and with it came such relief it was nearly palpable to her. But this story was different. This wasn't about someone shot or taken in the night. This wasn't about one of the countless atrocities committed by Franco and his generals. This was a smaller story than that. And it is bigger.

"My father, he did what he could, what he knew how to do. He would say it wasn't much, not nearly enough. But I will tell you that for those who survived, it was a heavy burden, and the cross eased it some. At least I hope it did." Manolo paused to point up at the Giralda, "you see, he was an artist, and it was too much to bear that his friends and coworkers were shot and killed like dogs."

The reporter asked if his father lost many friends in the war, and Manolo looked right into her eyes without blinking. "My father never stopped looking over his shoulder. He never stopped waiting for the men to return and take him back to the wall. He never stopped hearing their boots, their song, and the cold press of steel against his temple." Manolo paused for a long moment before continuing, "it might have been him, you see. There is no difference. It almost was him. But it wasn't. He survived and that, too, was a kind of death."

Before yesterday's late night Madrugá processions, I visited the cemetery where my *abuelo* had been taken and held captive, beaten and humiliated, before being released. I saw the place where men and women were made to stand and reckon with their last moments on Earth. The wall now is covered by carefully tended ivy. The city officials don't want the bullet holes visible. I saw the mass gravesite covered over now in marble. I saw the overgrown camellia tree that provides some shade for the grave but also partially obscures the cross. The ornate iron cross with no name is next to the monument that bears a poem by Alberti and the column that upholds the three-colored flag. My fingers traced the remaining flowers and leaves, searched out the rough edges and crevices, the places my grandfather's hands had touched. I counted the rusted iron roses and was grateful that the center heart was still intact. I imagined his back bent over the fire and his hammer pounding. I imagined the sizzle as his sweat beaded on his brow then bounced off the molten metal. I imagined our lives twining away from each other, twisting away from our truth like the iron tendrils climbing the cross.

Manolo looked away. He watched a young boy swinging on one of the enormous chains draped between ornate bollards that form a barrier separating the Cathedral from the street. He remembered doing the same when he was a boy waiting for his father to finish working on the *rejas* inside. "For many, many years my father witnessed the brutality against his neighbors and friends. Half our *barrio* was killed during the war years and for years after. He decided, with the help of a coworker, to collect, piece by piece, enough scrap iron to forge a memorial. This was very dangerous for him and they had to be very careful. The scrap was valuable and heavily guarded."

Eva signaled to the waiter for more coffee and took a moment to write in her notepad. Manuel took this time to recollect how his father had told him this story. He wanted to do it justice. "My father created the beautiful iron cross where he worked in the foundry at number 80, Calle Sol here in Sevilla. It took many years of collecting and then creating each flower, each leaf, each piece of the cross in secret, before he could forge it whole. When he finished, he placed the cross in a wheelbarrow and covered it with work clothes so it would remain hidden from anyone who might stop him or question him. It was early morning, before dawn, and he carted the cross to the cemetery and planted it in the sandy soil above the grave. There was no marble marker then. Just dirt. It was still a very dangerous time. It was the late 1950s, and he had been collecting the scrap and forging all the intricate pieces of the cross since 1936."

My uncle went on to explain that my *abuelo's* political leanings were leftist and that he had belonged to several covert organizations and unions; "his underground name was Lolo. He saw many of his friends and comrades taken, and all he could do to honor those who died was to create this homage, a tribute from his trade."

In her article, Eva concluded, "this is Sevilla's first homage, Sevilla's first remembrance. Beneath this cross, lie thousands of people waiting to be given a name. Every one of them with a story to accompany that name, and they are waiting for their story to come to light. This man, seeing all the injustices and atrocities, decided to pay tribute in his own way so that these nameless ones would not be forgotten."

My *abuelo* forged delicate six-petaled flowers and twining vines in secret. These he surreptitiously turned over the blazing fires to forge the cross. The homage took over 20 years to complete, from collecting the scrap to shaping each separate piece. The article concludes, "Lolo's Cross now has a name."

Until shortly before he died, my *abuelo* would go to the cemetery and right the tilted or toppled cross, plunging it again and again into Sevilla's yellow earth. After he died, my *tío* Manolo took over righting the cross. It now has a brick foundation to keep it true.

~

My parents begin to imagine a future together. They talk about their dreams and at the tender ages of 20 and 26, the possibilities are endless. He could decline to reenlist in the Air Force, they could settle in Spain. They could move to the United States, and he could go to college. Whatever they decide, he would not stay in the military. That much is certain. He appreciates the Air Force. It got him out of Oklahoma and helped him see the some of the world. But the military presence in Spain is heavy-handed and not particularly welcomed by those he has come to know and love. He wouldn't mind leaving that life behind.

Perhaps buying a small hotel on the Costa del Sol. They could cater to tourists, Americans who have not yet discovered all that Spain has to offer. They could take the money Bill has saved and purchase a small hotel. Dolores could cook, she certainly knows how. And Bill could handle the business side: marketing, the books, everything. They make plans to tap into the tourism market that may be slow at the moment but will grow, Bill believes. And then they would be in on the ground floor. They could do it.

The dreams start to seem truly viable and become plans they share with Dolores' family. Perhaps Dolores' sister could come too, and Manolo. It could be a family business. She imagines a new life away from the shadows of Sevilla under the bright warm skies of the Costa del Sol. All this talk of the future brings about the question of marriage.

Bill talks first with Manuel and Aurora. They are sitting around the dining table, and he rubs his sweaty palms across the tops of his thighs. He states his intentions clearly: his love for Dolores, for her family, and Spain. He explains that he does not want to take their beloved daughter away but wants instead to become a part of her life, all of their lives, here. "Will you have me?"

"You can marry at the church of la Macarena." And with that, Aurora has decided. She can see he has a good heart and as long as he doesn't want to carry Dolores away to America, she will bless their union.

"I am not Catholic. I'll have to take the classes."

"That shouldn't be a problem. But you *will* need to become Catholic. Dolores cannot become a Protestant. In *España*, if a Spaniard is not a Catholic, he is by all rights a card-carrying Communist. And Franco does not abide Communists. It's best not to carry that card with you." Manuel is firm on this. "At least not in such a public way." He winks.

But Bill is not arguing. He knows from the literature he received at the base when he first arrived in Spain that a protestant is not just a Christian who goes to a different church. In Spain, a protestant is someone who *protests* the established national religion - something that is not looked upon favorably in Franco's Spain. In Spain, no one is truly a protestant unless he claims it in front of a judge in a court of law, and this could mean the loss of his job, even the loss of his life. The literature went on to explain that Protestant wedlock is considered shameful, nothing short of living in sin. And Bill had seen the informative posters the Cardinal Segura posted all over town warning the young women of Sevilla about the Americans' carnal ways.

Before he and Dolores go to the church of la Macarena to find out what is required, they go to tell Euin who lives not far from the Alameda, near Dolores' neighborhood. Euin had recently gone back stateside and married his girl, Berta. The four of them have become great friends, and the dream of opening a hotel is generous and inclusive enough to include Euin and Berta. The four friends, along with Dolores' brothers and sister, could make this dream a reality. Dolores even imagines that her mother can ease her asthma by escaping the rainy cold winters in Sevilla. Maybe she could give to her mother in this way, she thinks. Dolores and Bill are both full to overflowing with their hope for their future together.

Euin and Berta are not home, and my father easily discovers the key hidden behind a wrought iron rose on their window's *reja*. My parents tumble into the tiny apartment giddy with excitement at telling their friends. Bill looks around for a piece of paper to leave a note as he pulls the government-issue ballpoint from his front pocket. But as he turns toward the kitchen, he sees Dolores fingering the framed wedding pictures, smiling in that inner way she has. Like a glimpse into a private world, like looking through the iron gates into a lush patio garden. He wants her to take him there. He turns the lock on the door and takes her hand in his. Turning her around and around in a gentle pirouette, he pulls her into his arms as they collapse onto the Moroccan rug.

~

Bill brings to the church his passport as well as letters of reference from his supervising officer and from friends. And Dolores, too, brings the forms that her parents had to sign so that she, an underage minor, can get married. Even though they plan for a wedding after she has turned 21 and after Bill has completed the religion course, she needs her parents' permission in order to begin the conversation with the priest. They are both still flushed and after they run from Euin's and Berta's apartment to the church of la Macarena, they are also somewhat breathless. It is June, and already there is no escape from the sun.

Bill and Dolores sit in tall, ornately carved chairs across from the priest and present all their papers. The office is cool and dark with the shutters pulled closed and just a small lamp burning on the desk between them. The priest takes his time, pulling first one and then another page from the stack, making notes in the margins, making only an occasional sound of affirmation. He puts the papers down and peers over the top of his glasses. "Oklahoma? This is in the United State of America?"

My father is nervous. He knows the priests don't like Americans, especially the servicemen. He is careful with his word choice and with his pronunciation. The Spanish language is coming easier and easier. "Yes sir, it is near Texas. Just north."

"Ahh, Texas. Yes." The priest then looks at Dolores, "do your parents approve of this American? A *protestant?*"

Dolores quickly nods her assent and points to the letter of reference her father wrote for Bill.

The priest scans the letter, "I haven't seen your father at mass in some time. And your mother? How is Aurora?"

Dolores tells him about the whole family, from Aurora's persistent cough to Manuel's work at the foundry, as well as her younger brothers' studies at school. She is nervous and talks quickly, telling him all the news she can think of. All the while, the priest seems to pay little attention, not even looking up as he shuffles through the papers again.

"And you've never been married?" he interrupts.

Dolores laughs abruptly and exclaims that she most certainly has not been married before.

But the priest only turns to Bill who is not sure he understood the question. He asks Dolores if the priest has asked him if he wants to get married, or if he has been married, or when does he want to get married.

After she explains, Bill answers somewhat sheepishly because he has not yet explained this part of his life with Dolores. "Yes. Yes, I was married for a short while. We divorced."

Dolores' eyes dart to him, glinting sharply before falling into shadow.

"Divorced?" the priest repeats.

"Yes. It was short-lived. It did not last. A mistake." All the while, Bill is looking at Dolores, seeking her forgiveness for not having told her.

"Are you sure you did not annul the marriage?" The priest is now looking directly at Bill who is still trying to find his future in Dolores' inscrutable eyes.

"What? No. No. It was a real divorce. That's good, right? It's completely severed. It was done in court, all the papers signed and sealed. With lawyers and a judge." Bill thinks the priest doesn't understand the nature of divorce. Most likely it is an uncommon occurrence in Spain. "I can get copies to show you." Bill reaches for Dolores' hand and finds it cool and dry to his touch.

The priest is silent for an uncomfortable period of time but when he speaks, his voice is quiet. "Marriages before God cannot be torn apart in a court of law. You are still married unless the marriage was annulled by the Church."

Both Bill and Dolores are looking at her tightly clasped hands on her lap. "But we weren't married in the Church. We were married by a justice of the peace. It was a mistake. It's over. I don't understand ... I should have told you. I'm sorry. I never thought it would cause a problem. It was nothing. Nothing. Dolores?"

The only thing she wants to know is the woman's name.

"Catherine. Her name was Catherine. And I never spent one night with her. Never."

"I'm so sorry. There is nothing I can do." The priest stands, straightens his robes, and opens the door for them to leave. "Dolores, please give my regards to your family."

Night finally brings a bit of cool, and my grandparents' bedroom window remains open for the scented breeze. "When we were young, lovers would whisper through the iron bars on the window. Remember? It was called *'Pelar la Pava.'* Boys would pluck the hen feather by feather, full of longing and anticipation, getting only a glance here, a smile there." Aurora's voice is just a hoarse sigh. What she knows to be true, she doesn't think her daughter has yet realized.

"I remember stealing kisses through that small window on your door. Do you remember, Aurora? You were such a brazen girl. Always defying your parents. Sneaking out." They are in bed whispering so they aren't overheard. It's the only place where they can talk in private.

"Me? Never. I was pure and chaste and only you could say different." She laughs a little before coughing. "But Dolores?"

Manuel pulls the covers up higher around Aurora as she likes the breeze only on her face. "He's a good man, and they made a mistake. I still believe his intentions are good. Can you talk with her?" He hands Aurora her inhaling medicine.

"I may not be the one."

"She loves you. You're her mother. Who else could she talk with?"

"Yes, I know that. But there is a space between us. Love yes, but also a space that cannot be bridged. I have never been able to talk with that one. She has so little patience for me. It's like we don't speak the same language." Aurora glances at the prayer card of la Macarena lying on her bedside table.

"She is just more practical. Dolores sees things clearly. Your world is too vague and magical for her."

"Vague and magical?" Aurora's eyebrows are lifted in challenge.

"You know what I mean, *querida*. You try to show her evidence of things unseen, and she looks for its shadow. There are things that fit into her world, and there are things that don't. But she is loyal to those she loves. And she loves us." Manuel knows Aurora sometimes feels as though she lost two children when Esperanza died: Esperanza and the daughter born into the devastating undertow of her sorrow.

"There is no room in her world for the surprises that life throws. I've seen her turn from what she doesn't want to see. I don't know how she'll take this."

~

Aurora doesn't have to say anything to Dolores. Just as my *abuela* stands in the kitchen rehearsing with la Macarena the words and phrases that will gently usher her daughter into this new world of motherhood, her daughter comes in and announces that she and Bill went to the municipal building to request permission to marry. They passed under the chiseled arrows and yoke of the *Falange* that is carved over the entrance and signed their names to documents embossed with Francisco Franco's name. They want a wedding in two weeks. It is clear to Aurora that Dolores does not want to talk about anything else.

They marry in the Episcopal church on July 28, 1957. The day is scorching hot, and Dolores in her white dress is nearly blinding to behold. Her radiant smile obliterates any raised eyebrows or questions. No one can deny her this beautiful day and her heart's desire.

My mother's younger sister, Esperanza, stands beside my mother. And the whole family is here to celebrate. Even la Macarena sneaks in to witness to the celebration, *"behold a new beginning, Aurora. Behold the hope in this. Behold the* esperanza *in this moment now."*

Aurora finds herself looking at Dolores, her smile and eyes bright and alive with all the future holds, and she imagines her first Esperanza. This is something else her firstborn will never know: the heat of a man's embrace, the soft urgency of his kiss, the scratchy rustle of crinoline under a wedding dress, the exchange of vows. All these things her first daughter will never know. And the baby within, Dolores' not Esperanza's. Bill mistakes the tears in Aurora's eyes for typical mother-of-the-bride tears of joy, but Dolores sees the shadow beneath, the ghost of her sister. Even here. Even today.

I know this because it is the same shadow that passed across my mother's face at my wedding. The same sense of loss, of underlying sorrow. That day my mother attempted to pull my sister into her experience, asking her if she ever wished she could get married, have a wedding, wear a white dress. In that moment, I held still, between breaths, invisible against the white painted walls of the church dressing room, with my unarticulated feelings of *even here. Even today*. My sister, though, broke the spell and laughed, revealing that in her life lived always in the perpetual gift of this present moment, these questions made no sense. As I turned to embrace my maid-of-honor, my beautiful sister who would walk down the aisle before me, I wondered if my mother could understand.

~

Aurora's first mention of the coming baby is to tell Dolores that all pregnant women should get what they want, whatever they want, or else the baby will be marked with the mother's longing."

"Mmm, like the rose, Mamá?" Dolores points to the blossom between her brows that is becoming rosier as the baby grows.

Dolores isn't surprised her mother knows about the baby. Aurora always seems to know things, even things Dolores tries to keep from her.

"Yes, the rose. Or if you want *boquerones*, you should have them or else the baby will come out like a little fish."

"My baby is not going to be a little fish. She'll be beautiful and smart. I have everything! I want nothing at all."

They are in the kitchen, and Aurora is chopping onions careful not to turn her full attention on her daughter. She knows that it is best to approach Dolores from the side, "be careful, *híja*."

Aurora tries to join her daughter in her high hopes for her baby and the new life she and Bill are building. She knows that this is what her daughter wants of her right now. But inside, Aurora holds a little back, just a little in case the gods are watching.

~

At the base-exchange, Dolores buys loaf after loaf of sliced, white bread and cans of Campbell's Soup. She buys smooth peanut butter, soft toilet paper, pre-packaged ground beef, and bottles of milk. There is so much for so little money. Just a few of the dollars Bill gives her for groceries buys so much food. She enjoys bringing armloads of plastic wrapped goods to her parents and to her brothers who eat and eat.

Her generosity feels good. To show her love this way, to provide for them this way, feels powerfully good. She wants her mother to stop taking in laundry and her father to cut back on some of his hours at the foundry. And though she is unconscious of one of her motivations, I know she also is attempting to blot out the sadness that still lurks in the corners of her family home by proving, tangibly with food, that she is more than her sister's shadowy ghost. It's a new day. There's plenty now, more than enough. She brought plenty to their table.

Being pregnant agrees with my mother. She does not feel at all sick. In fact, she's never felt healthier, more alive. Her face becomes fuller, she carries her weight all around and becomes pleasantly plump. Together, Aurora and Dolores make smocked tops for her growing belly.

The amount of attention Dolores gets is astounding. Rarely is she allowed to help in the kitchen. It's always, "It's too hot in here. Get off your feet or they will swell like balloons." Or, "if you stand or move too much, that baby is going to slip out." Or, "get as much sleep as you can so that baby knows how to sleep when he is born." She's not allowed to clean, carry, or concern herself with much at all, "you don't want to strain the baby; that baby is going to come early if you don't take it easy." The advice comes from family and neighbors and strangers alike.

Aurora watches her daughter grow. It is something she's never quite gotten accustomed to. Ever since Dolores passed the age of four, it has been astonishing. Not quite a second chance and always a blessing that she is so grateful for, but also painful in ways that she can only confess to la Macarena when they are alone in the kitchen.

"I can't help thinking that my first will never have this chance. I'll never see her marry. She'll never have children." Aurora sneezes at the scent of vinegar that she is using to wash her windows. She rubs and rubs at one stubborn spot.

La Macarena moves in a flurry of rose petals to the other side of the pane and scratches at the same spot. Her fingernail scrapes off the residue, and She returns inside. "*No. But Dolores will, and your second Esperanza will. Your sons, too.*"

"Did you feel this way? That with Your son lost, You lost also his children?"

"Yes, but then I remember he gained generations. Because of him, I can know you in this way. Ultimately, Aurora, it was his life. He needed to live it his way. He made choices that were not the choices I would have made for him as my son, but they weren't mine to make. I believe he chose the life he lived."

La Macarena stoops low to rinse Her rag in the bucket and sloshes a little onto Her robes. "Be careful." Aurora says as she places an apron over la Macarena's head and cinches up the ties. "Do you think Esperanza chose her life?"

"Perhaps. Perhaps she knew that her living the life she lived would be something sweeter for the shortness of it. Maybe she chose the sweeter. Maybe that was her gift to you. A chance to know the sweetness in every moment despite the war and hunger."

Aurora remembers Esperanza's intensity. She didn't allow you to be distracted. She demanded your attention to the moment she carried in her hand. "Still, it's hard to believe that she chose to die. To leave me. Our relationship was like no other. She saw me, and I saw her."

My *abuela* pats her runaway curls with her damp hands and continues on the window as la Macarena pours water into a large pot. "*And yet, look what she was able to give you in that short time. A full mirror to your soul, and she tapped into your hope and joy like none before.*"

"And none after. She was the essence of all I hoped for." Aurora hands the Virgin an onion and nods to the knife in the sink.

"But that was your *choice."*

Aurora tosses her rag into the bucket splashing them both. She laughs bitterly, "this too is a matter of choice? We choose the life we will lead, and we choose how we will be affected by losses?"

La Macarena stops chopping the onion and puts down the knife. She turns to Aurora, taking her by the shoulders, "*You can choose to resign yourself to a solitary moment in time – joyous or sorrowful – and be defined by that. Or, you can choose to live every new moment fully.*"

The onion is strong, and Aurora wipes at a tear. "And you think I am trapped in that one moment?"

"You have allowed one horrible time in your life to shadow many subsequent moments. That has been your choice."

Aurora turns back to the window, "we've had this conversation before. You expect me to forget she ever existed? To forget she ever lived and breathed and danced?"

"You think of it as loyalty to Esperanza, but your putting all your hope in that one fragile and mortal vessel kills the very passion that she inspired in you. It kills the spirit of Esperanza." La Macarena heats oil in the pan and drops in the onion, watching it dance. *"If you could move forward in your faith, that same passion could be rekindled in others and inspired by others, by even Dolores. It is not too late."*

~

On the morning of March 17, 1958, Dolores' daughter is born. My mother would say prematurely, but no one really asks. The baby girl is a healthy seven pounds, with dark curly hair and smoky eyes that seem to know Dolores through and through. Dolores finds herself looking away at first, such is the intensity of her daughter's gaze.

When Aurora sees her first grandchild, her breath becomes uneven and jagged. Manuel shows her to a chair and brings her a glass of water. After a moment, they bring her granddaughter to her.

Dolores watches carefully as her mother takes her into her arms.

"Mamá? Isn't she beautiful?"

"*Si, míja*. She is beautiful. I can't believe it." Aurora, shaking her head, turns to her husband, "look at her, Manuel. Look. She looks just like Esperanza did when she was born. It's uncanny. The same eyes. The same chin. Look at that, Manuel." Her fingers trace around the little ears and under her chin.

Dolores looks away from her mother, searching out first Bill who is still watching his baby daughter. Then she seeks out her younger sister, her father, her brothers. But no one sees her. All have eyes only for the baby. Once again, and even now.

My *abuelo* looks up and recognizes the familiar pain flit across Dolores' face before the mask descends again. "She is stunning. To me she looks just like Dolores. Where's Bill in this little one?" Manuel laughs at his own joke.

Bill shrugs, "yeah, I thought all babies were born with blue eyes. I guess hazel wins this time! I'm not complaining about that. She's perfect."

Dolores names her daughter Patricia. It is St. Patrick's Day, and Dolores is adamant that her daughter will not be named after any grandmothers. The family had all assumed, but Dolores says this is not the custom in America. She will have her own name.

Motherhood bestows a new life for Dolores. Becoming her own person in her own right. Dolores feels newly entitled to a full breath of air, filling her lungs for the ache of it, stretching, moving in the world as if she might own the ground beneath her feet. It is how she feels when she dances, but that is such a narrow stage compared to this. This act of naming is Dolores' second act of moving away from the shadows of the past. And Patricia is Dolores' beautiful daughter – her Noble One – to which her loyalty is now pledged. Her perfect *patria*.

~

On April 5th, Bill and Dolores take Patricia for *paseo* through the María Luisa Park. They have attended some of the processions over Holy Week, and they find the city somber and silent on this Saturday before Easter. The quiet is as welcome as a soft lullaby after the week of crowds pushing and pulling during the processions. The trumpets blaring and shouts of celebration coming from every corner was a wall of sound that was disconcerting to Patricia, only weeks old.

The orange trees throughout the park are leaping into blossom, emanating their deep perfume. The acacia and sycamore trees seem to burst into radiant leaf. Spent marigolds – the flower dedicated to the Virgin – have collected in the gutters, crushed remnants, after being carried then tossed as the various Virgins processed on Good Friday. Despite the cacophony of color, there is a hushed somberness to the city, as if it is truly in mourning. But Dolores and Bill sense none of this as they are over the moon with their beautiful daughter, this beautiful new life that heralds and entwines their lives together.

In a very real way, Patricia binds Bill to this culture and this country that he loves dearly. He now belongs to this family as father to the beloved granddaughter. Even more than as husband to Dolores, he belongs. And Patricia fortifies Dolores; no longer just her mother's daughter, no longer her sister's shadow, she is now her daughter's mother. Patricia gives her substance. She is a mother, barely 21 years old; she is a woman in her own right with custody of her own life, with custody of this little life as well.

Orange blossoms drift down like a snowfall Dolores saw once a long time ago. They fall into the carriage like confetti and dot

Patricia's blanket, catching in the curls of her hair and scenting the air all around them. As she looks up to the spreading branches, an orange blossom falls upon Dolores' birthmark, and she feels baptized into this new life and deliriously happy.

Patricia is christened in the church of la Macarena on a beautiful day in April. The entire family is in attendance, all standing to be *madrinos* to Patricia, all with outstretched arms to hold her. This little one has so many who will bless her and guard her and attend to her years.

~

Esperanza and Aurora visit often with Dolores and Patricia when Bill is at work. They dress my sister like a little doll and play little games, clapping hands all the while bouncing her on their knees and singing songs and reciting rhymes. Dolores, Esperanza, and Aurora sing every little song over and over, and there is only one that catches in my *abuela's* throat. As the months change the seasons from spring to summer then fall, it is clear Patricia has all she needs in the world. Two parents who dote on her and an extended family who magnifies the joy. The more people a child has who truly love her, the happier that child will be, and my sister's circle of love is ever widening. For the first months of her life, Patricia sees nothing but luminous smiles and hears nothing but bright, bright laughter and song. This is a new beginning for the entire family.

Dolores watches her mother with Patricia and tries to imagine how it might have been when she was an infant. As she holds Patricia close, she tries to remember her own mother's arms around her. But all she can recall is the fluttering fingers that tugged at her hair or swiped at a smudge on her cheek. Try as she does, she cannot remember the feel of her mother's touch, the warmth of her hands, or the lift of an embrace. All she can remember, as far back as she can remember, are the vague shadows lingering in the space between.

But now there is Patricia. Her daughter, who seems to be saying, "I see you. I know you. I understand," every time she looks at her. And Dolores finally knows what it feels like to be of consequence, full and tangible, alive.

~

There is an artist in town who takes and embellishes photographs. His work hangs in the homes of many of Bill's married friends. One that catches Dolores' eye hangs in Euin's and Berta's apartment. It is of Kay, their baby girl who was born shortly before Patricia. The portrait completely captures Kay's wide-eyed wonder and her curious personality. She's always moving from one thing to the other, and her emotions follow her, running the gamut. Dolores wants a portrait made of Patricia.

"She's at the perfect age, so alert, so engaged. She's changing every day, and I want to remember her always as she is now. Every day she gains new abilities ... she's growing so fast." Dolores and her mother are sitting between a load of fresh laundry.

"You can't capture her." Aurora takes a diaper and folds it into thirds.

Dolores blows a raspberry on Patricia's belly. A squeal of delight fills the apartment. "Of course, I can't capture her, but I can trace this moment. I can capture this moment. Look at her!"

"But will you embrace the next? She will not remain like this. She will grow into her own person," Aurora places the diaper on the stack on the coffee table.

"I know that. What else would she do? I just want to always remember this sweetness, this time in our lives. She is so perfect and beautiful and so, so smart." Patricia laughs at her mother's singsong voice.

"Yes. You are right."

"She's nearly standing now, on her own. She can move around the table holding the edge. Soon she won't sit still long enough to take a photo."

Aurora still worries about tempting the gods. She worries that if you love someone too much, she may be taken. Dolores knows she is remembering Esperanza, and she is grateful for Patricia who is evidence that she exists despite the shadows threatening to overtake the room.

"Nothing is going to happen. Don't be so superstitious. It's just a picture."

Later, when Dolores is retelling the conversation to Bill, she fumes over the old-fashioned haunted thinking that her mother clings to. Bill listens as Dolores pantomimes her mother, "it boxes life, frames it, stifles the breath ..." Dolores shifts her gaze from Bill to Patricia, "all I know is that she will not grow up with a mother who didn't want her, who looks right through her."

That last phrase hangs in the air heavy and portent, and I know buried deep within those words lay all the hurt and sadness that comes with being the child her mother could not want. My *abuela* was grieving the loss of Esperanza when my mother was born. That moment was filled with longing for the past, when Esperanza was alive and healthy, not with the blessing of a new life. There was no room within that all-encompassing grief for another child. I know the wound that is buried in those words because I heard them from my mother when she tearfully confessed to me that she never wanted a second child. She knew she didn't have the energy, the time, or capacity to nurture another child. She was busy. Her hands were full of the task at hand and her heart was heavy with grief. This is how I know my mother's pain at seeing her mother's grief. A pain that continued to ricochet like an errant bullet whittling away at what inner resources she had scavenged. I know how that shadow taints gestures and tarnishes intentions. And I know how it becomes the hidden shape within every attention, every neglect.

Pulling the beads until they nearly snap, I turn to la Macarena and ask, "how is it You accepted and embraced your child? It wasn't your idea. It wasn't what you would have chosen; a child out of wedlock, before you were ready. And then the grief? How did you accept that? You surrendered. But how? How do I move beyond this?" Our eyes meet, but there are no answers. She doesn't speak to me the way I know She did with my grandmother.

~

The photographer who arrives to take the photograph fills the small room with a smoky blue haze and the sharp acrid smell of exploded flash bulbs that remains for hours. From the chosen photograph, a beautiful portrait will be made of my sister. A hint of blush will bloom in Patricia's cheek. Gentle washes of color will sweep through her curls. Her dress is palest pink, and the photographer will tint the black and white photograph perfectly.

When I saw the portrait years later, what captivated me most were her eyes. My sister's eyes were vibrant, alive, and shining with an intensity evocative of some inner fire, a purpose beyond this moment here, beyond even herself. In the portrait, my sister is sitting upright with a delicately crocheted blanket draped behind her. She is staring intently at her mother who must have been standing behind the photographer; she is grinning mischievously. And I saw them both, intent on each other, eyes vivid with intimate knowing, fierce and tender love.

~

The questions the doctors at the base hospital are asking make no sense. Dolores cannot surface from the depths of this dream, this nightmare. What are they saying? What are they asking? They all talk at the same time.

"Did she fall?"

"Was there a car accident? Maybe a week ago, even two?"

"Has she been sick? Runny nose? Rash? Anything?"

"Could she have hit her head on something?"

"Check for ruptured blood vessels in her eyes."

"Yes."

"The fontanels?"

"Right."

"There may be some intracranial pressure caused by swelling?"

But Dolores just stands against the wall staring at the doctors as they work furiously on her near lifeless daughter. She doesn't understand what they are asking. She's not sure if they are talking to her or to each other, and the interpreter hasn't arrived yet.

"Are you sure ma'am? No accident?"

Dolores just shakes her head over and over. She doesn't know what to say and these urgent questions feel more accusatory than inquisitive.

"Is she walking? Could she have fallen?" The doctor is pantomiming, walking fingers across palms and then off the edge.

But Dolores doesn't know how to respond. She doesn't speak English. She doesn't understand. Their urgency scares her. Patricia's listlessness scares her. All she can do is ask over and over, "*¿qué pasa con míja?* Please help her. Help her!"

When Dolores first brings Patricia to the doctors at the base clinic outside of Sevilla, she thinks it may be connected to an earache her daughter had the week before because Patricia had been banging her head against the crib bars. That week had been particularly difficult with Patricia inconsolable, Bill away on temporary assignment, and her own patience running low.

The doctors ask if Patricia has vomited, does she have diarrhea, has her stomach been hard as though she has a cramp. "She doesn't seem dehydrated."

It seemed that along with Patricia's increased activity, her appetite was also growing. She was becoming more independent and more willful. Patricia was so smart and had definite ideas of what she wanted and when. Lately, having a headstrong nine-month old had been challenging for Dolores. On the one hand, she loved her daughter's willfulness, and on the other, she felt overcome, eclipsed by Patricia's energy.

One doctor is calling Bill's commanding officer to find out where he is. Another doctor is filling out paperwork. Two others are ministering over Dolores' daughter who lies lank across the examining table. A nurse brings in a chair for Dolores, but she can't sit. And they won't let her hold her baby. She doesn't know what to do with her hands.

My sister's fever is quite high, and it doesn't respond to the intravenous analgesics that the doctors are giving. Her head is floppy as if her neck has no muscle strength. She isn't crying and is only barely responsive to stimuli. Dolores stands in a corner of the hospital room and begins picking at a ragged cuticle until it bleeds. She watches her daughter not respond as the doctors knead and massage her, shine lights into her eyes, peer down her throat, check her small body as if they are looking for answers she can't give them.

Dolores is running through the past weeks searching for any detail that might help the doctors help her daughter. Patricia had been especially cranky a week ago. Bill has been away on an assignment that was to keep him away from home for several weeks. Dolores and Patricia have been alone. Aurora has not been feeling well, her asthma keeping her at home instead of over at Dolores' apartment cooing and playing with her granddaughter. Dolores' sister hasn't come to visit either because she was busy working and taking care of their mother. It seemed that the mustard packs that had been commonly used to treat asthma had scarred Aurora's lungs. Her breathing was always short and labored, but now when an attack came on, she could barely stand without getting dizzy, her lips turning a bluish color. That left Dolores all alone with Patricia who was becoming more and more active, more vocal; always wanting up, or down, and reaching for things she shouldn't have. Wailing if she didn't get her way. Aurora said it was normal for a nine-month old to get frustrated as her interest in exploring the world surpassed her ability to navigate it. Also, a nine-month old's ability to communicate fails to keep up with her desire to express herself. She was cruising around the furniture, and Dolores was always attentive so that if she fell, she didn't hurt herself. And lately Patricia was frustrated at her inability to walk without someone's hands reaching out to guide her. The doted-on first grandchild, used to getting her way, would bat her mother's hands away and squeal. But Dolores was always careful that Patricia not hurt herself. Emotions began to escalate in the tiny apartment. It wasn't uncommon, especially when Bill was away at work, for both Dolores and Patricia to cry. The world suddenly seemed a big and dangerous place, and Dolores was spinning trying to keep up with Patricia.

The interpreter finally arrives, and the doctors are urgent, "Ma'am, your baby is very sick. The doctors can't bring her fever down. They've tried everything and nothing is working. Perhaps a lumbar puncture will indicate what is going on so that they can treat it. But we don't have that capability here. Not for a little baby." This the interpreter tells Dolores just before she is whisked away to get an emergency U.S. Military Dependent's passport.

Bill's duty is in Morocco, and he can't return until the next night. The doctors at the small air base in Sevilla believe that a bigger hospital will be better equipped to diagnose the problem, and they don't believe Dolores should wait until Bill gets home. Patricia and Dolores are airlifted to an Air Force hospital in Germany that evening.

In Germany, the doctors barrage her again with questions, "there must have been an accident?"

"A fall? Even a week ago?"

"Nothing?"

"You say she's not been sick?"

With the help of an interpreter Dolores tries to answer, "She was cranky a week or so ago. I thought maybe she had an ear infection because she cried and cried. There was nothing I could do. I tried everything, but she cried all the time. I took her in to see the doctor because I couldn't stop her. She wouldn't be comforted. But the doctors in Sevilla said there was no ear infection."

"When did your daughter present listless like this? With no muscle tone, floppy like this?"

Dolores can barely make sense of what the doctors are asking, the interpreter is trying, but the urgency has everyone flustered. She hasn't slept, and the days are colliding into each other. "Today, I think. No, it was yesterday when I went to the doctor again. I thought she was finally better. She had stopped crying and seemed sleepy. That's okay, right? She was sleepy after all her crying. She had worn herself out. But her sleepiness didn't go away the next day. I couldn't get her to fully wake up. And she wasn't feeding. She's usually so active. So busy. And then she couldn't hold her head up."

The doctors order a spinal tap. They prepare Dolores for the inevitable pain Patricia will experience by showing her the needle and the spot where they will insert it. She'll need to keep her daughter from moving, keep her perfectly still. They tell her this several times, emphasizing the point by placing their hands over hers and clamping down on Patricia's body much more firmly than she would have done. The hardest thing Dolores has ever done is hold her baby daughter still as they jab that needle into her back, but what is worse is that Patricia does not flinch.

An IV is inserted. Nurses keep cold compresses placed across Patricia's forehead, under her arms, behind her knees, all in an effort to bring her temperature down. But it doesn't. The lumbar draw shows that Patricia does not have meningitis, nor any other infection. Her fever continues to climb, and my sister slips quietly into a coma.

Bill arrives the next morning and is trying to understand what has happened. Seeing Dolores' wan expression in the institutional green hallways of the base hospital delivers a blow that Dolores and the doctors will verbalize for him later. She hasn't slept, she hasn't eaten, she won't sit down or rest even though everything that can be done for their daughter is being done. "These are the best doctors outside of the U.S. Let's give them some time, a little room to help her."

But Dolores won't leave Patricia's bedside. She throws all the words that the doctors have been saying at him. Over and over he is pummeled with the same questions, but he is just as unable to answer. He wasn't home.

The impotence Dolores feels comes out as anger toward Bill. Anger that he was away when this happened. Anger that he's been away a lot lately, leaving her alone with Patricia for days, sometimes weeks. With her mother ill as well, she's had no help from anyone. She's been at her wit's end. She's panicked and hysterical, and she's blaming him.

And he accepts the blame. If it will help Dolores through this, if it will calm her, he will accept the blame, and he will apologize until she can hear him. It's just as well because he does feel this is his fault. He volunteered for the assignment in Morocco. But the two of them are always so self-sufficient, a twosome that sometimes feels exclusive to my father. And Dolores has her family nearby.

"It's a waiting game now." The doctor isn't looking at either Bill or Dolores.

"What do you mean? Waiting for what? Can't you bring her out of the coma?" Bill searches out the doctor's eyes.

"We've done ... we're doing all we can. But yes, it's in Patricia's hands now. Or perhaps, if you're a praying family, God's."

"Are you saying that Patricia has to choose to get better?" Now that Dolores has tapped into her frustration and anger, it's hard to put it down. "She's a baby!"

"Isn't there some medicine? Something?" Bill is pulling the doctor aside, away from Dolores.

"Sir, you need to know, your daughter has at most a 50-50 chance of making it out of this coma. Her fever ... you need to prepare yourself. You need to prepare your wife. If your daughter does make it through this trial, there will be others.

Bill braces himself on the wall beside the ICU where Dolores is standing over their daughter now with tubes taped to her arms and legs, coming out her nose and down her throat. He leans his forehead against the cool green wall listening to the bleeps of the heart monitor, the hum and mutter of the other gadgets that surround his baby daughter. "What do you mean?"

"If your daughter survives this coma, there may be some brain injury. This type of neurogenic fever is indicative of some swelling around the brain. Babies, especially those learning to walk, fall." The doctor holds up his hands, "I know. I know. There's been no accident. Nothing that either of you remember. But that is what this kind of fever tells us."

"What can we expect when she wakes up?" Bill is swallowing back bile and is fighting the darkened shadows that are encroaching upon his periphery.

"*If* she survives, most likely she'll have an injury that could manifest in some mental retardation, some moderate to severe motor dysfunction. We just don't know yet. Her fever is too high. The human brain cannot sustain these temperatures indefinitely." The doctor lets these words settle. He sees each word as it whittles away the young father's resolve to fix this untenable situation, ultimately revealing a brutal understanding. "We are helping her breathe and trying to keep the fever down ... at this moment we are doing absolutely everything we can, but we need to know how heroic you want us to be."

Bill moves to the threshold looking in where his wife and baby daughter are ringed in a halo of light under the industrial lamp hanging from the ceiling. They belong to each other more than any two other people on this earth. More than he belongs to either of them. Feeling at a loss, completely inadequate, this is all he can do to protect her. In this moment, one fact becomes crystal clear to him. And his answer to the doctor is just as clear. "You do everything, *everything*, in your power to save them."

Bill doesn't see the curious look the doctor gives him. He sees nothing but Dolores and Patricia surrounded by an intense white light.

~

Aurora sits in front of la Macarena. It has been some time since she's been able to come to the church. She's been so ill, and even though Esperanza had tried to help her cross the street, Aurora didn't have the stamina, the breath, to travel the distance. This is the first time in over a month, and she doesn't know how to begin.

Her rosary is worn from worrying. And as she begins the *Mater Dolorosa,* the beads slip from her grasp. For a moment, Aurora just sits there looking at the beads, a black puddle on the marble floor. She's lost. For the second time in her life, she is lost, and she doesn't know if she will survive this time. She's not that sure she survived the last time. "This is more than I can bear, *Señora*."

Aurora watches as la Macarena bends low, dropping to Her knees to pick up the rosary; the body of Christ has broken off the crucifix and only the hands and feet remain. La Macarena holds the beads in Her palm, not offering them back to Aurora, not getting up. La Macarena holds the beads and touches each one so singly, knowing each by heart. In just a whisper, She starts the *Dolorosa*, moving from the first sorrow to each devastating sorrow that follows: from the prophesy, through the flight and loss and grief.

At the fifth sorrow, the crucifixion, Aurora turns her palm up in her lap, and la Macarena pours the beads into her awaiting hand. The Virgin's hand closes Aurora's fingers around the beads, and She covers Aurora's hand with Her own. The scent of roses, like a momentary incense, drifts by, and together they pronounce the fifth sorrow. "*... woman, behold your ...*"

"I can't do this. She is my daughter. She has suffered enough.

All her hopes, our dreams, the future ..." Aurora pulls her hands away and leaves the beads draped across her lap in the folds of her dress.

"Of course, you can. We can together." La Macarena's face, despair and hope ensnarled.

"Wasn't it enough that Esperanza was taken? Dolores has already suffered from that loss. Don't take her daughter, too." Aurora is now kneading la Macarena's robes, pulling and tugging at the heavy brocade.

La Macarena takes my *abuela's* hands in Her own, *"Behold your daughter, Aurora. And here is an opportunity for Dolores to behold her mother. Your fates are intertwined. We are all connected."*

Aurora stares at the wooden pew in front of her. The grain runs in separate streams merging together and then separating around a knot, like an island. Rivers running through wood. "Bill tells me she is dying inside." Aurora is struggling with her words now, not able to draw a deep enough breath to speak a full sentence. "And I'm not there. She's all alone."

La Macarena releases Her grasp on Aurora's hands and adjusts Her robes as She rises up from Her knees. She removes Her heavy crown and arranges Her *mantilla* so She can sit down beside my grandmother. Embracing Aurora, She lifts her chin, tilts her head, and kisses her full on the mouth. The kiss is long and deep, and a taste of warm honey fills Aurora's mouth. But instead of leaving her breathless, Aurora is released refreshed. She can breathe.

Pulling away, la Macarena looks into Aurora's eyes. *"She is not alone. I am there with her. I am with her now, just as you are with her now."*

"But Dolores doesn't know that. She feels alone. I know it. She is in hell, and she feels alone." Aurora takes yet another easy deep breath.

"Yes, hell is despair without hope, and Dolores is in hell. But Aurora, it is her choice."

Aurora has enough breath now to let the full force of her words fall on la Macarena. "It is too soon. She hasn't surfaced yet. She is not in a position to choose anything."

"Soon she will begin choosing again. And what will she choose? Hope in vain? Despair without hope?" La Macarena holds out Her two hands, *"Life – eternal life – is the two entwined. Sorrow and Hope."*

"Together? At the same time? It is impossible to hold both at the same time." Aurora picks up the rosary and clutches it so the crucifix digs into her palm.

"I know it seems a leap, but it is from within this tangle of hope and despair that we can move forward and experience life. Both are gifts, both are necessary to fully live in this moment here and to live as though your life might be over in the next instant. Know this, Aurora, life that is fully lived is also fully consumed in every moment." La Macarena picks up Her crown and places it back on Her head.

Aurora stares down at her lap, at her hands clasping the beads. Turning her hand over she unclenches her fingers and discovers the slivered moons that are pierced into her palm. She looks at la Macarena's bloodied and bruised hands. Her nails bloodstained. Her knuckles raw. But Her hands are open. Her right hand is open and outstretched, nearly pointing forward as if showing the way. Her left hand is also open, but it is lifted, palm up, as if to assist in an inhale. It is a conductor's subtle gesture, ready, a new movement, a giving up and releasing what we cannot hold.

La Macarena's voice is so quiet, so cautious, as She tries once more to explain, *"the world is beautiful, Aurora. Beautiful, but also dangerous because our relationship to it is tenuous and transient. We can love only that which is fleeting and finite, that which changes in every moment because it is alive."*

Aurora lifts her eyes to la Macarena where she sees her own pain reflected so clearly. "Why do we risk it?"

The Virgin takes Aurora's face in Her hands, *"To love something safe, something that is unchanging, is to love an ideal, a philosophy, a political ideology, or an image. You once said, 'pictures are of things no longer.' And you are right. The moment the flash fades, that person is gone. We change in every blink of the eye. And our love comes alive and passes in every instant."*

Aurora is crying. Her tears are falling, and la Macarena captures them in Her palm. *"Aurora, Esperanza was beautiful, and she inspired a love that was vibrantly beautiful and equally dangerous precisely because she could die. Patricia was beautiful before, and she is beautiful still. She was lost and then found. Changed in an instant, but beautiful nonetheless."*

Aurora's hands begin to work the beads, one by one. Her lips begin to form words that no one can hear, no one except la Macarena. As she begins the *Mater Dolorosa* at the first sorrow, she thinks maybe she understands: loving someone is accepting them in every moment for who they are in that moment. Who they were in the previous moment is already gone, and holding on to that is a betrayal of that love. But with the next bead, the understanding is gone - it is that slippery - and she is left once again with her meager act of faith in the midst of doubt.

My *abuela* begins the fifth sorrow again, and la Macarena joins her to continue in unison, *"When Jesus saw his mother and the disciple whom he loved standing near, he said to his mother, 'Woman, behold your son.' Then he said to the disciple, 'Behold your mother.' And from that hour the disciple took her to his own home."*

I sit in my *abuela's* church, and the sun is lower now, streaming in through a window. An intense shaft of light slices across my arms severing my hands. I lift my hand and open it to capture the beam in my palm. Light so ephemeral, like nothing at all. I know my grandmother's pain and sorrow. I know it like my own. It is a grief that has traveled through the generations. Our silent song. Across lifetimes, bridging generations, spanning time. As I sit with my *abuela's* rosary threaded through my fingers, I imagine my grandmother's voice revealing the fifth sorrow: granddaughter, behold your mother.

~

The brown paper wrapped package rests against the wall just inside Dolores' and Bill's apartment when they return home. Euin must have delivered it. The windows are open and the curtains billow in the evening breeze. The kitchen has been stocked, and Bill moves through the apartment turning on lights. It has been almost a month since they've been home.

"She's asleep. Do you want to put her to bed?" Bill's arm hovers just at Dolores' shoulder.

"I'll hold her for now." Dolores turns away from Bill and moves into the living room.

The apartment looks the same as when Dolores left. A few toys are on the coffee table, a bottle is in the sink. All these things the same, yet everything is changed.

"You've been holding her since we left the hospital. The whole way. How about I take a shift and you get some rest. Maybe eat a little something and lie down for a while." Bill follows Dolores and reaches his hands toward her.

"You act as if this is a burden! She's not a burden. I can hold her." Dolores steps to the window and gazes out at the people running to get out of the sudden rain shower.

Bill turns from his wife and daughter and picks up the package, cutting the twine and ripping the paper, letting it fall at his feet. Beneath layers of protective packing material is the portrait. There are Patricia's eyes twinkling mischievously up at him. There is her smile, a little crooked as if she's ready to laugh, ready to blow a raspberry. There, in his hands, is a representation of all that she was. All the bright horizons, the infinite potential, the amazing possibility that she was.

"Put that away. I don't want to see it." Dolores' voice is hard and cracks under the force of her words.

But Bill can't look away. "She is just as beautiful, Dolores. It's still Patricia. Look."

"No. I can't. Get rid of it."

I imagine my mother struggling with guilt just as much as blame. Should she have gone to the doctor sooner? Was there a fall she didn't see? Did she want too much? Did she take everything for granted? Was she being punished? This felt like punishment.

The portrait stayed wrapped in an old baby blanket for decades, moved from house to house, from country to country, always in the attic or the garage or a closet, always tucked away where no one could see unless they go looking for it, as I often did.

~

The family rallies behind Dolores and Bill. They come with food and so much love. They listen as Bill and Dolores tell and retell their stories of what happened at the hospital in Germany. Their process is protracted and painful, but the family sits with the story and they hold it. Bill and Dolores also tell them the truth of what they can expect, and what they can no longer hope for. But the family can see for themselves. Aurora and Manuel see that Patricia is not as attentive. She no longer squeals in glee at their arrival. She's not cruising around the furniture. She is not playing the clapping games. Patricia sits, placidly, as her grandparents, uncles and aunt all hold her and coo to her and sing and play, always taking care to support her head as they did when she was an infant.

Dolores watches for a while, but she is overwhelmed with a grief she hoards and doesn't want to share. She leaves the room. It is too painful to watch as her brothers, her sister and her parents try to pull Patricia out from the faraway place she has gone inside. There is no comfort here. There is only more acceptance of the way things are, just like her whole life. Acceptance of the way things are, acceptance of all these tragedies, all these sorrows, all the not-enough. For a moment she wonders if she, too, can accept this. But in the next instant she realizes she doesn't want to. She'll never accept this. She doesn't want to do as her family has done all these years: silently muscle through, continue, move forward, always forward through the constant sorrow. No, she says to herself. Acceptance is giving up. She will fight this. She will never accept this diagnosis. Don't they understand? It would be disloyal to Patricia.

As Dolores walks to the kitchen, Aurora notices that Patricia no longer has eyes just for her mother. She is no longer tracking her every move, watching and mimicking her mother. She knows that this is the most devastating blow for Dolores. The daughter who mirrored her and learned to smile from her mother's smile, the daughter who beamed for her mother especially, is now changed. But change is a constant in this life, and she wishes she could help Dolores understand. Patricia is still who she is. Our love for her is still the same. None of us are unchanging. Patricia doesn't have to be perfect as she was. She is perfect as she is.

Dolores wants to ask her mother how she had continued, how had she moved on after Esperanza died. But she can't. Sometimes the guilt that she lived, when Esperanza didn't, rises in her breast, ready to be confessed and atoned for. And sometimes it's a curse nearly escaping her throat that she wants to fling at her mother and everyone. She knows she is a reminder. She knows that her mother remembers Esperanza when she looks at her and wonders what Esperanza would be like, what she would have done, who she would have married, about her children, about the ghost children of her firstborn daughter. It's an unspoken reality. It is as it has been. Shadows of loss and longing. She thought she had escaped.

Aurora wishes she could talk with her daughter about the soul. She wants to tell her daughter that in the end there is nothing to do but continue through each day as each day dawns. She wants to apologize for all the sadness in her heart. She wants to take responsibility for casting the long shadows that Dolores has claimed for her own. She wants to tell her the truth, that she misses her Esperanza and that she has never recovered from that loss; that sometimes when she looks at Dolores, she feels that loss all the more. But she can't say any of it. She does love her, though.

Aurora follows Dolores into the bedroom. "I know Patricia may never be all the things we wished for her. But everything is not lost. You still have her."

"Mamá, you don't understand." Dolores glances at herself in the mirror over the chest of drawers, she looks at her mother standing behind her shoulder. "She doesn't see me anymore. She looks right through me if I can even catch her roaming eye. It's as if she doesn't know me or recognize me. I could be anyone."

"I do understand, Dolores. I do. This child of yours knew you in a way no one has before. That much I do understand. And I'm sorry." Aurora is seeking her daughter's elusive eyes as they dart across their framed reflection.

"The doctors say there is nothing more they can do for her here. Perhaps in America."

The Sixth Sorrow: Buried

Taking the body of Jesus down from the cross: "I wait for the Lord, my soul waits, and in his word I hope; my soul waits for the Lord more than watchmen for the morning, more than watchmen for the morning. O Israel, hope in the Lord! For with the Lord there is steadfast love, and with him is plenteous redemption. And he will redeem Israel from all his iniquities."

Psalm 130:5-8

In the early spring of 1959, Bill books passage on the cargo and passenger liner, the SS Excalibur leaving from Cadiz on June 20, 1959, bound for New Jersey. The tourist-class tickets are expensive, and Bill will have to pull extra duty to make ends meet.

Once they get to New Jersey, he will reenlist at McGuire Air Force Base, and they will make their way to Clinton-Sherman AFB in Oklahoma. There, they will search out the doctors who can help Patricia. Dolores believes that in America there will be hope. She finds that she can face her mornings with her faith placed firmly in the doctors in America.

Bill tries to explain to Aurora and Manuel that the doctors in Germany knew Dolores was looking for any glimmer of hope. When she pressed them again and again, they finally conceded that perhaps in America there could be therapies and other opportunities for Patricia that were not available here. She didn't listen as they reiterated there were no guarantees. She didn't see the look that passed between them and her husband.

He knows Dolores' family doesn't want them to leave. And he doesn't want to leave. He doesn't want to abandon all the support for Dolores and Patricia he has in Aurora and the family. He doesn't want to let go the dream of a small hotel on the Costa del Sol, the dream of a family business that felt so real just months ago. And he doesn't want to reenlist in the Air Force. He hopes against odds that Dolores' family will help change her mind. He can see Aurora's desperation at losing her daughter and watches as she cajoles and pleads. And he is surprised when he sees Aurora resort to manipulation and guilt. But my mother's mind is made up; in many ways she has already left Spain. Dolores' jaw is set. And Bill knows there is nothing that he won't do for her. He'll do even this.

~

With tickets purchased and a few months yet to wait, Manuel and his sons take Bill to the Plaza de Toros in the Maestranza area of Sevilla. Bill had yet to go to *la corrida* to see a bullfight and although the family rarely went, this is one thing they want to do for him.

The ring shimmers as though made of gold, and their seats are on the less expensive *sol* side. Bill sees the fancy dressed spectators on the *sombra* side of the ring but doesn't envy them their shade. He wants the burning clarity that the severe Sevilla sun brings. On the combed yellow sand is a red band that encircles the ring. The colors of the city: hopeful gold juxtaposed with blood red. The architecture of the ring is dramatically intensified in the slanting sunlight. Brightest light against deepest shade. To Bill it seems always one or the other.

Manolo tells Bill as much of the lore as he can. What he doesn't remember, Manuel does. "Belmonte overcame the greatest odds to be one of the bravest and best."

Bill listens as Manolo goes into vivid detail about each kill, where each hand-picked bull came from, what maneuver, what sequence ... so much more than he'll ever remember, more than he cares to know.

"And Joselito went from never being so much as gored to being killed by a bull while thousands watched," Antonio interrupts wanting to show that he knows just as much as his older brother.

These bullfighters are held in the same esteem as baseball players back home, Bill thinks. He wonders if they collect cards and follow the stats.

"He got overconfident," Manuel says while watching his youngest sons animate the greatest battles in the ring; José playing *toro*, Francisco is the brave *matador*.

"But Manolete, the 'Knight of the Sorrowful Countenance,' was the one to watch, right, Manolo?" Antonio is adjusting his hat to block some of the sun blazing into his eyes.

"Why did they call him that?" Bill is closing his eyes and feeling the sun full on his face.

Manolo opens the program that shows thumbnail pictures of many famous bullfighters and shows Bill a picture of a man with eyebrows slanting down and eyes almost mournful. "His expression. You can see that he suffered for his art. They say he hated killing those bulls, but it's what his art demanded. And after each fight, he would imagine that there could never be another."

"He had no faith." Manuel says flatly. "And you and Antonio are being overly romantic."

But Antonio picks up the tale where Manolo left off, "It was just twelve years ago, in Linares. He and a bull from Miura agreed to kill each other." He leans forward in his seat trying to get a better angle, Bill is silhouetted by the sun.

"They agreed?" Bill's eyebrows are also slanting, but in indulgence and incredulity. He turns to watch Francisco and José dance around each other in the aisle between the seats, Francisco with an imaginary *muleta* and José using his fingers for horns.

Manolo interrupts Antonio because he sees my father's interest peaked. "What else could the bravest bull ever and the bravest *matador* do? They both came from right here in Andalucía, you know. And they were the bravest of all. After a long fight, they agreed to do the most noble thing for each other. Almost as though one would be diminished without the other."

"So, they killed each other?" Bill shakes his head and again opens the program to study Manolete's face. He can't imagine knowing anything so certainly.

My *tío* Manolo is smiling and his eyes sparkle in the sunlight. "Manolete and the bull from Miura stood, each facing the other, each exhausted from their time in the ring together. The *pasos*, they say, were magnificent, like dances. I heard you could see how even their breathing was synchronized. And it was then. Some even say they heard the agreement. They could die from exhaustion, or they could be the end for each other." He is weaving this fabled story for my father, to distract him, make him laugh again.

But my *abuelo* takes the story from here, "He finally lived up to his name. Manolete, the 'Knight of the Sorrowful Countenance,' decided then and there to take his own life by offering it to the bull. If you ask me, he had no faith. He couldn't believe that when one passion is taken, it will return in another form if you allow it."

"You mean there could have been another great bull?" Bill asks.

"Yes, it's possible. Anything is possible." My *abuelo* takes off his *boina* and runs his hands through his dark hair now tinged with steel at the temples. "But what Manolete did not understand is that we are never left completely bereft. We only need to stay open to what comes." He lights a cigarette, and his eyes narrow from the smoke and the sunlight. "Manolete resigned himself to believing that he would never again realize his dream, and so he ended it for himself. But he could have taught his art. He could have become a poet. A great chef. Who knows? He was as romantic as my sons who think love is something or someone they can hold in their hands. But it's not. Love is action. Love is the act of receiving and releasing. Manolete's only act was one of resignation."

Antonio shrugs his father's insults away, "there had never been another bull like that one from Miura for Manolete. He knew that any bull he fought after that one would pale in comparison."

"Then don't compare." Manuel shakes his head.

But Bill doesn't hear Antonio or Manuel. He is staring at the ring, the blood red circle drawn around the golden sand broken only by the sharply defined bisecting line between *sol* and *sombra*. His father-in-law's words etched on that line.

My parents and sister arrive in the U.S. late in the summer of 1959. As they drive from New Jersey across the vast farmlands of the mid-west, Dolores nearly suffers an agoraphobic response to the open horizons. There is nothing, save a grain silo, a haystack, or a windmill, to break the monotony of golden fields, green fields, brown fields. She watches as the state lines pass, wondering over the week-long journey, when and where and what is Oklahoma.

Now and then, they pass through a city, but mostly they stay on the highway, eating at roadside diners and sleeping in motels under blinking neon signs. Each town looks much the same from the road. And the motels all look the same. The pillows, the bedding, and the curtains all smell like stale cigarette smoke. The paper-thin walls of the motels shake as the roaring trucks barrel past.

In the car, Bill fiddles with the radio knob and skips over those stations preaching gospel. He finds other stations playing country music but often before a song is finished, the signal fades and the melody gives way to a crackling static. Bill lights another cigarette and reaches over, twisting the knob again.

Dolores holds Patricia in her lap, pointing out the window

at whatever she can, "blue car, black truck, oh, a motorcycle, restaurant, tree ..." There's not much to this land. Just a big blue highway cutting across the horizon. Patricia grabs her mother's pointing finger and places it in her mouth. When this doesn't satisfy, she finds her own thumb and rests her head on Dolores' breast. Dolores breathes in deeply the scent of her daughter. This sweetness hasn't changed.

They drive first for Bill's hometown. It is a small town that spreads haphazardly on either side of Highway 9. It's drier here, dustier. The peanut fields are full, and the tender green plants sprawl under the Oklahoma sun. Dolores listens as Bill tells her about dirt-devils and tornadoes and his family. "My father died in 1955 of liver and heart problems. He was in the boot, shoe and harness business and owned his own leather goods store right on West Main Street. He operated the shop until the economy forced him out in the 1930's."

Bill glances over at Dolores to see if she understands and how she's responding. It's always so hard to know. "My father then went to Texas to work at a shoe repair business there. He sent what he could home. He had some troubles, though." my father's right wrist drapes over the top of the wheel and his left flicks ash out the triangular vent window.

"Marguerite is the oldest and only girl. She's married to a great guy, Joe Bill, and I've lost track of how many kids she's got now. I think two, but she wants more. She went to college and was a teacher, but I don't know if she's still doing that with little ones running around." The radio returns to the in-between static, and Bill twists the knob back and forth before switching it off. "You're going to love her. She's a good woman, and I'm sure she'll love you and Patricia. She and her husband farm just a little way outside town."

Dolores nods and imagines faces to the names. She wonders how they will talk to each other. She hasn't learned much English yet. It's a difficult language.

"My oldest brother, Jack, is a teacher, too. And he's farming with our Uncle Carl and Aunt Effie. Together they work some acres out there. He's not yet married, but I hear he's got a girl. Then there are my two younger brothers, Jimmy and Joe Don. Jimmy is in college studying to be a pharmacist, and Joe Don has just finished high school." Bill can't see Dolores' face, and her silence makes him nervous. He fills up the quiet with words he hopes will ease her way.

"They are all good people. I'm sure you'll get on just fine with them. But you'll love my mother. She holds everything together. She's so strong. She's a retired teacher and now she teaches kids piano from home and sometimes sews curtains and things for neighbors."

Dolores tries to listen but is distracted by the nothingness that encroaches from outside. There is nothing. A singular street, cutting right through the middle of town, with additional streets jutting out at 90° angles from that central artery. A grid with no curve, no bend. Dusty cars line the streets, women walking around in shapeless dresses with kerchiefs covering curlers in their hair, men in shirtsleeves, cigarettes dangling from the corner of their mouths, newspapers tucked under their arm, eyes squinting against the rising smoke and the sun. It takes some time for Dolores to realize what is missing. Her eyes darting around, taking it all in, this new place, her new home, America ... it has no color.

Within minutes they have crossed from one end of town to the other. The main street nothing but a series of storefront windows covered in scrawled soaped-on words. The entire town is about one-square mile. Once they turn off onto 2nd Street, my mother notices how the small single storied clapboard houses, one after the other, seem to almost hide their faces in the shadows of the overgrown lacebark elm trees. Front porches lay lopsided, prostrate, and surrounded by leggy rhododendrons seeking sunlight. Each house was once white, this she can tell even though they are all now varying shades of earth.

My grandmother Lucile's house is just the same. Traces of disrepair are covered over by patches of fresher paint. An overturned bucket props up a porch railing that has rotted. The entire porch leans a bit to the left, and Bill reminds Dolores of the tornadoes that are common in this part of Oklahoma. He tells her not to worry because they have a root cellar accessible from inside and outside the house; a siren blows a warning.

They are all there. Lucile, the matriarch, all her boys, her daughter Marguerite along with her husband Joe Bill. There are some children running around, and Dolores isn't sure if they belong to the family or if they are neighborhood kids. Like children everywhere, they climb the trees and call out to one another above the heads of the adults. Dolores seeks out these similarities. These things that connect her frame of reference to her new reality. But this place is so foreign, and it feels unforgiving. Wiping the dust from her face, she opens her car door and takes a deep breath of the dry tasteless air.

The first person to embrace Dolores is a woman Bill calls Aunt Effie. She is small and lean, her face sunbaked, parched into soft feathery lines, her brown eyes moist like mud. She doesn't say a word to Bill but takes Dolores into her arms and says, "there, there honey. You're home now." Before they've completely pulled away from the embrace, Aunt Effie scoops Patricia out of Dolores' arms and starts cooing and clucking. As she walks toward the porch, the rest of the family comes and circles around Bill and Dolores.

My mother doesn't understand most of what is spoken. Their words are rapid fire and heavily accented in a way that slurs them one into the other. She can't tell the brothers apart except by age. She sees the family resemblance along their eyes, brows and forehead.

Marguerite, pregnant and due any minute by the look of her, is at her side, "Are you tired after your journey? Here, honey, have some lemonade."

One of Bill's brothers is grabbing his arm and leans in "Brother, you told us she was beautiful, but damn."

Bill embraces them all, answering the questions as best he can, stealing furtive glances at Dolores. He notices that his mother refrains from talking to Dolores at all, instead she talks about her as if she's not right there.

"Does she understand us at all?"

"Why, I didn't know she'd be so dark. She could be Kiowa."

"Are all her people Spaniards? She's got no one here?"

"So, is the girl well and truly retarded?"

"It's a shame, a real shame."

Later, Bill whispers in my mother's ear, "they've never been outside the state of Oklahoma, some not even venturing outside of Caddo County. They'll come around. They've never met a foreigner before. And it's taken us all some time to get used to what happened to Patricia."

However, there's not time enough in all eternity for my mother to get used to what happened to my sister. That's why they are here, in America, so that they can find a way to help her. So that they can find a cure. And she doesn't want Bill's family to know Patricia the way she is now. She doesn't want their pity. Dolores wants them to know and love the little girl Patricia was before she got so sick, when she was sparkling and quick and smart. Seeing her in this limited way isn't true, this isn't how things should be.

~

The town nearer the air base proves to be just as dusty as Bill's hometown. Perhaps more so because Route 66 passes through and so do all the trucks headed to and from California. My parents find a small house to rent. Bill calls it a "shotgun;" all the rooms are lined up one after the other. To get to the bathroom, they must pass through the living area and the kitchen. The pink-tiled bathroom is tucked behind the kitchen, the bedrooms behind that. There is a patch of brown earth behind the house where the two supporting posts for a wire clothesline stand like austere crosses. The wire will leave rust-colored stains, like wide slashing wounds, upon their clothes before Dolores replaces it with cord Bill buys at the Ben Franklin.

The house is furnished, and Dolores spends her first weeks in the house cleaning and washing everything. The sheets, the towels, the curtains, everything is so filthy. There is no crib for Patricia, but they manage with a single bed mattress on the floor. At least if she falls off, she won't fall far.

At the first doctor's appointment, Bill and Dolores meet with a pediatrician. He refers them to a neurologist who in turn suggests a child development specialist. It is clear, though, that each holds little hope for a better prognosis than what they heard in Germany. Their daughter is brain damaged. She most likely will be developmentally delayed. It will take her longer to learn things. There may be limits to how much she can learn. Some of the physical manifestations may be weak lips, tongue, trouble chewing and swallowing. They will need to watch for choking. She may have seizures, but since she hasn't had any yet, it's doubtful. Balance and coordination issues are common. She may have trouble speaking, difficulty with language like finding the *right* word. She may never be able to communicate. We just don't know. The list is long. The child development specialist explains services for families with mentally retarded children, but other than that, there is not much to do but wait and see. "She's still so young. We don't know what she'll be able to regain. And there are the institutions I've already mentioned."

"But how can you help?" Dolores asks through Bill. She is not so easily dismissed. "What can you do to cure her?"

Sensing Dolores' distress, seeing how worn she looks, how desperate, he offers the only thing he can think of. He shows them a new program that has shown some progress in brain-damaged children. "It is somewhat avant-garde. There's not a lot of research. But I don't see how it could hurt."

"What is it?" Bill is worried that this specialist is going to pass on false hope to Dolores who is so vulnerable to any glimmer.

The doctor points to photographs in the brochure with a sharpened pencil, "it is a patterning therapy. It starts by having the children crawl and move as they did at each stage of early development. It's an attempt to get them to learn or relearn missing skills."

"But Patricia was almost walking before. Now she needs to learn to crawl again?" Dolores' eyes go from the brochure to Bill to the Doctor's overly plump lips. His pasty face puckers as he sucks on his cigarette.

"At this age, the brain is still developing. We don't know what Patricia can relearn, how fast or slow. The Doman-Delacato

Method is a home-based rehabilitative program that parents and community volunteers implement."

"Doctors?" asks Dolores.

"No ma'am. These would be friends, neighbors, and your family members who get trained in the methods of respiratory patterning, crawling and creeping patterning, balance activities, and other exercises. There are flash cards that you can use later, as well as manipulatives. Here is the information from the company. It is called Institutes for the Achievement of Human Potential." He places the pamphlet in her hands and sits back in his chair behind his desk. He blows a steady thin stream of smoke toward the ceiling.

"Friends? Family? No, no. What can you do? What can American hospitals do?" Dolores is furiously asking Bill to translate, but she can see his eyes. She knows.

The doctor sighs and opens another pack of cigarettes. He fidgets with his lighter. "Explain to your wife, there is no scientific support for this method, but I am of the opinion that it can't hurt in a situation like this. There is little the medical community can do, but I would never underestimate the power of an involved, supportive family and community. If you choose to keep her at home, Patricia is going to need a lot of hands-on physical and mental stimulation. The two of you are not going to be able to do this alone whether you use this method or not."

"Is there anything else? Any advice?" Bill asks as a delay tactic. He doesn't want to translate these words for his wife.

"I believe it would be best if only one language was spoken at home. One language will be difficult enough for Patricia. It's best not to confuse her."

Bill thinks about his family. Each of his siblings busy with their lives, his mother also busy in their lives. They haven't embraced

Dolores and Patricia as he had hoped. He thinks of Aurora, Manuel, Esperanza, and all the brothers who held, played with, tickled and teased Patricia. Silently he mourns the separation from a family who not only embraced him but poured their love and attentions on Patricia before and after the fever.

Dolores takes the brochure from the specialist and opens to a picture of a smiling family holding the hands of a two-year old who is obviously taking one step forward. The testimonies inside the pamphlet are more optimistic than the doctor was. Bill reads the caption that Dolores points out to him, "parents around the world have helped their children labeled as mentally retarded to move along the path to wellness."

"Wellness!" Dolores holds this idea like a beacon. "This will help her get better."

Bill will suggest later that day and again in a week or two that they return to Sevilla. He talks about Aurora and Manuel often in hopes of pulling Dolores into his dream of returning to the supportive arms of her family. But Dolores has placed all her hope in America. She has a new allegiance now. If this is the recommendation, then this is what they will do. She doesn't need family support, Bill's or her own. She doesn't need friends. She can do this. Bill will be working, but she can do this. She will do this.

My mother will speak only English now. She will forsake her country and language. Convinced that she has to live like everyone else on their street, she watches her neighbors and pays attention. They purchase a refurbished television, and she watches the jealous and tormented lives on *As the World Turns*. She buys TV dinners and Palmolive dish soap. She wears pedal-pushers and chews Doublemint gum. She sings along with American Bandstand and eventually her cultural and linguistic dislocation will be complete.

My sister will never again hear the language of her first lullabies.

~

For many years, the exercises and methods as prescribed by Institutes for the Achievement of Human Potential are Dolores' focus. She tapes a straight line down the hallway – now grateful for the long corridor their shotgun house provides – and holds Patricia around the belly while maneuvering her arms and legs in the patterning method she prays will help.

Slowly, much too slowly, there is progress. The doctor notes that Patricia will be walking soon and that her gross- and fine-motor skills have improved. But Dolores can't see it. She can't see that Patricia can now sit up alone, that they don't have to put pillows all around her in case she tumbles. All Dolores can see is that Patricia is three-years old and needs help with her coordination and the patterning of crawling; she can't feed herself, she still wears a diaper, and she isn't yet speaking in sentences like the other children in the neighborhood.

It is clear that Patricia is not coming back to the precocious child she once was. And whereas Dolores is just beginning to wrap her mind around this fact, she doesn't want anyone else to admit to it. When Bill alludes to any progress or lack of progress, she just puts her head down and works all the harder. She clenches her jaw as she bends and holds and adjusts Patricia's limbs. Her jaw is set even in sleep.

There are times when Bill hears a sound much like an exhalation escaping Dolores. A sigh really. Not of contentment or of relaxation, but resignation. Her sadness has become a way of life. A punishment, a penance, they both must suffer. In her sighs and with just that breath, she once again puts herself aside to attend to Patricia. She moves through the necessary exercises with her arms and her hands, holds up picture flashcards and repeats the applicable words: House, Tree, Flower, Girl, Boy. Bill doesn't know that while she pushes through the exercises with Patricia, her thoughts cross oceans and continents and years to a twirling brown-skinned tomboy spinning beneath lemon trees humming to herself. But sometimes her humming creeps into this moment, the present moment, and he glances at her just briefly wondering if this time she might return to him and also, perhaps, inhale.

Patricia's pediatrician recognizes the strides they are making together and praises Dolores for all her hard work. But Dolores feels there is still so far to go. She sees the other children. She wants Patricia to catch up. The doctor senses Dolores' pain, her frustration at the limitations that are beginning to be undeniably evident through her comparisons with other children. He also sees that depression is settling in deep and confides to Bill that there needs to be more to her life than the exercises and work she is doing with Patricia. "Surely someone in your family can come help her. Do you get a babysitter, ever?"

"She won't think of it." Bill can't remember the last time they went out. The last time they laughed together. The last time they made love. He sees the disappointment in her eyes. He feels it, too. He sees that she is giving up hope because she cannot have this one thing she has hoped for.

~

I remember the Doman-Delacato exercises. I remember the brightly colored flashcards, the outlined pictures of fruit, and the vestibular activities to help with balance. I remember the strip of masking tape down a different hallway in a different house in a different city. I remember my mother on her hands and knees, working with my sister. I thought it was all a game following that tape like a train on a track, but it wasn't. It was a lifeline. My mother's lifeline.

Day after day, I watched my mother and sister work together, crawling and eventually walking along the tape: left knee, right hand, right knee, left hand. And I would do the exercises, too. I would do them alone. Without help. The picture flashcards were colorful, and I would call out answers. But what I saw fleeting and ghostlike in my mother's eyes scared me, so I became silent. Her pain palpable in her set jaw, her bitten lip; her sadness only barely beneath the surface, evident when she looked at me. And I internalized my mother's pain as she watched me creep then crawl, walk then run. The gritty salt I inadvertently rubbed into her wound reminded her everyday of what was forever lost.

~

Though light spills in through the west facing windows, where I sit in the church is in shadow, and the dimness feels like a comforting and familiar blanket. I wonder if my mother sought to leave Spain in part because she, too, believed she was the cause of her mother's pain. Did she try to escape the sadness that showed through even when my *abuela* was trying to express love? Even when she was smiling?

This city should feel like home. I so wanted to find some inheritance here in the meandering streets and cadence of conversation, in the pageantry of Holy Week, in this pew as I hold my grandmother's beads. But somehow the rosary has become knotted, a jumbled mass of black beads and silver beads all snarled together, and I see now that my inheritance is not here. It's in the silence and secrets of those abandoned and those who abandoned hope. As I tease out a strand and try to loosen the tangle, I wonder if my forsaken inheritance is buried with those yet to be claimed.

Holy Saturday is supposed to be the day we are all claimed,

each of us by name. But my name is swallowed by silence. The rosary unknots suddenly, spilling open in my hands. I knit the beads between my fingers and start again at the sixth sorrow: "I wait for the Lord, my soul waits."

~

The Friday morning when Bill's childless Aunt Effie comes to take Patricia to the farm with her, Dolores has to sit down with her head between her knees. Bill had talked with Effie and arranged for her to take her for the weekend. He's worried about Dolores, the circles under her eyes, her weight loss, her hands that rattle the coffee cups. She's up with Patricia often in the night, and though he tries to help when he's home, she rarely lets him. It's clear, she's not taking care of herself.

Effie gets a cold washcloth and places it on Dolores' neck, clucking her tongue at how this proves her point. "Girl, you are going to kill yourself if you don't take a bit of a break now and then. No one, not even God can go at it twenty-four hours a day and seven days a week. Let's get you a Sabbath day of rest."

Dolores doesn't really understand what Effie is talking about and feels bullied by Bill and Effie. Both are telling her not to worry, that Patricia will be watched like a hawk, that she'll be safe and sound and returned in just three days.

It is so hard for my mother to watch Effie drive away with Patricia in the backseat. Though my mother's arms are empty, they feel leaden. It's as though she's undergone an amputation but what limb? What organ? She's not whole, this she knows with every breath she pulls deep into her lungs. She stands on the front lawn waving long after the car has turned the corner.

She remembers words Effie whispered to her before she drove away, "There is no blessing in what happened to Patricia, but she will be your child forever. In my book, there's a blessing in just that."

Effie made her want to scream. Or cry. Or run. Yes, there's a blessing in Patricia being alive, but Dolores can think only of what is lost. Effie doesn't know all that Patricia was before the fever. She doesn't understand what was burned away. She wants to scream out loud so everyone will finally understand how much she feels cheated. She wants people to understand what she lost in that damned fever. But she can't seem to surface to the light of day.

My mother stands on the lawn looking down the street well after Bill leaves to return to the base. She stands on the lawn until a neighbor comes out and asks if everything is all right. My mother nods absentmindedly and turns to the house, moving her legs up the steps and through the door.

Inside, there are the rooms where she's lived for nearly two years. The kitchen is sunny and bright, polished clean. The strip of masking tape runs down the hall connecting the two bedrooms with the bath, kitchen and living room. The flashcards are stacked neatly on the coffee table, and the other manipulatives are in their box on the kitchen table. Dolores picks up Bill's coffee cup and the saucer he insists on drinking out of. She turns the heat off the percolator and pours the boiled coffee down the drain before rinsing the sink. She opens the window to freshen the air.

Next she collects the ashtrays from the bedroom and living room and empties them, wiping them with a tissue. After taking the wash off the line, she folds and refolds the towels, stacking them on the shelf in the bathroom. She takes a shower, washing her hair slowly, soaping the length of her body under the steady stream of scalding water. She dries with a freshly washed towel. She hadn't snapped the stiffness out of the towel, and she rubs her arms and legs roughly with the coarse unyielding fabric. She slips into

Patricia's room, into Patricia's bed and breathes in her scent as she falls into a dreamless sleep that is undisturbed until Bill rouses her that evening when he returns home from work.

All day Saturday, Dolores is at a loss. Bill mows the lawn, and neighbors are all out and about, but Dolores keeps wiping at the counters. She wipes the beige and white Formica kitchen table, at the ring there that will never come out. She scrubs at the hard-water stains in the bathroom sink and tub. Later, standing at the living room window, she takes in a deep breath that smells of the fresh cut lawn still so new to her, such a sharp green scent. She breathes in again and doesn't notice when Bill sidles up and suggests they go dancing.

The full force of what he has just suggested hits my mother. She realizes without any regret, without any hope or wish for other, that she is never again going to be that girl my father married. Something her mother once said rises to her consciousness, the words gnaw in her stomach, "when one is simply trying to survive, there is no room to love."

She can't go out dancing, but she does. And it wrecks her. She dances and dances, and she smiles and talks with the other wives, and she shakes so inside she thinks she must be sick. And later, she can't make love with her husband, but she does. She sees his hands upon her, but she doesn't feel, can't feel anything at all. She can't survive without Patricia, but for three days, she does.

~

The pediatrician has slowly been trying to help Dolores adjust to the reality of Patricia's prognosis. She will not catch up to her neighborhood peers. She will not attend school, though there are some programs through churches. "There has been progress. Yes, it has been slow, but that is to be expected. The therapies help, and you should continue, but there needs to be some balance." His office is overly warm, smells of antiseptic, and is painted a sickly shade of green. Under the fluorescent lights, everyone looks ill.

"Everything is fine. I am fine. We need to help Patricia." My mother is dressing my sister who sits squirming on the examining table. The glossy green walls are starting to close in. She is feeling suffocated and there are pinpoints of light pricking at the edges of her eyes.

"You have lost more weight. You're anemic. Your blood pressure is too low. Bill tells me you have dizzy spells and headaches. Are you getting any sleep?" His prescription for the family, to bring some balance, to bring a new focus, a new perspective, is to have another baby. "You will take care of yourself if only for the baby."

"What?" Dolores can't imagine having another baby. Where would she find the time? If he is so worried about how tired she looks, how does he think she'll look when there's another baby to take care of? Where does he think she'll find the energy? Her every breath is for Patricia, to help her learn and catch up, to help her get better. Another child will only be more work, more washing, more feeding, an unwanted distraction from her work with Patricia. How many arms does this doctor think she has? How will she care for her daughter if there is another child to tend? "No. No more children."

Turning to my father the doctor shrugs, "another baby could help. A brother or sister perhaps? A new life to celebrate?" The doctor watches Dolores as she stares vacantly out the window and fusses absently over Patricia.

"No. I can't. Another baby? No." My mother remembers how tired she was during her pregnancy with my sister, especially those first months. And what if she got the morning sickness like so many women? And how could she lift Patricia and hold her during her exercises when she gets so big at the end? "It's impossible."

"Your daughter has really made strides. Look at her. She's alert and active. She's toddling now! You have done an amazing job with her these past two years, but as your sole purpose ... perhaps another child could help the family find some meaning beyond Patricia's diagnosis and her therapies. You could meet other mothers. Go to the park." The pediatrician lights a cigarette and looks at Bill now, "here's another way to look at it: a sibling might help encourage Patricia, provide an example, maybe even help out eventually. If you won't consider an institution, you still need to consider Patricia's future. Who will take care of her when you no longer can?"

Bill shakes his head, "I don't know. Our hands are pretty full as it is." But the idea finds purchase and takes root in Bill. Maybe this could help Dolores return to him. A baby might save their family.

Over the course of weeks, he imagines a new beginning, another chance, and now and again he mentions the idea to Dolores. "Do you think the doctor knows what he's talking about? Could he be right? About another baby?"

She wonders if this could truly help lift her out of her fog. Would another baby help them feel like a real family, connected, and happy? Eventually Dolores is worn down and accepts the prescription. My parents place what little remaining faith they have in what the pediatrician says will help them all and perhaps save Dolores from her despair, perhaps save them all. Another baby, new life.

The Seventh Sorrow: Anointed

"Now there was a man named Joseph ... and he was looking for the kingdom of God. This man went to Pilate and asked for the body of Jesus. Then he took it down and wrapped it in a linen shroud, and laid him in a rock-hewn tomb, where no one had ever yet been laid ... The women from Galilee followed, and saw the tomb, and how his body was laid; then they returned and prepared spices and ointments."

Luke 23:50-56

On the day I am born, Dolores lifts her second-born daughter and presents her to the empty hospital room, "*míra, Mamá.* Her name is Cristina."

As far away as Oklahoma is from Sevilla, Dolores believes her mother can hear her. If anyone could hear her, anyone at all, it would be her mother.

~

Peering into the eyes of the elaborately jeweled and clothed statue, my grandmother beseeches, "*Señora,* she is all alone there. Her letters reveal nothing. I think she is trying to protect me. "My grandmother pulls in a ragged breath and reaches out to the Virgin.

"She has chosen a path, Aurora." The Virgin's voice is soft as She lifts the hem of Her heavily embroidered robes and climbs down from Her high altar. The scent of desert roses fills the sanctuary, and Aurora pulls in a deep breath. Once again, and as always, la Macarena comes to sit beside Aurora, to wrap Her youthful hands around the rough and thick-boned hands of my grandmother.

La Macarena's hands are warm and soft, and Her caress eases the ache deep inside Aurora's own hands. "But now there is a new baby. She already has so much to worry about." La Macarena nods as she rubs Aurora's rough knuckles and kneads her calloused palms. "Another baby will not save her from her sorrow."

"You are thinking of your own life now, Aurora. This is your daughter's life, and her daughter's." The Virgin knits their two rosaries around

their entwined fingers.

"I was not the mother she needed," Aurora looks up. "I grieved too long."

"Grief knows no time. She will find her own way through the seven sorrows. Just as you have."

They sit in silence, and my grandmother remembers when her hands were as smooth and her fingers as tapered as la Macarena's. So many years have passed since they first sat together like this. So many years and still the same bottomless aching grief. "Promise me You will stay with her." My *abuela* searches la Macarena's face, Her stormy eyes, for the answer she needs to hear. "Please, promise me."

"Siempre, Aurora. Until you yourself can." La Macarena stands and arranges her robes and *mantilla* before turning and making Her way toward the slanting rays of the setting sun. Aurora hears a whispered *"Always,"* just as She disappears in the day's last light.

~

Two weeks after Dolores comes home with their new baby, Bill turns away the Methodist minister. Several days later he closes the door on the Church of Christ preacher. The rector from the Episcopal church and the pastor from the local Presbyterian Church suffer the same indignity, coming no farther than the welcome mat at their front door.

My father doesn't ask them in or offer to take their hats that they turn and turn in their fingers. He doesn't offer a cup of coffee or a glass of iced tea which is the custom. He holds the front door open, his hand on the jamb, but leaves the screen door clasped. He stands just inside the threshold with Dolores behind him in the shadows. He withholds the curses he thinks as flies invite themselves in through the tear he meant to fix last fall.

These men of God are in the habit of looking in the Daily

News each Sunday morning for the listings of weddings, births, and deaths before they head off to church. Being a small town, and a fairly close and God-fearing community, the pastors of the four churches come to call after Cristina is brought home.

"I don't understand, Bill. You named her after our Savior, after the risen Christ. You named her Cristina. Why, she was even born over the Easter weekend. I know your family. I know you are a good Christian man." The reverend holds his hat in his hand, working the brim round and round, searching my father's eyes for a way in.

"What I am or am not is none of your concern, Reverend." Bill looks tired. And whereas the reverend knows new babies can do that to a parent, this man's fatigue comes from a deeper place.

The reverend is perplexed, and his brow is furrowed from mid-day sun and the stubborn nature of this man before him. He's met with down-hearted men, lost men, men in the throes of grief, and men who even say they hate the Almighty, but he's never been faced with a man who is a Christian yet won't baptize his new daughter. "But son," he begins again, "you must believe that Christ died for our sins and that through our baptism we are born into new life, we are in fact, saved from our sin. Why would you deny her her very namesake?"

It would seem that these men of God believe that it is unthinkable to allow a child to remain without a church home or the sacrament of holy baptism. As if these are rites that mark entry into the human community; rites that separate the civilized from the barbarian. To deprive an innocent child of these sacraments, which are necessary for survival and ultimately salvation, is considered cruel. But it is of no use. Each of the four men eventually bid my father goodbye, turn, and make their way to their car. Bill decides that Cristina will not be baptized. She will not be raised in any church. And this has nothing to do with his faith.

"What faith she comes to will be hers alone," he tells Dolores. "She will have to find a faith that sustains her, one that is true for her. Something that is not the predigested pablum of these preachers."

The Spanish proverb that Aurora sometimes said, and that Dolores repeats now – take holy water and eventually you will become a believer – is enraging to him. What has such faith served? Where is the strength of conviction? His wife still cries in her sleep. His firstborn daughter will never be all they dreamed for her. He feels trapped in a life he didn't want for himself or for his family. The fever will forever be the dividing line between his life filled with *alegria* and this life filled with a longing for something that will never be. He sees no new day, no blue skies, no salvation anywhere.

But still, Dolores feels that Cristina should be baptized, just in case. "What if ..."

"We're not placing bets here! We're not playing that 'what if' game!" Bill is practically yelling, and Dolores shushes him before the neighbors hear. He feels stuck. Hedging bets is exactly what he sees all around him. Insurance policies. Knocking on wood. Farmer's Almanacs and phases of the moon. All of it amounting to no more than weather reports and crossed fingers. How has that helped them? How has that helped Patricia? How has that sustained their marriage? How will that protect this new daughter? He pours his hot black coffee into the saucer and drinks it down while Dolores looks at the clouds gathering in her cup.

A simple old-fashioned saying from his childhood parish returns to him, and he repeats it to his wife, "a little religion brings you to the porch of the church, some protection from inclement weather at most. But true faith means facing a storm of relentless and uncompromising agony." Bill's voice is unwavering, "she will have to find her own home."

~

Dolores reads in a letter from her mother that Sevilla is asking Pope John XXIII to confer the Canonical Coronation on "Our Lady of Hope Macarena." She reads that three volumes of documents applying for the coronation are presented at the Vatican. "Imagine that," Aurora writes, "our own Macarena de Esperanza."

Later, in the fall, our family moves to San Antonio where my father has been transferred. Soon after, the Pontifical brief by His Holiness grants the Canonical Coronation. Aurora writes this time of the beautiful new cloak hand-embellished especially for the coronation by the famous embroidering shop started by Elena Caro. Dolores turns the letter over for any news of her family. She longs for her mother's voice, but the writing is only of the celebrations, the processionals, the glory that belongs to la Macarena. Dolores then remembers, all this about the Virgin *is* her mother's voice. She doesn't know that her mother is trying to protect her from news about which Dolores can do nothing.

My *abuela* can't leave the house anymore as she is nearly bedridden. She sleeps more and more and slips seamlessly between dreams that seem more vibrant than her waking encounters. She finds most comforting those where her own mother, young and robust, is waving, beckoning. There's the dream where she feasts at a glorious banquet with her lost Esperanza safe and warm while a violent thunderstorm rages outside. And she dreams of me, of an urgent message she must tell me. These she shares with Manuel as he places cool cloths on her forehead.

The letters Aurora receives from America contain photographs of the small family, but she can see the vast disappointment, the dreams gone, even hope – that which was still alive when Dolores left Spain – dead. It's as if life itself has hardened her beautiful daughter instead of softening her heart. She looks afraid, resentful, resigned. Here is a photograph of a woman moving through her day, muscle, tendon, and sinew focused on the tasks before her but without joy, without one flicker of hope in her eyes. Aurora tells her other children, "we have each other. We can help each other, but Dolores is alone. She is all the way in America without her family and friends. It is Dolores we should worry about. Don't concern her with our troubles. Don't tell her just yet."

Aurora shares her worries about Dolores with la Macarena who is always near. The Virgin sits on the bed just as she did when Aurora's babies came. The balm she rubs onto Aurora's neck and chest warms but no longer opens her lungs. "*Señora*, she is wan, skin and bone. She needs us but won't ask. She says all is well, but these photos show otherwise."

"*She is a stubborn child. Like her mother.*" La Macarena smiles knowingly.

"Yes, but at what cost? We've offered to pay for them to come home. We could collect enough money. She says no. She says she can't leave the possibilities that are there for Patricia." The light in the room is soft, and amber, and Aurora works at inhaling and exhaling.

"*I will stay with her.*" La Macarena sweeps Aurora's sweaty curls from her brow and a sweet scent envelopes her.

"And the baby? Her mother ..." Aurora wheezes, "is this what I did to Dolores?"

The Virgin places her cool hand on Aurora's forehead. "*We can only do our best in any given moment.*"

"But too late. I was too late to salvage a real relationship with her. By then all she could see was what she had seen day after day her whole life: my sadness, my grief, my fear of losing her like I lost her sister. She couldn't wait to leave. Is that why she won't come home?" Aurora's voice is barely audible. But la Macarena hears.

"Our tears are not words. Silence has a price."

"And now Dolores is silent. Her grief all her own. She won't share it with us. But Cristina will see. She will know. Daughters do."

"I will stay with her."

"Promise me."

~

One afternoon while we are living in San Antonio, another envelope with blue and red diagonal bars along the edges arrives. Although I am too young to remember, I do. My sister is next to my mother, and I sit propped in the corner of the nubby brown and gold sofa. The crinkly paper is filled border to border with cramped writing. My mother is crying. She turns the page over and starts again from the beginning. Her tears fall slow and thick, smudging the thin translucent paper. Her hand trembles, the fine bones like the spines of an ivory fan, or like a sparrow's wing. The letter falls to the floor as she buries her face in my sister's long dark hair.

The cicadas throb their afternoon rhythm, a call and response between neighboring elms. Through the venetian blinds, wispy clouds slip across horizontal slices of sky. Dust motes appear and disappear in turn. My pulse thrums within, deeper and deeper. And quiet. She does not see me, and I don't try to become more tangible to her. This is my first knowing, the first of many, that I am ephemeral and can make myself invisible at will, a ghost child or a shadow. With just the right breathing, I can melt into the room, sink into this couch, disappear into that bed, even an embrace. I wield this gift that has been bestowed, like a blessing, my inheritance.

I see my father try to comfort her, but her grief is angry right now. She feels she should have been there. She feels guilty for her feelings and for wanting an escape. She feels torn. She feels yet another layer of guilt and grief blanket her. I know my grandmother has died. Having not met her, I miss her more deeply because I know she would have seen me, even when I'm invisible.

It is my sister who brings some solace to my mother. Patricia had known her grandmother. They shared their lives, the three generations together for a brief joyous time: Aurora, Dolores and Patricia. My mother holds Patricia longer. She whispers secrets into her ear. Together they are an embrace. Self-contained and beautiful. Each night and sometimes until morning, my mother sits on my sister's bed and helps her calm and unknot her muscles and breathe while June bugs bounce against the screen. Our twin beds are separated by a nightstand. A lamp with a pink gingham shade casts a soft light. I watch as they breathe together, slowly in and slowly out. My mother massaging Patricia's chest and belly, rubbing lavender oil in slow pulses to match their breath. Together they breathe in unison, a slow two-step, a duet in the round, until my sister falls asleep. I know these rites help soothe my mother as well. *Mater Dolorosa* and child in the whisper-soft rosy-hued light.

She doesn't come to me. It's alright, though. I already know how to breathe. The breezes taught me. And the sheer curtains showed me as they rise and fall, billowing across my face as I lie in bed. I sleep beneath the window, and my breath mingles with the soft humid breeze and flows through the filmy curtains and wraps around the earth. A blanket, a veil, a *mantilla* most sacred. The clouds gently part with my breath and in the moonlight, dissipate, vapor from my mouth. The roiling seas within finally calm. And I sleep until I see the sun open like a chrysanthemum, petal on petal, casting long slanting rays over another land. Aurora, the dawn, is spreading her warmth, fingers reaching.

The recurring dream always just before waking and in a lilting soft language I somehow understand, "Aurora is the dawn, and she births each day filled with both *esperanza* and *dolor* – hope and sorrow. Hope recedes but also revives. Eventually *dolor* gives birth to love. Remember these names. Remember always, you are that love."

The curtain falls over my face, and this brings my body back to me. San Antonio, the curtain rising and falling, tracing the contours of my face like a shroud or my own gossamer *mantilla*, and a gentle scented breeze from the climbing rose outside beckons. I roll over and rise to the new day.

The church is dark now. Candles at the various altars flicker and dance light across the walls and across la Macarena's face. More people have arrived and are sitting, turning their beads as they hold vigil these last silent minutes before Easter. My back is no longer aching; it is numb from the day spent wondering and waiting. I look at all the faces and marvel at their faith, persistent despite the daily news, despite their own tragedies, and unvoiced sorrows. I wanted these beads to link me to my grandmother and to her love of la Macarena. I wanted the processions to bring some clarity. I wanted to be claimed, and to find a home in Sevilla.

I hear the old woman next to me quietly speaking the words of the Dolorosa. She is dressed head to toe in black and wears a black lace *mantón* over her iron gray hair. She moves easily from one sorrow to the next, her beads clicking against the nails of her gnarled hands swollen with arthritis. Her phrasing is aligned with each breath. I wait and listen as she moves through the first, second, third. I am sensing the rhythm and feel the pulse pulling me into my own story, a story from what facts I know, a constellation that could just as well be some other pattern formed by connecting these same dots in some other way. And it pulls me into an understanding that does not lead to forgiveness. Instead it leads to a compassion that reveals there is nothing to forgive.

Intoning the fourth, fifth, and sixth sorrows, my neighbor's voice joins mine, lending me strength. In the quiet, our two voices blend with the voices of others also sitting vigil with la Macarena. I see now not only old women, but men, and some younger people, even children. Slowly the church has become filled with people coaxing sound from silence. Listening as they whisper, their voices alone almost silent, but together there is a crescendo, an audible murmuration. And the seventh sorrow swells: "the women from Galilee followed, and saw the tomb, and how his body was laid; then they returned and prepared spices and ointments."

I surround myself with all these gentle voices, like heady spices and anointing oils, like a balm. Our own *cante jondo* – our song too deep for words. My family, all these here with me and their families, all those beneath my *abuelo's* cross, and all those who left Spain to make another home far from home. And all their children and grandchildren and great-grandchildren. And me holding my *abuela's* rosary.

Suddenly church bells start to ring out, and the black veil that has been draped over the cross is finally lifted. I see that the basilica of la Macarena is now filled to capacity. The hush is accented with the cadence of breathing. More candles are being lit, and the light is warm, golden. I feel wide awake despite the hour and despite the hours of sitting through Holy Saturday. I know now. This story is not true. But it is truth enough.

As I pull my *abuela's* rosary over my head like a necklace, it seems I can almost smell the boiled rose petals from which the beads were made. Tucking the crucifix with only the hands and feet of an ebony Jesus inside my shirt, I gather my jacket and bag and stand to leave. The woman next to me smiles and turns her legs to the side as I weave my way past her and through all the many faithful who came to celebrate the Easter Vigil Mass.

I was born on Holy Saturday. Some say it is the one and only day God is dead, but maybe it is not a day filled with impotent waiting as I had thought. It is the day that my *abuela* believed Jesus completes his most important work. On this day, he descends into hell to claim, each by name, the souls waiting there, and to carry them home. *This* is what we were doing here in this church during these last minutes of Holy Saturday. And *this* is what is being done all over Spain. We are going to the tombs and bearing witness to how the bodies were laid, the thousands and thousands of bodies. And we are preparing spices and ointments. And we are calling their names.

Acknowledgements

History has always been recorded by those with power and the means to tell the tale. Thanks to Spain's 2007 Historical Memory Law - the long overdue response to the Pact of Forgetting imposed after Franco's death in 1975 - stories of what happened during the Spanish Civil War are finally starting to emerge like moths seeking light. The atrophy of memory from decades of silence has made the telling of this particular story a collection gleaned from news articles, fragmented family memories, photos, dreams, and ultimately much imagination.

I wish to thank my family in Seville, especially my Uncle Manolo, for tenderly holding my grandfather's deathbed confession. And on behalf of many of Spain's grandchildren and great-grandchildren, thank you to Eva Ruiz, for giving my uncle, and so many others a means to share their stories. I have done my best to weave with integrity and compassion the strands of story and historical record into a whole (albeit moth-eaten) cloth.

Thank you to my earliest readers and those who helped me tease out this story: John, Kris, Dawn, Heather, Lisa G., Leah, Sarah, Tracy, and Laurie. And thank you to my writing group for their early encouragement: Melody, Shelley, Lisa T., Kelli, and especially Dawn for all those days at The New Deal Café and her gentle but firm pressure to keep at it.

I have so much gratitude for Portland's Attic Institute and to Cheryl Strayed for the memoir workshop. The nurturing insights given in that warm and encouraging space were more than I could have hoped for. Thank you also to the Portland Buy Nothing Group for the translators and beta readers I found there who volunteered their time in support of this project: Sandra, Ana, Sam, Suzy, Carol, Thia, Debra, John.

To my husband's family who welcomed me into the home I always longed for, thank you. To my family who nudged me along when I thought I needed to nap instead, I love you. Thank you for believing in and accompanying me through this tricky and tender terrain.

And finally, I thank all who chose to give this story your time and attention. Any fault in the tale lies firmly in the telling.

About the Author

As an author, C. Vargas McPherson is interested in the intersection between truth and historical record, where efforts to derive personal meaning from life are as valued and pertinent as those crystalline facts that serve as starting points. C. Vargas McPherson holds degrees in Philosophy and English Literature from the University of Texas, Austin and Philosophy of Existential Faith from the University of Houston. She has studied at the C.G. Jung Institutes in Küsnacht, Switzerland and Boston, Massachusetts. C. Vargas McPherson now lives in Portland, Oregon, with her family and a cat named Simon.

Glossary

Abuela .... grandmother
Abuelo .... grandfather
Alegria .... joy
Anda. .... go
Barrio. .... neighborhood
Bocadillo. .... snack
Boina .... felt beret
Boquerones. .... anchovies
Bota .... wineskin
Bularías .... songs detailing the sorrows of our daily existence
Calamares. .... squid
Calle .... street
Camarona. .... shrimp
Camiseta .... shirt
Cantaor(a). .... singer
*Cante jondo*the most profound and moving variety of flamenco
Capitaz. .... foreman
Casar .... to marry
Caseta. .... canopy/tent
Caudillo. .... boss
Cazuela de mariscos .... seafood stew
Centimo. .... penny
Cerverza. .... beer

Churros — fried dough
Cine — movie
Communista — Communist
Cómo se llama? — what's your name?
Conejitos — weeds that have a little hooded berry
Confradía — a brotherhood or confraternity
Corrida — bullfight
Cosa del día — next thing of the day
Costaleros — bearers
Cuide a su hermana — take care of your sister
Dolors — sorrow; the Seven Sorrows of Mary
Dulces — sweets/candy
Encarnado — incarnate
Esperanza — hope
Feria — fair
Falangistas — Spanish fascist party
Finos — type of sherry
Gitana — gypsy
Gracias por todo — thank you for everything
Guapa — beautiful/pretty
Guapísima — very beautiful
Guardia Civil — civil guard/police
Hermandad — brotherhood
Hermano Mayor — big brother
Hermosa — beautiful
Hija — daughter
Hombre — man
Iglesia — church
Jamón Serrano — cured ham
Jerez — sherry
Lejos — far
Madrina — godmother
Madrino — godparents

Madroños .... arbutus "strawberry" trees
Madrugá .... early morning/early rising
Mañana .... morning
Mantón .... shawl
Mantilla .... lacy head scarf
Matador .... bullfighter
Mater Dolorosa .... sorrowful mother; Seven Sorrows prayer cycle
Mija .... contraction of 'my daughter'
Míra .... look
Mudéjar .... Islamic-influenced style of architecture and art
Muleta .... matador tool
Nazarenos .... confraternity members in the procession
Ni muerto .... 'not even when dead;' Republican cry
Olorosos .... type of sherry
Panadería .... bakery storefront
Paseo .... walk or stroll
Paso de Palio .... processional float and canopy
Patas Negra .... finest Iberian ham from pigs with black hoofs
Patria .... homeland
Peseta .... small unit of money
Pipas .... sunflower seeds
Puerta del Perdón .... door of forgiveness
Pulpo .... octopus
Polvorones .... crumbly almond cookies
Putana .... prostitute
Querida .... dear one
Queso .... cheese
Rejas .... iron bars usually over windows/doors to protect
Rejero .... ironworker/maker of rejas
Reredos .... large altarpiece or screen behind altar
Retablo .... religious painting
Rojo .... red/communist
Saeta ...... "arrow," a song to religious effigies during procession

Salida..exit
Sardinas..sardines
Saya...skirt
Seguidilla.............folksong and dance form in quick triple time
Semana Santa..holy week
Señoritas...young ladies
Sevillana..........woman from Seville; traditional regional dance
Siempre..always
Sin vergüenza...without shame; shameful
Sol...sun; sunny side
Soleares.........................songs expressing a more existential ache
Soledades..................songs of the solitude of an anguished lover
Sombra...shade; shady side
Tapa..snack served with alcohol
Tía...aunt
Tío...uncle
Tocando Palmas.........................percussive clapping in flamenco
Toro..bull
Toreador...bullfighter
Traje de Luces...bullfighter costume
Traje de Mantilla..........full mourning dress with comb and veil
Turrón...almond candy
Un dedo..a finger/measure of beverage
Un Hombre Bueno...a good man
Vecinos...neighbors
Vestida de Flamenco...flamenco dress
Vino Tinto..red wine

Made in the USA
Las Vegas, NV
03 September 2022